Mexico's Mandarins

Mexico's Mandarins

Crafting a Power Elite for the Twenty-First Century

RODERIC AI CAMP

University of California Press

BERKELEY   LOS ANGELES   LONDON

University of California Press
Berkeley and Los Angeles, California

University of California Press, Ltd.
London, England

Library of Congress Cataloging-in-Publication Data

Camp, Roderic Ai.
  Mexico's mandarins : crafting a power elite for the 21st century /
Roderic Ai Camp.
    p.   cm.
Includes bibliographical references and index.
    ISBN 0-520-23343-3 (cloth : alk. paper).—ISBN 0-520-23344-1 (pbk. :
alk. paper)
    1. Elite (Social sciences)—Mexico.   2. Social networks—Mexico.   3.
Leadership—Mexico.   4. Mentoring—Mexico.   5. Elite (Social
sciences)—Mexico—Interviews.   I. Title.
  HN120.Z9 E433   2002
  305.5'2'0972—dc21   2001003643

Manufactured in the United States of America
11   10   09   08   07   06   05   04   03   02
10 9 8 7 6 5 4 3 2 1

The paper used in this publication is both acid-free and totally chlorine-
free (TCF). It meets the minimum requirements of ANSI/NISO Z39.48–
1992 (R 1997) *(Permanence of Paper).*

To Emmy

Contents

Tables

Acknowledgments

I would like to thank Tulane University and the Roger Thayer Stone Center of Latin American Studies for their financial support in the early phases of research for this project. I would also like to thank the Gould Center for Humanistic Studies and the Kravis Leadership Institute, Claremont McKenna College, for summer support in revising the manuscript. Finally, criticisms and suggestions from many colleagues enhanced the calibre of this work, including those from Daniel C. Levy, Kevin Middlebrook, John Baily, Miguel Basáñez, David Lorey, Kathleen Bruhn, and William Beezley. I would also like to offer a general thanks to my seminar students in comparative elites whose own insights contributed to interpretations expressed in this work.

Part I

POWER ELITES, MENTORING, AND NETWORKING

1 Mexican Power Elites: Do They Exist?

This is a book about how leaders are formed. It is based on the notion that elites exist, that they matter, that they function in all areas of society, and that they exert a crucial influence on their replacements, acting as mentors to successive generations of younger leaders.[1] This work explores and identifies numerous features of Mexican leadership, and more broadly, reveals qualities which exist in numerous Third World settings, including many outside the Western hemisphere.

This study focuses on four central, interrelated issues. First, it establishes the existence and importance of a power elite in Mexico. It describes the composition of that group and illustrates differences between the present versus the future generation, establishing prototypes for both groups. Second, it identifies the extent of and the means by which power elites are linked to each other within and across their respective groups. It explains in detail the importance of informal as well as formal sources of networking, and networking's role in creating power elites.

Third, it provides evidence, for the first time anywhere, of mentors and their influence on the formation of power elite circles, including networking and recruitment. Finally, it analyzes extensively the sources of socialization in the formation of elite ideas and attitudes, including the impact of mentors within family, careers, and education, focusing strongly on the last variable in Mexico and abroad.

No theme ever has been more crucial to understanding a society's internal workings than the way in which institutional decisions are made

---

1. As George Moyser suggests, Vilfredo Pareto was one of the original theorists who viewed elites as involved in every branch of human activity. See Moyser's *Research Methods for Elite Studies* (New York: HarperCollins, 1986), 8.

and how their substance and process change over time. Consequently, the composition of leadership, which individuals achieve positions of influence, how they come to exercise power, and what agents determine their ideological concerns, remains a significant topic into the next millennium. In fact, Edward Muller and Mitchell A. Seligson recently argued that survey researchers have concentrated too heavily on mass views, and instead should shift their focus because "elites have greater opportunity and ability than the general public to influence the kind of regime a country will have," precisely the issue I hope to address.[2]

The composition of a society's leadership is complex and far-reaching. Most studies which have examined leadership in the twentieth century are highly compartmentalized, often focusing on a single group in society, and more typically, on a specific career type within a chosen group. Government officials and leading capitalists have attracted the most attention from analysts; on the other hand, intellectuals and religious leaders have received little serious examination. Two of the leading American analysts of power elite theory, G. William Domhoff and Thomas R. Dye, make this same point.[3] This omission alone limits the value of most studies of national leadership in the United States.

All societies boast influential decision makers, individuals whose decisions determine the allocation and application of important resources and citizen attitudes and behavior. By focusing on "measurable consequences" of elite decisions rather than on elite ideas and values, which in the long run may be more influential on both elites and non-elites, elite studies have ignored an essential ingredient in the leadership stew.

Leadership takes on added importance in those societies where institutional and organizational features are weak. Mexico can point to important institutions, such as the presidency, but most observers characterize its institutional development as sparse, and its decision-making structure as heavily reliant on informal linkages, centralized in the hands of few individuals.

No country is devoid of institutional influences. Basically, Mexico is a hybrid of institutional, structural, and informal influences, as is true of all societies. These influences may come from abroad as well as from within

---

2. Edward Muller and Mitchell A. Seligson, "Civic Culture and Democracy: The Question of Causal Relationships," *American Political Science Review*, 88, no. 3 (September 1994), 647.

3. G. William Domhoff and Thomas R. Dye, *Power Elites and Organizations* (Beverly Hills: Sage, 1987), 14. National and cross-national comparisons of religious leaders are practically negligible.

a nation. The degree to which informal agents exercise greater impact than institutional and structural conditions is the feature worth noting. Among Mexican political leaders, for example, the president has exercised extraordinary influence on state development.[4] Moreover, given the relative weakness of the private and cultural compared to the public sector, the presidency has exerted an extraordinary impact on society extending well beyond the immediate political realm.[5]

Mexico's general institutional setting for most of the years this study examines could be described as semi-authoritarian. The state was governed by a revolving, single-party elite affiliated with the Institutional Revolutionary Party and its antecedents beginning in 1929. Prior to 1989, when opposition parties succeeded in obtaining significant representation in the national legislative branch, and for the first time began to win state gubernatorial elections, individuals associated with this party and the governing elite controlled the allocation of state resources. The most influential political institutions could be found within the boundaries of the executive branch. The legislative and judicial institutions remained structurally weak, underfunded, and politically impotent compared to the national bureaucracy.[6]

The state grew in scope from the 1930s until the 1990s. Its influence over the economy, and its formal and informal control over many non-state actors such as business groups, labor unions, and cultural institutions, further distorted the state's impact. The predominance of the state in Mex-

4. To understand the sources of presidential influence, see the helpful overview by Jeffrey Weldon, "The Political Sources of *Presidencialismo* in Mexico," in Scott Mainwaring and Matthew Shugart, eds., *Presidentialism and Democracy in Latin America* (Cambridge: Cambridge University Press, 1997), 225–58.

5. For insights into some of these trends historically, based on a case study of elite pacts accomplished in the critical year 1928–1929, see historian Alan Knight's interpretation of the centralization of power and the growing influence of the center against the provinces and the elites against the masses. "Mexico's Elite Settlement: Conjuncture and Consequences," in John Higley and Richard Gunther, eds., *Elites and Democratic Consolidation in Latin America and Southern Europe* (Cambridge: Cambridge University Press, 1992), 129–34. Knight concluded that the elite settlement of 1928–29 "fostered a consensual unity among the revolutionary elite such that elite divisions were fudged, accommodated, and conciliated, and the temptation to resort to force, confrontation, and extraparty rabble-rousing was much reduced."

6. For some insights on why, see Jeffrey Weldon, "The Political Sources of *Presidencialismo* in Mexico," in Scott Mainwaring and Matthew Shugart, eds., *Presidentialism and Democracy in Latin America* (Cambridge: Cambridge University Press, 1997), 225–58, and Luis Carlos Ugalde, *The Mexican Congress: Old Players, New Power* (Washington, D.C.: CSIS, 2000).

ican society weakened the private sector. It also weakened the ability of non-state actors, for example, the media, to seek out other resources and achieve greater autonomy. The relative lack of plurality in the decision-making process in many spheres of society enhanced the importance of elites generally and government elites specifically, and the characteristics associated with elite behavior.

Mexico slowly began, following the global pattern occurring elsewhere in the region, to decentralize control in the early 1990s, having witnessed for the first time in many decades a hotly contested presidential race in 1988, which provoked deep divisions within its own political leadership, and within society. As Mexicans began to take hesitant steps to implement a more competitive electoral process, and to shift some political control from the executive to the legislative branch, they also began to reduce the size of the state in the economic sphere, thus strengthening Mexico's private sector. The private sector, which had remained heavily protected by high tariff barriers for decades, faced up to new competition from abroad, as Mexico and the United States joined Canada in 1994 in a regional economic bloc, the North American Free Trade Agreement.

These broad political and economic changes paved the way for other actors to expand their values and express, in more visible terms, their views. In addition to the traditional political and economic elites, religious, cultural, and military leaders involved themselves in new tasks and missions, many of them critical to political liberalization or to political stability and legitimacy.

The Catholic Church, led largely by a group of bishops, began to criticize openly and indirectly the political and economic failures of the regime. As early as 1986, prominent intellectuals joined with northern bishops, an unheard of alliance, to publicly accuse the government of electoral fraud.[7] The armed forces attempted to fill in a vacuum created by the inability of civil agencies to cope with drug trafficking, making this mission the number one issue of national security in the 1980s and 1990s, until the military was forced to confront the executive branch failures leading to the notable Zapatista uprising in January, 1994, followed a year later by a smaller but more aggressive guerrilla movement, the People's Revolutionary Army (ERP).

Today, Mexico is deeply engaged in the process of a democratic transformation. That process is likely to alter, in the first decade of the twenty-

---

7. For a detailed account, see Vikram Khub Chand, *Mexico's Political Awakening* (Notre Dame: University of Notre Dame Press, 2001).

first century, many of the institutional relationships which dominated the country for most of the previous century. This work seeks to show that the broad political setting described above contributed to specific characteristics of Mexican elites. It also seeks to shed light on how and why elites in recent years have contributed to altering those well-established societal patterns.

ELITE SELECTION PROCESS

In order to identify those qualities characterizing Mexico's influential personages and their peers from other Third World societies, I have carefully selected 398 figures who represent its most notable politicians, military officers, clergy, intellectuals, and capitalists from 1970 through 2000.[8] These individuals have been examined in depth through published biographical accounts, correspondence, and personal interviews. These Mexicans were carefully chosen from revised, broader samples of leading figures analyzed by the author in five previous studies covering three decades of research.[9] In some cases, for example, intellectuals, individuals were selected because they published their ideas in Mexico's leading cultural venues, or were chosen by their peers as having exerted the greatest in-

8. *Politicians* are individuals who determine government policies and the allocation of state resources. They can be prominent figures from interest groups such as labor. *Military officers* are the individuals who have the most influence in civil-military relations, internal military policy, and who are in direct command of large numbers of troops. *Intellectuals* are leaders who create, evaluate, analyze, or present transcendental symbols, values, ideas, and interpretations on a regular basis to a broad audience. They come from a broad range of professions, including academia and the media. *Capitalists* have the ability to determine the long-run policies of Mexico's most influential firms; and *clergy* are the Catholic religious ministers who exert the greatest influence over the Conference of Mexican Bishops' pastoral and spiritual tenets and on the laity of important individual dioceses. Where appropriate, I have included so-called celebrity elites, individuals who have used the mass media to exert "an enormous impact not only on the wider public but also on decisionmakers in politics, business, and science who experience popular culture through them." See Suzanne Keller, "Celebrities as a National Elite," in Moshe M. Czudnowski, ed., *Political Elites and Social Change: Studies of Elite Roles and Attitudes* (DeKalb: Northern Illinois University Press, 1983), 12–13.

9. *Crossing Swords: Politics and Religion in Mexico* (New York: Oxford University Press, 1997); *Political Recruitment across Two Centuries: Mexico 1880–1995* (Austin: University of Texas Press, 1996); *Generals in the Palacio: The Military in Modern Mexico* (New York: Oxford University Press, 1993); *Entrepreneurs and Politics in Twentieth Century Mexico* (New York: Oxford University Press, 1989); and *Intellectuals and the State in Twentieth Century Mexico* (Austin: University of Texas Press, 1985).

fluence on societal values and symbols during the period under study. In other cases, they are persons thought to have held the most influential institutional positions, such as the ministers of government, treasury, and programming and budget in the public sector. Many were chosen because scholars and expert analysts have considered their contributions to their respective professions as significant.

According to the criteria set forth footnote 8, the selected elites were culled from 460 political figures, 320 officers of the top rank in their respective services, 290 leading capitalists, 183 intellectuals, and 160 bishops whose careers spanned 1970–2000. The sample of 398 consists of 100 politicians, 100 officers, 100 capitalists, 50 intellectuals, and 48 clergy. The latter two groups are smaller because they represent smaller, initial universes, and because combined they can be viewed as a secular and religious cultural elite. The samples for politicians, capitalists, intellectuals, and clergy are essentially drawn from complete universes for those groups in the specified years. The data set on the Mexican military is the most complete anywhere, but a lack of access to complete background information limited the original scope of that universe. If complete information were accessible, I would estimate the military universe at approximately 470 officers. There is no reason to believe, however, that the 380 officers from whom the selections were made is not representative of that group.

The elites have been selected from pools using well-established reputational, relational, decision-making, and positional criteria in elite literature, all of which are described in detail in my earlier work.[10] This select group does not imply that other individual Mexicans are or were not equally significant during these decades, only that each individual included, according to the criteria used, would appear on most anyone's list of influential persons.

It will become readily apparent that few women appear among this pool of elites. Only a small number of Mexican women have achieved influential positions in major national institutions, which is also the case in

10. To summarize briefly, *positional* = people occupying key roles in important organizations; *decisional* = actors who wield influence in the decision-making process; *reputational* = individuals believed by knowledgeable observers to have actual or potential power to influence society; and *relational* − persons who maintain important relationships with the other three sets of actors. See David Knoke, "Networks of Elite Structure and Decision Making," in Stanley Wasserman and Joseph Galaskiewicz, eds., *Advances in Social Network Analysis* (Thousand Oaks: Sage, 1994), 280–81.

most postindustrial societies.[11] Mexican women are rarely represented among capitalists, and not at all among clergy or the military.[12] A handful of women do appear among influential cultural figures and politicians, but they are exceptional.

ASSUMPTIONS OF EXPLORING MEXICAN ELITES

This work differs substantially from the author's previous explorations of Mexican leadership. Those earlier efforts sought to identify important variables and to offer some modest models of socialization and recruitment for individual elite groups, especially political, and to compare findings with other Latin American and Third World societies. This analysis goes well beyond that in subject matter, breaking much new ground about mentoring and networking. Equally important, it examines for the first time a broad sweep of leaders from most influential categories, making it possible to identify and analyze representative qualities of Mexican leadership rather than a narrow component of elites.

Students of leadership have sought to make elite studies more empirical, replicating trends found elsewhere in the social sciences. As a basis for this empiricism, theorists have offered numerous definitions of elites.[13] Some of the most insightful recent analysis is by Lowell Field, John Higley, and Michael Burton. They provide a perfectly useful definition of political elites which can be broadened to incorporate elites generally as individuals "who are able, by virtue of their strategic positions in powerful organizations, to affect national [religious, military, economic, etc.] outcomes regularly and substantially."[14] However, a bias exists in this definition. In postindustrial societies, where organizations exercise influence in every possible

11. A recent study in the political sphere is Victoria Rodríguez, *Women's Participation in Mexican Political Life* (Boulder: Westview, 1998).

12. For example, women were formally incorporated into the Mexican armed forces March 21, 1938. The first group of women enrolled in the Military Medical School in 1973, and three women completed the tough paratrooper course in 1975. In 1977, the army offered its first basic course for women at the Heroic Military College. The first female officer, a graduate of the Military Nursing School, was promoted to general in 1994. As of 1997, 8 percent of the army was female.

13. According to Alan Zuckerman, a conceptually valid definition of an elite is possible; the problem stems from disagreements over the level of inclusiveness. See his "The Concept 'Political Elite': Lessons from Mosca and Pareto," *Journal of Politics*, 39, no. 2 (1977), 344.

14. See their "A New Elite Framework for Political Sociology," *Revue européene des sciences sociales*, 28 (1990), 152.

realm of activity, a strong rationale exists to require an elite to hold an organizational post.[15] In Mexico, and other Third World countries, using selective, positional, organizational-based criteria might inadvertently exclude many influential actors.

Such structural biases long have existed in sociological and political science literature. They explain why "family relations, world views, and praxis (or tacit 'rules of the game') in the activities that define groups as elite have not been systematically treated by those who have studied American elites."[16] This bias is explained by the fact that early students of elites pursued a theoretical path laid out by Vilfredo Pareto and Gaetano Mosca, rather than a conceptualization of elites offered by the distinguished sociologist Karl Mannheim. Mannheim in essence argued that elites could be distinguished from non-elites on the basis of their mental culture, their worldviews, and outlooks.[17]

During the last half century, elite theorists and students have argued heatedly about the importance of certain features in defining elites, and ruling or power elites. It is not my purpose to revive this debate, and go over old, well-plowed, theoretical ground. However, a number of arguments should be clarified. As G. William Domhoff concludes from his decades of research on American elites, the role of social class, a Marxist analytical emphasis, and the role of institutions, which C. Wright Mills stressed, are both important in understanding power. Simply put, the "ruling class could not exist without the institutions, but the institutions are infused with class [elite] values."[18]

In this study, in terms of the general literature on elites, my research examines three assumptions. First, I am interested in how social status and parental characteristics affect individual elite values and elite access to other elites. Expressed more succinctly, social background variables exert

15. For example, see the recent work of David Knoke, "Networks of Elite Structure and Decision Making," 277, in which he argues that "a power elite is established at the intersection of three social formations: a class-conscious upper social class of wealth holders, interlocked directors of major corporations, and a policy-planning network of foundations, research institutes, and nonpartisan organizations . . ."

16. George E. Marcus, "'Elite' as a Concept: Theory and Research Tradition," in George E. Marcus, ed., *Elites: Ethnographic Issues* (Albuquerque: University of New Mexico Press, 1983), 18.

17. Ibid., 14.

18. G. William Domhoff, *Who Rules America Now? A View for the 1980s* (Englewood Cliffs: Prentice-Hall, 1983), 217–18.

an impact on elite socialization.[19] Michael Burton and John Higley suggest that studies of Third World nations demonstrate that elite social composition may be relevant to political change, but inadequate for explaining major policy changes.[20] However, this unproven causal relationship may be due to the unavailability of adequate data and to the fact that data on social class values are difficult to evaluate empirically.

A second argument incorporated in my approach is the belief that in spite of the importance of an elite's origins, background, and related sociological characteristics, these alone do not explain the level of interaction or integration which occurs within and among leadership groups.[21] Instead, personal linkages, in the form of extensive networking, occur through many organizational and non-organizational settings, of which family is only one contributor.

A third point which has become transparent in the literature from both Mexico and the United States is that pluralist theorists are correct in arguing that numerous mini-groups exist within any leadership elite. Students of elites have exaggerated their level of cohesion, especially studies examining leading capitalists.[22]

Keeping these three general assumptions about elites in mind, it is also necessary to address bluntly the existence of a power elite as distinct from elites generally in Mexico. The assumptions of this work about a Mexican power elite, however, incorporate very specific parameters.

A MEXICAN POWER ELITE

Does Mexico have a power or ruling elite? The answer depends largely on how one defines a power elite. The definitive answer is also limited by

19. This is a point well made by Samuel J. Eldersveld, *Political Elites in Modern Societies: Empirical Research and Democratic Theory* (Ann Arbor: University of Michigan Press, 1989), xiii.

20. Michael Burton and John Higley, "Invitation to Elite Theory: The Basic Contentions Reconsidered," in G. William Domhoff and Thomas R. Dye, *Power Elites and Organizations* (Beverly Hills: Sage, 1987), 230. Indeed, most of the empirical studies I have evaluated over the years are highly sophisticated methodologically speaking, but extremely weak and incomplete on the substantive data, thus making the results and assumptions questionable.

21. Peter Y. Medding, "Ruling Elite Models: A Critique and an Alternative," *Political Studies*, 30, no. 3 (1982), 404.

22. The opposing views between and among pluralists and elite theorists are nicely handled by Philip H. Burch in his exhaustive *Elites in American History*, 1 (New York: Holmes and Meier, 1981), 3–22.

access to information, access which is far more restricted in societies like Mexico compared to the United States, where a proliferation of information exists. But even in the United States, the paucity of empirical information about influential individuals remains a central obstacle to elite theory, which only a handful of scholars have attempted to redress.[23] Much of the actual functioning of elite decision making is informal and "off the record," thus limiting access from outside observers.[24]

If we think of a power structure as a network of organizations and roles responsible for maintaining the general social structure and shaping new policies within a society, and the "power elite" as a small set of people who are the individual actors within that power structure, who also share direct, informal access to other elite actors in their sphere of influence, then it is possible to identify a clear Mexican power elite.[25]

If a power elite is thought to be made up of a group of people who hold overlapping positions or play influential roles directly in two or more sectors of society, for example, political and economic, then it is clear that Mexico does not have a power elite.[26] My data reveal that only one religious or intellectual elite among the forty-eight and fifty, respectively, selected for this study occupies an influential role or position within the other three leadership categories. The exchange between Mexican political and economic leaders is represented by *only one individual* from two hundred in the combined categories.[27] The only reason five military officers

23. See, for example, John Bendix's review of G. William Domhoff's *The Power Elite and the State* in *Society*, 28 (May/June 1991), 90–91.

24. Lowell G. Field and John Higley, "National Elites and Political Stability," in Gwen Moore, ed., *Studies of the National Structure of Elite Groups* (Greenwich: JAI, 1985), 2. I discovered this personally when on several occasions, after years spent examining Mexican leadership, I received fresh, significant insights after being allowed to witness elite interactions, rather than attempting to reconstruct them after the fact.

25. This conceptualization is adapted and borrowed from G. William Domhoff and Thomas R. Dye, *Power Elites and Organizations*, 9.

26. Robert Scott, an early analyst of Mexican politics, claimed that Mexico was "governed by a power elite of interlocking political, economic and status leaders whose interests and attitudes overlap sufficiently to assure a considerable degree of cooperation, but it is neither a closed nor a functionally specialized elite." While the last part of the statement has been well documented, no evidence exists to support an interlocking relationship. See his "Mexico: The Established Revolution," in Lucian Pye and Sidney Verba, eds., *Political Culture and Political Development* (Princeton: Princeton University Press, 1965), 380.

27. Scott's argument that the economic and political elite were interlocking is contradicted by Peter H. Smith's analysis, *Labyrinths of Power: Political Recruitment in Twentieth-Century Mexico* (Princeton: Princeton University Press,

are represented among notable political leaders in Mexico and vice versa is that by law officers must hold the top military cabinet post, national defense.

No other elite overlaps exist. Collectively, 7 out of 398 elites, a minuscule 2 percent, exercised direct influence, organizationally speaking, across any two elite groups in the last three decades, convincing evidence against the existence of positional, institutional elite interlocks across Mexican leadership categories, and this type of a power elite.

The level of interlock among the five leadership categories in Mexico is influenced by different criteria within each category. For example, almost no theoretical literature exists on where or how such linkages might take place between cultural or religious and all other elites, economic, military, and political. In Mexico, most religious leaders are members of the Catholic hierarchy. It would be theoretically possible for a cleric to rank among top Mexican intellectuals since elite intellectuals are measured according to the influence they exercise on Mexican values, not solely according to organizational positions held. One member of the Mexican clergy, internationally recognized bishop Samuel Ruiz of Chiapas, might be considered politically influential without having held any office (canon law bans Catholic priests from doing so anyway). His role in recent political events involving the emergence of the Zapatista Army of National Liberation (EZLN) on January 1, 1994, has been thought to be crucial, more influential than the bishop himself would admit.[28] Even Ruiz's critics would agree that he has exercised a tremendous influence in the mediation process between the guerrillas and the government.

The most examined interlock empirically, based on highly developed theoretical arguments, involves the exchange between leading capitalists. The United States literature on this type of interlock considers the following approaches. The management control model, which argues that corporate board membership is insignificant because professional managers, not capitalists, control firm decision making.[29] This approach has little relevance in Mexico since leading capitalists or their children directly manage most of the powerful Mexican-owned firms.

1979). That person is the late Carlos Hank González, an influential politician in several administrations and a leading capitalist.

28. Personal interview with Samuel Ruiz, bishop of San Cristóbal de las Casas diocese, Lago de Guadalupe, México, April 20, 1992.

29. For discussion of this approach, including criticisms, see Marvin G. Dunn, "The Family Office: Coordinating Mechanism of the Ruling Class," in G. William Domhoff, ed., *Power Structure Research* (Beverly Hills: Sage, 1980), 32–33.

The second approach argues that businesspeople who sit on corporate boards influence policy decisions beneficial to their own firms. This model, as we shall see, is highly relevant to Mexico since numerous capitalists and their nuclear family members sit on multiple boards of Mexico's leading firms.[30]

The third approach is the financial control model, which simply suggests that banks control firms, and therefore they are the most influential firms. In Mexico, holding companies bought up the most powerful banking chains after President Carlos Salinas (1988–94) introduced a dramatic privatization program. Mexican holding companies, controlled by leading capitalist families, are the most influential firms. This too was the case before nationalization in 1982.

Finally, neo-Marxists advocate the class hegemony model, which argues that a small upper class controls corporate wealth. Their argument is relevant to Mexico. Unlike in the United States, in Mexico when a board member dies or retires, he is typically replaced by a member of the same influential family, producing decade after decade boards composed largely of capitalist stockholders.[31]

The existence of a Mexican power elite, as defined above, affects the importance of elite decision making in Mexican society. The fundamental transitions which have occurred structurally and ideologically in macroeconomic policy and political development since 1970 are a product of both

30. As James Bearden points out, owner-controlled firms tend to have boards composed of "inside" directors, company executives, and representatives of the controlling group. When stockholders become dispersed, outside directors tend to replace insiders. The New York Stock Exchange, for instance, requires that listed companies have at least two outside directors. Mexican firms, even when family controlled, could easily meet that requirement by having a family member of a different firm sit on the listed company board. See his "Social Capital and Corporate Control: The Singer Company," *Journal of Political and Military Sociology*, 14 (spring 1986), 141.

31. Thomas Koenig, Robert Gogel, and John Sonquist, "Model of the Significance of Corporate Interlocking Directorates," *American Journal of Economics and Sociology*, 38 (1979), 174–83. In the United States, corporate control and interlocking characteristics are quite different. Furthermore, influential businesspersons are well represented among the boards of prominent cultural foundations and institutions. For discussion of these patterns, see Mark S. Mizruchi, "Why Do Corporations Stick Together? An Interorganizational Theory of Class Cohesion," in G. William Domhoff and Thomas R. Dye, eds., *Power Elites and Organizations* (Beverly Hills: Sage, 1987), 207, 210.

changing citizen attitudes and elite preferences. Lowell Field and his colleagues have made a well-supported case for elite influence on the direction of societies, specifically on major political and policy changes. They have argued that elites can be described as disunified, consensually unified (i.e., structurally integrated and unified on the rules of the game), or ideologically unified (i.e., structurally integrated on both the rules of the game and policy issues).

In the last three decades, a strong case can be made for Mexico having transversed all three categories, from ideologically to consensually unified, to in the 1990s consensually unified to disunified. With the electoral victory of Vicente Fox in 2000, Mexico is now somewhat in limbo between the latter two categories as it strives for a fresh consensus on the political and economic rules of the game.[32]

Elite decisions contribute heavily in determining the success and legitimacy of a political model. Mexican democracy after 2000 will have to make room for all important elite groups to participate in the decision-making process, as well as their agreeing on the rules of the game and worthiness of political institutions, a goal which electoral reforms have contributed to in a positive way.[33]

Members of Mexico's political power elite performed crucial roles and made influential decisions which transformed its political system from a semi-authoritarian model in 1970 to a full-scale electoral democracy by 2001. The electoral victory of Vicente Fox, for example, could not have been achieved without the 1996 electoral reform laws, hammered out in negotiations among leading representatives of the three major political parties.

Political elites, assisted by capitalist allies, also encouraged and put into place a policy agenda which significantly altered state control over the economy, strengthening the domestic private sector vis-à-vis the state and opening the economy to global influences. These fundamental structural changes in the 1980s and 1990s were accompanied by underlying ideological shifts which provided a fertile setting for fresh political and economic directions.

Catholic bishops throughout the 1980s and 1990s were committed to

---

32. G. Lowell Field, John Higley, and Michael G. Burton, "A New Elite Framework for Political Sociology," *Revue européene des sciences sociales*, 28 (1990), 155, 178.
33. John Higley et al., "Elite Integration in Stable Democracies: A Reconsideration," *European Sociological Review*, 7, no. 1 (May 1991), 35.

electoral democracy, aggressively pushing the laity to participate in the voting process. Their efforts increased markedly after 1992, when political elites, directed by President Salinas, eliminated and revised constitutional restrictions on Catholic priests and the church. Numerous pastoral letters, issued by bishops, called on Mexico's citizens to exercise their voting rights, labeling abstention a sin. Catholic bishops played a pivotal role in reinforcing grass-roots demands for fair elections and political accountability. Bishops were also the loudest critics of government macroeconomic policy failures in the 1980s and 1990s, providing an articulate resistance to advocates of economic globalization.

The officer corps, the least visible Mexican power elite actor, nevertheless has exercised a silent veto over political elite leadership in spite of subordination to civilian elites. Again and again throughout the last three decades, presidents have sought out their support in times of political crises to maintain regime legitimacy. Without the officer corps' open acquiescence and public support, the political model would have faltered sooner than 2000. Their expanded security missions have also made clear the political elites' reliance on the armed forces to maintain Mexico's internal stability in face of the failure of civilian institutions to perform those tasks.

Mexican intellectuals, through books, the print media, and the classroom, constantly reinforced the liberalizing political direction beginning in the 1970s. Many of Mexico's prominent political elites have attributed their own values, in part, to the ideological influences of intellectual mentors. Intellectuals also contributed strongly to the grass-roots democratic landscape, writing numerous editorials and columns on the necessity for expanded political space and electoral integrity. Intellectuals founded new magazines like *Vuelta, Nexos,* and *Este País*, as well as newspapers, to convey their message to elites and non-elites alike. They contributed importantly to changing the public debate, and even on occasion found themselves publicly allied with Catholic bishops.

Many capitalists, generally timid political reformers, collaborated with the technocratic political leadership, reversing the bank nationalization and state ownership of numerous businesses. In the 1990s, after the initial success of the National Action Party at the state and local level, some prominent capitalists, with ties to the power elite, began to give financial support, and in some cases, personal support, to opposition parties, strengthening electoral competition.

Five power elite groups, politicians, intellectuals, clergy, military officers, and capitalists, were the most influential elite actors in Mexico during the last three decades. They are the groups who must be examined in order to understand elite contributions to the transformation of Mexican society, and as critical contributors to the directions Mexico will take in the twenty-first century.

2   Mentoring Mexico's Power Elite

The formation of a power elite depends on many variables and influences. In seeking out how power elites acquire their values and make professional and educational choices, and how they network with one another, I discovered that in the Mexican case, mentors play a crucial role. The most original contribution of the present study is the striking evidence it provides to support the belief that mentors are crucial actors in determining many characteristics of the power elite. Incredibly, no other available studies were discovered which document their role or their group characteristics.[1]

A MENTORING MODEL

All societies and all organizations at every level feature conditions which encourage a mentoring process between an accomplished worker and a potential protégé. Craft guilds for centuries passed on their skills and established quality controls through formal apprenticeship processes. Elites in all categories and professions perform similar functions, but those functions are rarely structured, especially in societies where institutional qualities are less mature.

Many elites or potential elites seek out disciples and mentors for a variety of reasons. Some are practical. Potential disciples hope to develop the skills that will enhance their success within a profession or organiza-

---

1. The serious lacunae in theoretical and substantive literature on mentors makes it difficult to draw important comparisons. Some scattered literature exists in psychology, but it is not elite oriented. Other literature can be found in the business world, but it is neither particularly sophisticated nor broadly conceived, focusing primarily on career advancement.

tion. The disciple may also be seeking companionship from an older figure who may substitute for an individual's parent.[2] The mentor is also motivated for a combination of reasons. Many mentors seek out talented disciples in the belief that they can pass on their formal and informal professional knowledge and enhance the ability of their chosen student to succeed, perhaps eventually to replace them.[3] Disciples are also important, especially in an organizational setting, as sources of information and intelligence.[4]

Mentors also seek potentially successful disciples in hopes of maintaining and enhancing their own influence.[5] For example, a well-placed cadre of powerful Mexican political disciples can lead to a former political elite reviving a career if one of those disciples were to become president. Repeated examples of this exist in recent decades, as illustrated by the fact that President Carlos Salinas de Gortari appointed his early political mentor as majority leader of the chamber of deputies during his administration.[6]

In Mexico, one would expect mentoring to be more entrenched than in the United States. The lack of institutional protection, and the level of informal politics in many spheres, encourages Mexicans to seek out an individual protector. In the broader society, this personalized protective vehicle has been described and analyzed by anthropologists as a patron-client relationship. I am not suggesting that an elite mentor functions as a patron does in the general social system, but that the presence of well-established patron-client patterns in many Third World countries, Mexico included, provides a fertile environment conducive to other forms of mentoring.[7]

2. For the importance and meaning of the psychological factors, see Daniel J. Levinson, *The Seasons of a Man's Life* (New York: Knopf, 1978), 97 ff.

3. This seems to be especially true in academia. See Robert T. Blackburn et al., "'Cloning' in Academia: Mentorship and Academic Careers," *Research in Higher Education,* 15, no. 4 (1981), 315–27.

4. Michael G. Zey, *The Mentor Connection* (Homewood: Dow Jones, 1984), 10.

5. Zey recognizes the benefits to the mentor of a protégé in his work on business. Ibid., 78.

6. The mentor was Gonzalo Martínez Corbalá, who did not share the president's neoliberal economic views. Salinas served as his aide while still a student in economics at the National University. Nevertheless, he repaid Martínez Corbalá for his initial boost to his career, also appointing him as interim governor of his home state, San Luis Potosí, in 1991.

7. Merilee Grindle recognized this connection in the political world in her "Patrons and Clients in the Bureaucracy: Career Networks in Mexico," *Latin American Research Review,* 12 (1977), 37–66.

The general literature on mentoring in postmodern societies concludes that collectivist cultures like Mexico give stronger support to mentoring than individualistic, organizational cultures, and that mentoring is a "key resource for the development of power in organizations," affecting a protégé's rank, career track, and position of power.[8] Beyond that, some cultural analysts actually believe that in numerous societies, notably in the public arena, power is measured by the acquisition of friends, not the acquisition of capital.[9]

THE LEVEL OF MENTORING AMONG ELITES

I argued above that incumbent elites play a crucial role in admitting and choosing their replacements within elite circles, regardless of the activity in which they are engaged. I believe elite mentors serve as crucial agents in determining numerous characteristics of elite disciples who become the next generation of elite mentors. Strangely, we know little about elite mentors. This is a major omission in understanding the nature, recruitment, and socialization of leadership in any society, including Mexico.

The few serious studies of mentoring in the United States have focused on the process within the business sector. C. Edward Weber, who authored an insightful essay on the topic, found a similar lacuna twenty years ago. His analysis of the scant available literature in the business world suggested four major points. First, most mentors of business executives had mentors themselves. Second, based on a case study of the Jewel Tea Company, "everyone who makes it has a mentor." Third, mentoring is not a "mere superior-subordinate relationship," but leads to the growth of leaders. Fourth, the age differential most conducive to establishing a relation-

8. Belle Rose Ragins, "Diversity, Power, and Mentorship in Organizations: A Cultural, Structural, and Behavioral Perspective," in M. M. Chemers et al., eds., *Diversity in Organizations: New Perspectives for a Changing Workplace* (Thousand Oaks: Sage, 1995), 116, 125.

9. Glen Dealy, in *The Public Man: An Interpretation of Latin America and Other Catholic Cultures* (Amherst: University of Massachusetts Press, 1977), 10, is the most outspoken advocate of this interpretation, which he applies to all Latin cultures: "The currency of public power is friendship. For the public man friends are used as currency in the identical sense in which capitalists speak of money and currency as synonymous terms. . . . One should think of friendship in a parallel manner. Though perhaps sometimes less tangible than money in a bank, friends can be accumulated, saved, and spent in much the same way."

ship between mentor and disciple was half a generation.[10] To what extent do elite Mexicans from all professional backgrounds share these qualities found among United States business executives? Are elite Mexicans the product of elite mentors?

Mexico's power elite in the last three decades is overwhelmingly the product of elite mentors. Only one out of seven of our power elites had no known elite mentor. Furthermore, most of the mentors were either members of their same small power elite circle or members of elite circles prior to 1970.[11]

These figures are extraordinary for two reasons. First, the fact that nearly half of Mexico's most influential figures were disciples of their own peers during a thirty-year period suggests the rapidity of elite dynamics on one hand and the ability of a narrow group of leaders to choose their replacements on the other. Second, although having an elite rather than an "ordinary" mentor is not a requirement for achieving super elite status, in more than eight out of ten cases it is the norm. Thus, those talented individuals in Mexican society with leadership ambitions are not likely to achieve membership in Mexico's power elite without the assistance of an elite mentor. Having such a mentor does not guarantee achieving elite status, but rather it is a typical characteristic among those Mexicans who achieve such influence.

Among the broad groups making up Mexico's power elite, important differences exist among the numbers of mentors who come from their ranks, and their membership in the contemporary or past power elite (pre-1970). (See table 1)[12] Clergy stand out among the five groups as having the largest percentage of mentors who are from the older power elite. This is explained by the fact that typically a future leading member of the Catholic clergy is selected by an incumbent bishop while still studying in the diocesan seminary. Because most priests do not become bishops until they are in their forties, their protégés will not reach elite status, specifically power elite status, until after their mentors have retired. On the other

---

10. C. Edward Weber, "Mentoring," *Directors and Boards*, 5 (fall 1980), 17–24.

11. Elite status or elite circles prior to 1970 were determined using the same criteria detailed in chapter 1 for identifying members of the 1970–2000 power elite. Thus, except for the dates, they exerted a similar influence on Mexico in earlier periods.

12. Unless otherwise indicated, information in this and subsequent chapters is based on a comprehensive data bank of detailed background information about each of the 398 members of the power elite in the sample.

hand, few leading clergy managed to achieve power elite status without an elite mentor, who, in nearly all cases, was someone already within the church hierarchy.

Mexican military officers share certain similarities with Catholic clergy in the mentorship process. As table 1 illustrates, top officers overwhelmingly are products of an elite mentor–disciple relationship. In fact, they are the only group among the power elite to have no known members who have joined that exclusive circle without an elite mentor. They also are the group most likely to have been mentored by someone who is a member of the present power elite.

Why is this the case among three-quarters of influential officers? Many officers encounter their initial mentor while they are students at the Escuela Superior de Guerra or the equivalent Higher Naval War College. Instructors at both institutions generally are only a rank or two above the first lieutenants and captains or their naval equivalents who are completing the staff and command program, usually essential to achieving the rank of general or admiral. Therefore, mentor and disciple are not very far apart in age, increasing the potential that if both are highly successful they will become influential officers during the same era.

Mexican intellectuals and capitalists share a common feature in their mentorship patterns; a large minority achieved their status without elite mentors. Among intellectuals, two explanations appear to apply. First, as Carlos Monsiváis, a leading cultural figure, has argued, younger intellectuals are no longer disciples of older figures. He bluntly suggests, probably exaggeratedly, that mentoring died with the late Octavio Paz, Mexico's Nobel prize-winning poet, who he claims was "the last leading intellectual to mentor a younger generation."[13] Second, among all power elite groups, intellectuals' upward mobility is the least structured and institutionalized. By their very nature and activity, intellectuals are independent personalities who typically work alone. Consequently, it is not surprising that many can succeed, and can be recognized, without the guiding hand of a prominent, well-established mentor.

A sizeable number of capitalists also prospered without elite mentors. Despite the closed nature of many characteristics describing Mexico's capitalist class, it is evident, especially in the late 1980s and the 1990s, that the dynamic quality of the economy allowed a number of ambitious, unconnected Mexicans to join the wealthiest circles without a prior entrée

13. Personal interview with Carlos Monsiváis, Claremont, California, November 18, 1998.

Table 1. Power Elite Mentors Who Were Members of Mexico's Power Elite

	Mentor Power Elite Membership		
Type of Power Elite	*Present Elite (%)*	*Past Elite (%)*	*Neither (%)*
Political	51	45	4
Intellectual	22	41	37
Capitalist	25	49	26
Military	76	24	0
Clergy	38	59	3

NOTE: *Present elite* indicates mentor is a member of the present sample of the power elite (1970–2000). *Past elite* indicates an individual would have been a member of the power elite prior to 1970 using the same criteria to place a Mexican in the present power elite sample. *Neither* indicates the known mentor has never been a member of the power elite, past or present. (*N* = 398)

among the power elite. Some evidence exists to support a relationship between having mentors and achieving upward career mobility in the private sector, but no studies exist for leading capitalists.[14]

The importance and durability of elite mentorship in Mexican society can be further pushed by asking the extent to which elite mentors are products of other elites. In other words, to what degree is the mentor–disciple relationship a multiple, generational pattern extending beyond that of a single mentor–disciple linkage? In this study I traced two generations of elite mentors.[15] The information in table 2 illustrates elite mentor continuity in Mexico. Among military officers' elite mentors, for example, nearly two-thirds were themselves disciples of mentors who belonged to power elite circles. Among all power elite mentors, more than half were mentored by individuals who were members of the past power elite (pre-1970), and a fourth were mentored by current power elites (1970–2000). Again, this suggests an intertwining of power elites and

14. See Terri A. Scandura, "Mentorship and Career Mobility: An Empirical Investigation," *Journal of Organizational Behavior*, 13, no. 2 (March 1992), 169–74; Susan Kogler Hill and Margaret H. Bahniuk, "Promoting Career Success through Mentoring," *Review of Business*, 19 (spring 1998), 4–7; and Gerard R. Roche, "Much Ado about Mentors," *Harvard Business Review*, 57 (January/February 1979), 14–16.

15. In the data bank, using extensive published and unpublished sources, the author attempted to identify a mentor or mentors for each power elite. Since six out of seven mentors were power elites at some time from the 1920s to 2000, I was able to take that information one step further, and identify the original mentor's mentor.

Table 2. Power Elite Mentors' Mentors Who Were
Members of the Power Elite

	Mentors' Mentors' Power Elite Membership		
Type of Power Elite	*Present Elite (%)*	*Past Elite (%)*	*Neither (%)*
Political	13	65	22
Intellectual	7	59	33
Capitalist	7	47	46
Military	61	39	0
Clergy	13	87	0

NOTE: *Present elite* indicates mentor is a member of the present sample of the power elite (1970–2000). *Past elite* indicates individual would have been a member of the power elite prior to 1970 using the same criteria to place a Mexican in the present power elite sample. *Neither* indicates the known mentor has never been a member of the power elite, past or present. ($N = 398$)

power elite mentors, and the narrow chronological space (three decades) in which they are linked.

The most comprehensive characteristic of power elite mentors in Mexico is that they too are power elites, past and present. Therefore, they share the same general characteristics of that power elite. Most members of the power elite served as mentors, performing tasks to which they were exposed as disciples. Because of this extensive overlap, power elite mentors cannot be easily separated from power elites generally.[16]

I have established the importance of elite mentors among multiple generations of Mexican power elites. Other than the individual elite group with which power elites are identified, do other factors exist which affect the presence of such mentors among prominent contemporary leaders, and their continued influence into the next millennium?

Over time, one of the patterns which appears to be important is the proportion of mentors who belonged to the same power elite circle as their disciples. The earlier finding from U.S. business leaders that mentors are typically only ten to fifteen years older than their disciples is confirmed in Mexico by the fact that the youngest power elite members draw a dis-

16. Most Mexicans who fail to achieve power elite status are likely to have had mentors, too. But those individuals may not have had a mentor who already was a member of the power elite, or a mentor who through skill and good fortune rose to power elite status, or did not wish themselves to become a power elite.

Table 3. Changing Generational Patterns among Power Elite Mentors in the Power Elite

Power Elite Date of Birth	Mentor Membership		
	Present Elite (%)	Past Elite (%)	Neither (%)
Pre-1900	0	64	36
1900–09	5	74	21
1910–19	44	44	12
1920–29	42	46	12
1930–35	51	37	12
1936–40	41	53	6
1941–45	72	22	6
1946–50	75	5	25
1951–	60	10	30

NOTE: *Present elite* indicates mentor is a member of the present sample of the power elite (1970–2000). *Past elite* indicates individual would have been a member of the power elite prior to 1970 using the same criteria to place a Mexican in the present power elite sample. *Neither* indicates the known mentor has never been a member of the power elite, past or present. (*N* = 398)

proportionately large percentage of mentors from the 1970–2000 power elite.[17] (See table 3.)

Even more striking is the fact that members of the power elite born after 1946 are twice as likely to have no known elite mentor–disciple relationship as those who were born before 1946. Nine out of ten of the older elites could claim mentors who themselves were power elites. Elites who are least likely to have encountered an opportunity to connect with a mentor who was part of the Mexican power elite, past or present, are those Mexicans born abroad, who are at a great disadvantage in meeting such a person early in their careers.

This generational information on elite mentors suggests two major changes taking place in the Mexican mentoring process. Younger elites compared to their older peers are operating in a chronologically more compressed elite setting in which their career spans are shorter and their achievement of elite status occurs at a younger age. This same pattern was replicated historically from 1910 through 1929, when many leading Mexicans were the product of revolutionary, military careers. Violence pushed

17. C. Edward Weber, "Mentoring," 17–24.

individuals up the leadership ladder at a fast clip. Mentoring relationships, because of the circumstances, also occurred among peers.

Older power elite members, who achieved influence in the 1970s and 1980s, took longer to achieve a recognized place among power elites, and consequently their mentors, when members of that self-same power elite, already had left the fold by the time their disciples arrived. The other important explanation for this pattern is that mentoring itself has shifted to cohort mentors, for example, when a mentor–disciple relationship is established through higher education it might typically occur among co-students or a young professor and student instead of older professors and younger students.

The most striking trend revealed in the mentorship patterns generationally is their decline. The youngest group of power elites, in their forties and fifties, have relied less on mentors as they make their way to elite status. Is the trend away from mentors that Carlos Monsiváis described among recent intellectuals generalizable to the next generation of power elites? It is difficult to know for sure, given the availability of information.[18]

Mentors play multiple roles among power elites. Those roles are often overlapping, and therefore they need to be specified. It is also essential to make the point here that members of the power elite often have more than one mentor over the course of their careers. Some of the tasks performed by these mentors are crucial to career success, and ultimately help disciples secure their places in the power elite. Other tasks help elites perform their own duties. Mentors in Mexico, and elsewhere, can be viewed as playing three often interrelated roles, each of which will be examined in detail. A mentor is an individual who influenced a person's career choice, professional and ideological values, and professional achievements. Mentors were identified by elites through interviews, published sources, and documentary evidence. For purposes of statistical figures, when multiple mentors are identified, the mentor determined to have been the most influential on a person's career was the individual used.

In general terms, however, the mentor can be described as an individual who establishes a close professional and personal relationship with a subordinate or peer. The mentor uses his knowledge and skills to support a disciple's career interests. The mentor also uses his persuasive powers to

18. A methodological explanation for this pattern is that less background information is available on younger versus older power elite members, therefore producing distorted figures generationally on known mentors.

encourage an individual to pursue a similar career trajectory, or to stay in that career. Finally, the mentor creates a strong bond of trust between himself and his disciple, and that bond of trust may be life-long or short-lived, depending on the evolution of the relationship.

These characteristics of the mentor are reinforced in post-revolutionary Mexico by comparatively weak institutional developments, and the importance of personal trust in political, business, and other professional relationships. The traditional absence of established rules, merit systems, and a culture of law, combined with the collapse of political stability immediately prior to 1920, resulted in a reliance on personal bonds to accomplish career goals and implement agreements.

In Mexico, the mentor has functioned as a recruiter, as a networker, and as a socializer. The *mentor as recruiter* is the task about which we have the most information, even though a mentor is almost never identified specifically as an agent of recruitment. The mentor typically performs a recruiting task in one of two ways. He may recruit an individual into his profession, thus serving as an *initial* recruiter. For example, many Mexicans were recruited into the priesthood by a Catholic bishop, who takes a proactive approach to identifying lower seminary students as likely candidates, encouraging them to continue in the higher seminary schools. Religious members of the power elite also have made it clear that bishops were instrumental in giving them access to credentials favorable to their success within the religious hierarchy. Bishops who served as initial recruiters also chose the most successful upper seminary students to continue their education abroad, an opportunity available only to small numbers of seminary students each year.

The second task involves networking. A well-established mentor may use his influence and prestige to help his disciples make contacts with other equally influential persons in his profession or in other professions. For example, the small number of Mexicans who completed higher education, especially education at a select number of public and private universities producing a disproportionate percentage of Mexican elites, created a setting where instructors and students both could establish close ties to students who became prominent figures in their respective professions, especially in the political, economic, and cultural worlds. Many mentors who were part- or full-time teachers used their classrooms to identify prospective disciples, creating important networks of individuals within and across professions. They in turn used those personal relationships to bring together future power elites.

In Mexican political life, mentors often have formed groups or cliques known as *camarillas*. These are small, informal groups whose most successful member advances the careers of his own circle, whose advancement depends on the leader's own professional mobility. Camarillas are often built on mentor–disciple relationships, but they tend to be exclusive to public life, and they do not perform socializing functions.[19]

The least examined mentoring role is that of the *mentor as socializer*, contributing to the ideological and attitudinal formation of future power elites. Mentors perform this task in numerous settings, familial, educational, and professional. It is possible that the same individual who performs this task could also perform both the recruitment and networking tasks, but it is not likely. The mentor as a socializer, however, often serves in a networking capacity, linking his disciples ideologically within their career professions. The individual who performs the socializing task can mentor a disciple either in Mexico or abroad. The foreign mentor, as far as the socializing task is concerned, became increasingly influential among the post-1970s generation of Mexican power elites.

SOURCES OF ELITE MENTOR–DISCIPLE CONTACTS

Elite literature always has considered the social composition and backgrounds of elites as indicative of certain social prerequisites of influential leaders and the advantages class and other background variables give to specific groups. If mentors play such an important role in the rise and formation of power elites, it is essential to understand how mentors and disciples meet, and if mentors' characteristics enhance some individuals' ability to make those contacts.

If we examine the three broad categories that foster mentor–disciple relationships—education, career, and family—we discover some interesting characteristics of the mentoring process. In the first place, none of the individual categories stands out as a breeding ground for elite relationships. In general, disciples are equally likely to find an elite mentor in family, career, or educational settings.

This mentoring pattern changes significantly when each elite group is considered separately from the entire power elite. As the information in table 4 illustrates, nine out of ten Mexican capitalists were mentored by family members, the highest rate of any power elite group, and nearly three times the norm for all power elites. Comparable studies do not exist,

---

19. See my "Camarillas in Mexican Politics: The Case of the Salinas Cabinet," *Mexican Studies*, 6 (winter 1990), 85–108.

Table 4. How Mentor–Disciples among Mexican Power Elites Meet

	Source of Mentor–Disciple Relationships		
Type of Power Elite	*Education (%)*	*Career (%)*	*Family (%)*
Political	45	42	13
Intellectual	76	15	9
Capitalist	1	5	94
Military	31	69	0
Clergy	63	25	11

NOTE: *Education* refers to a mentor–disciple contact which occurred in any educational setting, typically between a student and a professor, between any two students, or between professorial peers. *Career* refers to a mentor–disciple contact which took place in an occupational setting, typically between two individuals working in an organizational bureaucracy, often in a superior–subordinate relationship. *Family* refers to mentor–disciple relationships established within the immediate family, including mentors who were grandparents, in-laws, aunts and uncles, or parents. (*N* = 398)

but an examination of leading Cuban-American entrepreneurs in Florida concluded that family mentors, among other credentials and skills, played a leading role in enhancing their career success.[20]

Given the high incidence of prominent Mexican capitalists who are the children of capitalists, it is logical to assume that a future member of the power elite whose father was a member of that self-same group would mentor his child. Furthermore, capitalists intermarry with other leading families more than any other power elite group. This fact increases their chances of being mentored by a powerful relative other than their father, a common pattern among capitalists. For example, Alfonso Romo Garza, billionaire CEO of Grupo Pulsar, a leading holding company, borrowed the money from his father-in-law, a prominent member of a capitalist power elite family, to buy a controlling interest in Empresa La Moderna, after having been a failure early in his career. He also attributes a strong influence on his mission and values to his grandmother, niece of Mexico's revolutionary president.[21]

Some children of leading capitalists are mentored by others.[22] This ex-

20. Mark F. Peterson, "Leading Cuban-American Entrepreneurs: The Process of Developing Motives, Abilities, and Resources," *Human Relations*, 48, no. 10 (October 1995), 1193–1215.
21. *U.S./Mexico Business*, January 1996, 56–57; *Integratex*, July/August 1997, 33. Alejandro Laguera is his father-in-law and Carolina Madero his grandmother.
22. *Expansión*, April 26, 1995, 23. Andrés Sada Zambrano, a current member of Mexico's power elite whose father, Andrés G. Sada García, co-founded Grupo

ceptional pattern occurs among other power elite groups too. Jesús Silva Herzog, former treasury secretary, was the son of one of Mexico's leading intellectuals, a power elite member prior to 1970, who also held influential political offices, serving as the first director general of the nationalized Petróleos Mexicanos in the 1930s. Although he became an economist like his father, he was a disciple of Rodrigo Gómez, director of Mexico's Federal Reserve bank, the Banco de México, and one of the most influential financial figures in the second half of the century:

> No doubt, Rodrigo Gómez was like a second father to me. I was sort of his personal assistant as head of the technical office of the director in his last years at the Bank of Mexico. He was extremely intelligent, honest, with no formal education; but he taught me to put ideology aside and to recognize when 2 plus 2 equals 4. I traveled frequently with him to the United States and Latin America. He encouraged me to go to Yale because he believed strongly that Mexicans in the bank should improve their technical skills.[23]

Among top military officers, most met their mentors through a position they held in military institutions and organizations. Intellectuals, on the other hand, typically met their mentors at school, either at the preparatory or university level. This is not surprising because most intellectuals in Mexico have taught, and most intellectuals have begun their intellectual activities, including writing and painting, while in school, activities shared with their most talented peers and their teachers. Catholic bishops, like intellectuals, encountered the majority of their mentors in an educational environment, almost universally in their local seminary. Politicians, interestingly, are the most balanced of elites in acquiring mentoring contacts among all three categories.

As a source of contact between elites and elite mentors, family connections do not seem as important as education and careers. The notable exception to this pattern occurs among leading Mexican capitalists. However, an individual Mexican's social origin becomes significant in determining the influence kinship ties play in elite mentor–disciple relationships. Among all power elites who came from influential families, eight out of ten were mentored by a family member. Among power elites raised in

---

Cydsa, one of Mexico's influential holding companies, recently admitted that "he and I didn't talk about business frequently. Between us was Miguel Arce [co-founder], who was my only boss during my entire life."

23. Personal interview with Jesús Silva Herzog, University of California, Riverside, November 19, 1998.

modest social and economic circumstances, only a minuscule portion, one out of ten, were influenced by a family member in their upward career trajectory.

Class origins also impact the importance of educational linkages as a source of influential mentors since such contacts occur far less often among self-made Mexican elites than among those who came from middle-class circumstances. For example, one-fifth of all working-class Mexicans who reached power elite status did so without the assistance of an elite mentor.

As social conditions in Mexico change, one would expect institutional forms of contact to increase among potential elites, especially those within educational and career settings. In fact, the percentage of power elites born after 1946 who acquired an elite mentor within their family actually increased slightly, which suggests the continued importance of kinship ties in Mexico's elite mentoring process.

Five decades of research on elites have made clear that an individual's birthplace can affect opportunities in many areas including level of education, discipline studied, and career choice. The source of contact among elites and their mentors, as indicated above, is roughly balanced among three categories: education, career, and family. But as is the case with an elite's social origins, place of birth has significant consequences for the sources of mentor–disciple relationships.

Most power elites originate from urban settings, but those who are rural born generate contacts with mentors in patterns quite different from their urban-born peers. For example, half of all rural-born elites acquired their mentor through a professional setting. This figure is much higher than the distribution found among all power elites.

Lower numbers might be explained by the fact that rural-born power elites are at a disadvantage when it comes to having an important family member who is already an elite or in a strong position to push a relative into an elite sphere. Typically, a person would not be born in a rural setting if his parents already boasted power elite credentials. The fact that birthplace does *not* influence the impact of educational institutions as a source of mentors suggests that education functions as an equalizer for those Mexicans who share certain disadvantageous characteristics.

An elite's place of origin is even more influential on the mentor–disciple relationship than on their source of contact with a mentor. Rural-born Mexicans rarely make it into power elite circles *without* an elite mentor. This was the case for only one out of ten such Mexicans. Nearly twice as many urban-born elites were able to achieve this vaunted status without the help of an elite mentor.

Rural-born potential elites need all the advantages possible to compete against their urban-born peers, and an elite compared to a non-elite mentor mitigates some of the other existing disadvantages. To make contact with an elite mentor, the potential elite more often than not needs to move to the capital city. This is necessary because two-thirds of all elite mentors reside in Mexico City, thus strongly favoring the capital as the urban locus for establishing power elite mentor–disciple relationships.

Who are the mentors of future members of the power elite? Specifically, *how* do future elites actually come into contact with a mentor as distinct from *where* the contact takes place? Generally, one of three types of relationships produces a mentor–disciple pattern: familial, peer, and superior-subordinate. Their importance varies from one power elite group to another.

As suggested above, family is the dominant locale for mentor–disciple relationships among capitalists; consequently a kinship connection produces this linkage. Among politicians, military officers, and clergy, in four out of five cases—including Jesús Silva Herzog's circumstances—an individual's boss serves as a mentor, which suggests the importance of institutional or organizational settings and established superior-subordinate relationships. Peers, who provide the smallest number of mentor–disciple linkages of the three types of relationships, occur most commonly among military power elites. They mentored one out of five leading officers. None were mentored by a family member.

A power elite's family background is significant in the formation of a mentor–disciple relationship for another reason; it often determines whether or not the mentor is a member of the present or prior elite. My analysis demonstrates that individuals whose family members played prominent roles in leadership circles are 50 percent more likely to rely on elite mentors who are members of the previous influential generation of leaders.

Elite family history and its importance to mentoring extends well beyond parents. Analysis of power elites' maternal and paternal grandparents' and great-grandparents' relative status indicates that leaders with prominent family roots, whether Porfirian (anti-revolutionary) or revolutionary, are products of elite mentors. Even power elites with Porfirian antecedents, which for most of the post-1920s decades might be viewed as a disadvantageous heritage, were more likely to acquire influential mentors in their upwardly mobile careers.

MENTORS' INFLUENCE ON POWER ELITE FORMATION

It is apparent that Mexicans rely heavily on influential mentors to achieve their elite status. These mentors perform significant tasks in the development of Mexican leaders. Individual testimony from specific leaders suggests ways in which mentors might influence their values and behavior. But beyond the unique influences which characterize every individual mentor–disciple relationship, do mentors produce generalizable effects in the Mexican setting and elsewhere?

As I will demonstrate in the following chapters, mentors are critical actors in the networking ties among power elites. But mentors also determine the choices that potential power elites make early in their careers. Within Mexican power elites in the last third of the twentieth century, mentors were critical influences on disciples' choice of educational discipline and source of education.

This book argues the importance of preparatory and higher education as a determinant of changing power elite values in the last three decades. A significant catalyst to introducing altered patterns of education among top leaders can be traced to elite mentors.

The narrative reveals a powerful linkage in Mexico between influential leadership and mentors. Power elites—defined in this chapter as individuals who influence policy in their own areas and, in many cases, network with influential elites in other realms—function in other societies as well. It is very likely that mentoring is an essential ingredient in their formation and establishment, and that elite mentoring is also a dominant feature.

Why is this the case? In societies where Weberian influences have impacted the mentality of social scientists, a strong tendency exists to believe that individuals rise to the top of the decision-making structure on the basis of their merits. Ability alone rarely explains individual success, although it may explain it more commonly in some societies than others. In postmodern societies, where opportunities are broader, deeper, and fairer, informal agents play lesser roles.

In Mexico and most other less industrialized countries, personal linkages influence opportunities at every step of the way, opening doors which otherwise might remained closed. The emphasis on this pattern distinguishes Third from most First World countries. It is a major distinction, and its consequences deserve greater attention from scholars and theorists. This is not to say that some highly developed countries do not rely on these same informal patterns. This is the case for Japan, for example. In Third World countries, however, this pattern is universal.

Any analyst of a Third World country knows the importance of personal networking in everyday life and in achieving goals extending beyond the normal individual's day-to-day existence. Power elite circles are the products, in part, of a sophisticated form of networking at the highest levels of society. The crucial task of allowing access to this leadership group, given the weaknesses of institutional and organizational channels, falls on the shoulders of mentors.

Most future power elites cannot rely on just any mentor. They must acquire a mentor who already is or will become a member of the existing or previous power elite. Skills alone, even when learned from the most talented mentor, cannot push a disciple through the barriers surrounding elite leadership. Only through personal access, which facilitates contact with other power elite members with the resources to assist or encourage their careers and opportunities, can disciples become elites.

3 Networking within Power Elite Circles

I have made the blanket statement that a power elite, if it is thought of as a group of leaders who through organizational positions and roles are responsible for maintaining societal structures and shaping policies, exists in Mexico. I also maintain that a power elite, defined as individuals *directly* exercising influence in two or more sectors of society, does not exist in Mexico. Evidence for both of these statements is revealed through a careful exploration of elite networks.

Students examining the interrelationship between decision making and power elites argue that "access is the single most important resource in decision making."[1] How power elites achieve that level of access is crucial to understanding their structures, especially those structures not represented in established institutional ties, which are relatively transparent. Students of "power" structures argue that the personal networks which exist within them, and the location of actors in the networks, affect the exchange of information and resources which influence individual and group objectives.[2] In small groups, it has been suggested that frequent contact leads to development of a subculture—"a set of values and ways of solving shared problems . . ."[3]

It is often forgotten that information and influence are inextricably linked. It has been suggested that "differences in the distribution of knowl-

1. John Higley et al., "Elite Integration in Stable Democracies: A Reconsideration," *European Sociological Review*, 7, no. 1 (May 1991), 47.
2. David Knoke, "Networks of Elite Structure and Decision Making," in Stanley Wasserman and Joseph Galaskiewicz, eds., *Advances in Social Network Analysis* (Thousand Oaks: Sage, 1994), 290.
3. Michael P. Farrell, "Artists' Circles and the Development of Artists," *Small Group Behavior*, 13, no. 4 (November 1982), 452.

edge are a source of power, and power may be used to generate and maintain differences in the distribution of knowledge. Knowledge, then, is a scarce resource."[4] Networking within and between power elites contributes to sharing information, and that activity, with the exception of mentoring, is its major contribution. Of course, networking produces other, sometimes unique consequences. According to Ferdinand Kroh, East German elites used it to great advantage to survive the dismantling of socialism.[5]

Chapter 1 makes it clear that individuals do not hold influential positions in multiple sectors. This does not mean that elites are not closely linked to others *within* their own spheres of responsibility, but only to other circles of influence. The general literature on the formation of these linkages, which has come to be known in sociology and in the popular vernacular as networking, has been tested empirically by academics largely on the basis of institutional, positional points of contacts.

Here again, the North American bias toward institutional analysis contributes to a profound theoretical lacuna in measuring and understanding networking in other cultures. Gwen Moore, who has contributed substantially to advancing our knowledge of networking among elites, argues that personal interaction is probably "the crucial dimension" of their integration, and that understanding the actual structure of elite networks is a central concern in assessing elite cohesion.[6] Many points of contact in other societies may not occur on the basis of assigned organizational positions. A recent study of the Soviet Union which examines twenty regional first secretaries demonstrates the interconnectedness of informal ties to organizational positions, and their policy consequences.[7]

Institutional linkages are important for Mexican elite and non-elite networking, but other, *informal channels* are also important. Family, friends, place, and shared educational experiences, or combinations of those variables, frequently substitute for institutional and other more visible formal forms of networking, the most common of which would be career contacts within the same organization. Among the most careful students of American elites, Philip Burch recognizes this acute limitation:

4. Albert Hunter, "Local Knowledge and Local Power," *Journal of Contemporary Ethnography,* 22, no. 1 (April 1993), 36.
5. "Cliques and Old Boy Networks: Power Retention Strategies of the Former East German Power Elite," *Aussenpolitik,* 43, no. 2 (1992), 144–52.
6. Gwen Moore, "The Structure of a National Elite Network," *American Sociological Review,* 44 (October 1979), 674.
7. Gerald M. Easter, *Reconstructing the State: Personal Networks and Elite Identity in Soviet Russia* (Cambridge: Cambridge University Press, 2000).

One matter that is often slighted in elite studies is that of key family and kinship ties. There are very few references to such links in the general literature on the subject, certainly not in the work of Keller, Lasswell (and his research associates), and, surprisingly, even Bottomore. Indeed, if one looks at the essentially sociological analysis of C. Wright Mills and most other scholars, one searches in vain for any examination of kinship ties among elite figures in American business and government.[8]

Recent students of elite networks view their structures as overlapping circles. These researchers have used numerous organizational positions to test their assumptions in post-industrial societies, discovering a core of tightly interconnected individuals from each circle, in close contact with other elites inside and beyond their immediate circle and group.[9] This description fits the Mexican case nicely; it is essential to understand the relations and interactions among various elite groups.

The importance of additional contacts among Mexico's power elite can be illustrated in the linkages identified by a single power elite member. This individual examined the names of all other (397) individuals representative of Mexico's power elite from 1970 through 2000. Based on his age, elite category (intellectual), family background (middle class), and prominence within his own category, this person potentially had only average access to fellow power elite members. I asked this respondent three questions: Did he know the person listed, how strong was their relationship, and by what means was their relationship initially established?

The answers are remarkable for the insights they provide about elite leadership in Mexico. To what degree is Mexico's power elite linked through personal friendship? Our single respondent actually knew 117 of the 397 other members of Mexico's power elite, or 29 percent. This overall percentage would be typical for someone from the intellectual and capitalist elite, larger than the response from a religious elite, and smaller than that of the average political elite. Of these individuals, he described his friendship with 8 percent of them as strong, 28 percent of them as moderate, and 64 percent as weak. Within his own elite group, intellectuals, he personally knew nearly half of his peers. Even more remarkable, he knew nearly a third of Mexico's leading capitalists and more than half of the most influential politicians of his time. Two groups remained very much

8. Philip Burch, *Elites in American History,* 1 (New York: Holmes and Meier, 1981), p. 25.
9. John Higley et al., "Elite Integration in Stable Democracies," 39–45.

outside the purview of his personal networking circle: clergy and the military, of whom he only knew 4 percent.

The only other study that closely examines elite networking on a personal level is that carried out by Frank Bonilla and his associates in Venezuela. They obtained information on 164 individuals across occupational categories. The average person in that group claimed to know 89 percent of his fellow elites, one fourth of whom were friends. The elite giving the lowest response was 46 of 164.[10] These higher percentages for Venezuela are not surprising given its much smaller general population and the date of the survey.

Our respondent's sources of friendship break down into six categories: career posts (organizational bureaucracies), civic positions (voluntary organizations), family, social, education, and place (usually childhood residence). For our respondent, these responses reveal that career was most important, providing 41 percent of his contacts, followed by social at 24 percent, family at 19 percent, and civic and educational sources responsible for 8 and 7 percent, respectively. If we combine together the institutional positional sources used in most networking analysis (career and civic) in postmodern societies, it is apparent that they provide only half of this person's important contacts to other power elites.

This individual's responses reinforce the importance of non-institutional networking as an alternate channel of contact between and among Mexican power elites. It is definitely the case that influential Mexicans do not occupy formal positions of influence in multiple areas of power elite responsibility, at least as I have conceptualized them in this study. It is also true that without occupying such organizational positions, many elite Mexicans are able through informal networking in non-organizational channels to express their views. Indirectly, they exercise an influence on their society's values and policy.

The existence of such contacts and venues for discussion does not prove that Mexicans are using that access to influence policy.[11] But studies of the United States, the United Kingdom, and Germany demonstrate that political, social, and business leaders with extensive interpersonal networks are more influential and active in the formation of national policy than peers without such networks.[12]

10. Allan Kessler, "The Internal Structure of Elites," in Frank Bonilla and José Silva Michelena, eds., *A Strategy for Research on Social Policy, Vol. 1: The Politics of Change in Venezuela* (Cambridge: MIT Press, 1967), 230.

11. David Knoke, "Networks of Elite Structure and Decision Making," 276.

12. Gwen Moore, "Women in the Old-Boy Network: The Case of New York

INFORMAL NETWORKING SOURCES
WITHIN POWER ELITE GROUPS

The single example above only suggests the probable interconnectedness of Mexico's power elite. It is important to evaluate linkages collectively to determine the extent of similar networking sources among all power elites. For example, analysis of the sources of networking among Mexican capitalists reveals that they network as frequently through *informal* linkages, such as family, often initiated by an influential mentor, as they do through *formal* organizational or institutional linkages. (See table 5.) Family and social friendships are networking sources which play a significant role in the way individuals are linked to each other. Can this frequent pattern of networking in Mexico be explained?

Networking through kinship ties occurs more commonly among Mexican capitalists than among any of the four other power elite groups. This is also likely to be the case in Brazil or the United States. Two explanations stand out. In the Mexican, Brazilian, and (to a lesser extent) American examples, top business leaders, especially capitalists—Bill Gates prototypes aside—were raised in upper-class business families. Michael Useem reports that the inner group of American executives is "disproportionately drawn from the ranks of the wealthy and from among financial executives."[13] As Domhoff suggests, business families comprised only a tiny fraction of the families of the era.[14]

Among leading Mexican capitalists, 60 percent came from wealthy families, a group which accounts for fewer than 6 percent of the parents of all other power elites combined. In the United States, only half as many capitalists came from families in possession of large wealth.[15] Because Mexican capitalists so often follow in the footsteps of their parents and grandpar-

---

State Government," in G. William Domhoff and Thomas R. Dye, eds., *Power Elites and Organizations* (Beverly Hills: Sage, 1987), 65.

13. Michael Useem, "The Inner Group of the American Capitalist Class," *Social Problems*, 25 (1978), 237.

14. G. William Domhoff, *Power Structure Research* (Beverly Hills: Sage, 1980), 67. The classic, most detailed work of the social origins of American businessmen concluded that in the 1930s 10 percent of the American population produced 70 percent of its business leaders. See Carl S. Joslyn and Frank Taussig, *American Business Leaders: A Study of Social Origins and Social Stratification* (New York: Macmillan, 1932), 241.

15. Allen H. Barton, "Background, Attitudes and Activities of American Elites," in Gwen Moore, ed., *Studies of the Structure of National Elite Groups*, 1 (Greenwich: JAI, 1985), 182.

Table 5. Power Elite Networking Sources
among Capitalists

Source of Contacts	Known Sources (%)
Family	45
Corporate Boards	37
Business Partnerships	7
Career	4
Educational Institutions	3
Civic Organizations	2
Social Engagements	2

NOTE: Based on 299 known networking contacts among the 100 leading capitalists in the power elite database (N = 398). *Family* refers to a
networking relationship established within the immediate family, including power elites who were grandparents, siblings, in-laws, aunts and uncles, or parents. *Corporate Boards* refers to holding a position simultaneously on a corporate board with another power elite. *Business
Partnerships* refers to two members of a power elite co-founding a business together. *Career* refers to a networking contact which took place in
an occupational setting, typically between two individuals working in an
organizational bureaucracy, often in a superior-subordinate relationship.
Educational Institutions refers to a networking contact which occurred
in any educational setting, typically between a student and a professor,
between any two students, or between professorial peers. *Civic Organizations* refers to two power elites making contact in voluntary organizations. *Social Engagements* refers to power elites meeting in a social
setting, such as a party or country club.

ents, whom they typically identify as their mentors, taking over well-
established family firms, they are more likely to share those resources with
extended family members and with other capitalist families. Peter Mc-
Donough found this pattern in Brazil, where businessmen were more
likely than other elites to come from prominent industrial and banking
families, what he called a "father-to-son quality" in the transmission of
class.[16]

A second explanation for the importance of family networking among
capitalist power elites is that a huge majority of leading firms are closely
held by Mexican families. The multi-generational control of families over
Mexico's most powerful financial institutions and corporations exaggerates
the importance of family ties as a means of networking with other capitalist

16. *Power and Ideology in Brazil* (Princeton: Princeton University Press, 1981),
59.

figures. It is fair to say that the ownership structure affects the source of networking.

A third reason for the importance of family networking among capitalists is the multiple linkages among social class origins, elite club memberships, corporate board memberships, and status as leading capitalists. Useem discovered that the inner circle of American capitalists, defined by the number of corporations on whose boards they served, was "two or three times more likely to be drawn into club life than business leaders attached to a single company."[17] He also found that these capitalists had "more cohesion than other members of the capitalist class as measured by their acquaintanceship networks in exclusive social clubs."[18] In turn, upper social class status among American business elites is best measured by their membership in elite clubs.[19]

Mexican capitalists not only come from wealthy backgrounds, but almost exclusively from fathers who were wealthy or upper-middle-class businessmen. Among all the power elites who were capitalists (sixty-three), all but five had children who became capitalist members of Mexico's power elite.[20]

Club memberships among leading Mexicans are difficult to come by. But even a largely incomplete listing of capitalists alone suggests the potential for contact among wealthy Mexicans. Raúl Bailleres, a co-founder of the Bankers Club and mentor to other leading capitalists, met friends on a regular basis to play canasta until 7:00 or 8:00 in the evening.[21] Mex-

17. Michael Useem, "The Inner Circle and the Political Voice of Business," in Michael Schwartz, ed., *The Structure of Power in America: The Corporate Elite as a Ruling Class* (New York: Holmes and Meier, 1987), 148.

18. Michael Useem, "The Inner Circle and the Political Voice of Business," 237; according to G. William Domhoff, research in sociology and social psychology demonstrates that constant interaction in small-group settings leads to social cohesion. *Power Structure Research,* 50. In the only in-depth sociological study of America's wealthy class, Edward D. Baltzell explains how the linkage between wealth, influence, and exclusive club memberships came about in the first half of the twentieth century. *Philadelphia Gentleman: The Making of a National Upper Class* (Glencoe: Free Press, 1958), 385.

19. Allen H. Barton, "Determinants of Economic Attitudes in the American Business Elite," *American Journal of Sociology,* 91 (1985), 72.

20. Suzanne Infield Keller's comprehensive *The Social Origins and Career Lines of Three Generations of American Business Leaders* (New York: Arno Press, 1980), 150, concluded that "the sons of men who had themselves been businessmen had a greater number of channels through which they could enter the world of big business."

21. *Expansión,* April 13, 1994, 38. Anibal de Iturbide Preciat, a member of the

ican capitalists who work together on corporate boards and socialize through their professional and social clubs establish closer personal contacts and expand their range of personal networks beyond the day-to-day corporate setting. Leading capitalists in Mexico's top regional centers, such as Monterrey, also share numerous memberships in locally prominent clubs. In fact, one of Mexico's largest banking chains, Bancomer, was originally founded by a capitalist after conversations with various friends at the Casino of Chihuahua, the leading social club in this economically important northern state.[22]

Given the social background of Mexican capitalists and the ownership structure of Mexican firms, are the informal networking ties of Mexican capitalists and mentors exceptional in their extensiveness, or do the other four groups share some of these same characteristics? To what extent are ties within each of the five groups based on informal linkages, and what explains differences among each of the groups?

The group about which the most extensive networking data are available are power elite politicians. I was able to trace more than 500 networking sources among these politicians. The data in table 6 reveal important differences in the networking sources of capitalists and politicians. In the first place, informal friendships account for an overwhelming proportion of the networking contacts among politicians. Friendships established in a school setting between fellow students or students and professors alone are responsible for nearly two-thirds of those contacts. In interviews and memoirs, politicians identified the vast majority of these professors as influential mentors. Kinship ties within the immediate family provide a much smaller networking source among political figures, only one eighth the number of influential family ties that existed among capitalists.

What is important to keep in mind about the universe of top politicians' networking sources is that informal linkages through family and friendship combined account for seven out of ten contacts, while positions in formal organizations, political and civic, account for fewer than a third of

---

power elite and one of Mexico's most prominent bankers in the twentieth century, went to work as an office boy at Equitable Trust of New York, in Mexico City, where Bailleres was employed. Bailleres was nine years older than de Iturbide Preciat, and after he founded the Banco de Comercio, de Iturbide Preciat became the bank's general accountant and then general manager. They remained intimate friends until Bailleres's death in 1967.

22. The individual was Eloy S. Vallina. See his biography, José Fuentes Mares, *Don Eloy S. Vallina* (Mexico City: Editorial Jus, 1968), 49–50.

Table 6. Power Elite Networking Sources among Politicians

Source of Contacts	Known Sources (%)
Educational Institutions	61
Career	28
Family	7
Social Engagements	2
Civic Organizations	2

NOTE: Based on 510 known networking contacts among 100 leading politicians in the power elite database ($N = 398$). *Educational Institutions* refers to a networking contact which occurred in any educational setting, typically between a student and a professor, between any two students, or between professorial peers. *Career* refers to a networking contact which took place in an occupational setting, typically between two individuals working in an organizational bureaucracy, often in a superior-subordinate relationship. *Family* refers to a networking relationship established within the immediate family, including power elites who were grandparents, siblings, in-laws, aunts and uncles, or parents. *Social Engagements* refers to power elites meeting in a social setting, such as a party or country club. *Civic Organizations* refers to two power elites making contact in voluntary organizations.

those sources. Moore found this pattern to be true of women government administrators in the United States.[23]

Family is much less important as an informal source of contact among politicians than among capitalists because politicians do not come from wealthy families, and wealth does not determine the acquisition of influential positions among the political elite. Political elites begin networking when they are young, and these networking contacts are reinforced through social and professional relationships throughout their careers. Ex-president Luis Echeverría Alvarez recently commented on his personal experience: "I graduated as a lawyer with a companion who always was an exemplary student, who is one of the best lawyers in Mexico, Arsenio Farell Cubillas, whom I have known since high school, along with another very distinguished Mexican, Luis E. Bracamontes, who favored me with his collaboration as my secretary of public works and since the first year of high school I could observe them as exemplary students."[24]

The stellar example of political power elite networking through adolescent contacts in high school and college is that of former president Miguel

23. Gwen Moore, "Women in the Old-Boy Network: The Case of New York State Government," 71, 83.

24. *Excélsior*, March 17, 1997, A1. Both Farell and Bracamontes are members of the power elite sample.

de la Madrid, who could claim friendships with one-tenth of his fellow political elites on the basis of school-crafted social ties. Four of those friendships occurred in the classroom as a student of President José López Portillo, his predecessor, political mentor, and the individual who designated de la Madrid as his successor; Jesús Reyes Heroles, an intellectual mentor who served as de la Madrid's secretary of public education; José Campillo Saínz, who directed the federal housing program during his administration; and Hugo B. Margáin, under whom the president served when Margáin was treasury secretary in the 1970s.[25] De la Madrid taught a fifth member of the power elite, his successor and political disciple, former president Carlos Salinas de Gortari. The remaining five were schoolmates, two of them from preparatory school. This educational networking pattern was replicated by presidents José López Portillo and Carlos Salinas de Gortari.

Such networking contacts are not confined to future presidents. An elite who presided over the Institutional Revolutionary Party as president and served in three cabinet posts in the 1970s and 1980s recalls crucial friendships from his high school and college days:

> I completed my secondary and preparatory at the National Autonomous University of Mexico [UNAM] schools. I was only sixteen years old when I began my first year at *prepa* [National Preparatory School, ENP], and therefore seventeen when I graduated. Mario Moya Palencia [power elite member], who was six months older, came from CUM [Centro Universitario de México]. José Juan de Olloqui [ambassador to the United States] came from a school in New Orleans, and Carlos Fuentes [power elite member] enrolled too, but from a school abroad, and Carlos del Río, the president of the supreme court, was part of our group.[26] Other ENP students included Patrocinio González Blanco [power elite member], Jorge de la Vega Domínguez [power elite member], Carlos Jongitud Barrios [power elite member], and Pedro Vázquez Colmenares, governor of Oaxaca.
>
> The students from CUM arrived with a stronger discipline for studying than those of us from ENP. They were a good generation, but they were not the best students. In terms of overall cultural preparation and ability, the teachers at ENP were better than those from CUM. Other schools which were important, but much smaller, included the Colegio Aleman, which was even more disciplined. The Colegio de Francés Morelos is the antecedent to CUM, and was

25. Personal interview with Miguel de la Madrid, Mexico City, July 20, 1984.
26. Interestingly, Carlos Fuentes and Miguel Alemán Jr., who have been friends since their school days, are also connected through their fathers, who both attended the Ramos sisters' private school in Veracruz when they were children in the 1900s.

converted in 1948. Other CUM students included Porfirio Muñóz Ledo [power elite member] and Miguel Alemán [power elite member].

The law school really was a mixing pot for students from the different preparatory backgrounds, rich and poor alike. It was an influential social experience. We had students who barely had anything to eat. The legal texts we used weren't great, but passable. During the first year at law school [1950], we did not mix very well with the students from CUM. Part of the explanation was physical proximity. The old ENP was across the street from the law school. So we already knew some of the people from law school and felt comfortable. A unifying factor in our generation was the *Medio Siglo* publication, which brought many people together, including Sergio García Ramírez [power elite member], Miguel González Avelar [secretary of public education], and others.[27]

Intellectuals in the Mexican power elite share certain similarities with politicians in the way in which they meet each other. (See table 7.) Like politicians, intellectuals seldom meet through civic organizations and family. Most establish friendships through education, through collaboration on intellectual journals, many of which were initiated at the university, and through career contacts. Most of the "career" contacts occur in the publishing world, between editors and authors, among newspaper editors, reporters and editorial writers, or between general editors and editors of cultural supplements to influential newspapers.[28] Many of these editors served as mentors to younger intellectuals. The other large percentage of professional contacts occur in higher education among intellectuals who teach, the vast majority at the National University or at the smaller, more cohesive Colegio de México.

The importance of education as a locus of intellectual networking and mentoring in Mexico is not surprising, given the extent of intellectuals' involvement in higher education. What is significant about the structure

27. Personal interview with Pedro Ojeda Paullada, Mexico City, December 14, 1998.

28. The classic example of such contacts can be found in Carlos Fuentes's career, even though many of his networking relationships were cemented in school, at the Colegio Francés Morelos and at UNAM. But Fuentes, even in school, reinforced strong friendships through student publications, in his teens. He was the co-founder and editor of the *Revista Mexicana de Literatura* in 1956 with Emmanuel Carballo (power elite member), co-editor of *El Espectador* in 1959 with Luis Villoro and Jaime García Térres (power elite members), and editor of *Política* in 1960 with Fernando Benítez and David Alfaro Siqueiros (power elite members) and numerous other cultural elites. See my *Intellectuals and the State in Twentieth Century Mexico* (Austin: University of Texas Press, 1985), 138 ff.

Table 7. Power Elite Networking Sources
among Intellectuals

Source of Contacts	Known Sources (%)
Career	33
Journal Staffs	31
Educational Institutions	22
Social Engagements	6
Family	6
Civic Organizations	2

NOTE: Based on 270 known networking contacts among the 50 leading intellectuals in our power elite database ($N = 398$). *Career* refers to
a networking contact which took place in an occupational setting, typically between two individuals working in an organizational bureaucracy,
often in a superior-subordinate relationship. *Journal Staffs* refers to networking contacts through joint positions on editorial boards or magazine
staffs. *Educational Institutions* refers to a networking contact which occurred in any educational setting, typically between a student and a professor, between any two students, or between professorial peers. *Social
Engagements* refers to power elites meeting in a social setting, such as a
party or country club. *Family* refers to a networking relationship established within the immediate family, including power elites who were
grandparents, siblings, in-laws, aunts and uncles, or parents. *Civic Organizations* refers to two power elites making contact in voluntary organizations.

of education for intellectual networking is that it serves as the primary
source for friendships established between students and between students
and professors, for intellectual collaboration, for the creation of cultural
publications (whose founders join together in successive enterprises at later
points in their careers), and for institutional career contacts as college professors.

The two groups among Mexico's power elite who operate within the
most institutionalized structured setting are military officers and the
clergy. The military is the most difficult Mexican group to research, when
it comes to establishing accurate networking linkages, because officers
rarely discuss their careers publicly and they purposely avoid making career data, especially the dates of their activities, available.[29] Keeping in
mind the limitations secrecy produces, it is possible to examine the im-

29. For example, in the five official government biographical directories published from 1984 through 1994, after which they were discontinued, unlike the
hundreds of civilian politicians included, positions held by officers are not set off
by the dates they held these posts. See *Diccionario biográfico del gobierno mexicano* (Mexico City: Presidencia de la República, 1984, 1987, 1989, 1992, 1994).

portance of educational experiences and professional career contacts as two important sources of friendship among military power elites.

Exploring just the networking connections among each of the national defense secretaries and the naval secretary during the last three decades reveals their impact as mentors and the influence of shared educational experiences and staff career experiences at national headquarters. The pattern is similar in both services. The Heroico Colegio Naval Militar Antón Lizardo in Veracruz (HCN) performs the same role among top naval personnel as does the Heroico Colegio Militar (HCM) and the Escuela Superior de Guerra (ESG) for the army and air force. The difference between the two services is that the navy has two academies which recruit cadets for career military service, one in Mazatlán and the other in Veracruz. Both are well represented in the careers of top naval officers, but the fact that the naval officer corps is quite small and that cadets are divided between two schools means that graduates from respective individual generations are acquainted with all of their peers.

Top military officers are also linked through their professional training. Air force officers are enrolled in the Escuela Superior de Guerra, where they come to know their army colleagues. Naval and army officers come to know each other during lengthy joint training missions as cadets and junior officers.[30] Perhaps the most important link among all three services occurs among those navy, army, and air force officers at the rank of colonel or higher (or its equivalent) who are selected for the one-year course at the Colegio de Defensa Nacional. Since 1982 their classes have rarely exceed two dozen officers, and each individual selected is on a fast track to two- and three-star rank.

Educational networking (66 percent) appears to be more common than career linkages (34 percent) in an analysis of top officers, but this may be a consequence of the paucity of available information rather than reflecting actual contacts. It may also be explained by the fact that the "average Latin American military professional, since World War II, spends more of his or her career attending professional schools than any world counterpart."[31] Extracurricular activities also contribute to extensive contacts at the Her-

30. For example, Admiral Mario Artigas Fernández, commander of the training ship *California*, met division general Antonio Ramírez Barrera when Ramírez Barrera was assigned to sister ship *Tehuantepec*, as an Escuela Superior de Guerra student during a long mission in 1965. See Enrique Cárdenas de la Peña, *Educación naval en México*, 2 (Mexico City: Secretaria de la Marina, 1967).

31. Russell W. Ramsey, "Forty Years of Human Rights Training," *Journal of Low Intensity Conflict and Law Enforcement*, 4, no. 2 (autumn 1995), 255.

oico Colegio Militar. The American-style football teams of 1928–31 and 1934–38 produced many future leaders in the army, and three of these officers are in the power elite.[32]

What is apparent about subordinate–superior relationships among officers who reach the power elite in the military is that the vast majority occur in staff positions at the secretariat of national defense or through the presidential *estado mayor* (presidential military staff). These contacts are more frequent in the career networking of influential officers in part because such posts are considered plum assignments, and officers whose careers concentrate in staff rather than field positions in the forty-one military zone commands are promoted at faster rates and reach more influential commands.[33]

To illustrate the importance of staff duty in the networking among the 100 officers in the power elite, I have created a chronological listing of the known national defense staff assignments among Mexico's leading army officers What is apparent from this list is the high proportion of top officers who have held these posts early and midway through their careers, and the importance of specific staff assignments, primarily section 1 (personnel), section 2 (intelligence), section 3 (operations), and section 5 (plans).

Mexico's top clergy share certain structural characteristics with the inner core of the officer corps. They are typically trained within their own educational institutions, and spend their careers within a closed bureaucracy largely populated by their fellow priests. This is equally true elsewhere in the region, for example in Colombia and Venezuela.[34] They are almost always mentored by an older fellow bishop. But, contrary to popular belief, many structural elements exist within the Catholic Church which facilitate decentralization in the clergy's preparation and institutional advancement. For example, if one were to look for networking linkages among top bishops in the curia in Mexico City, the search would be in vain.[35]

32. They are generals José Moguel Cal y Mayor, Salvador Revueltas Olvera, and Julio Monroy Aguila. See *Revista de Ejército y Fuerza Aérea* (January 1987), 23–26.

33. Roderic Ai Camp, *Generals in the Palacio: The Military in Modern Mexico* (New York: Oxford University Press, 1992), 199 ff.

34. See Robert H. Levine's outstanding study, *Religion and Politics in Latin America: The Catholic Church in Venezuela and Colombia* (Princeton: Princeton University Press, 1981), 103.

35. Roderic Ai Camp, *Crossing Swords: Politics and Religion in Mexico* (New York: Oxford University Press, 1997), 185.

Most bishops spend their entire careers in one or two, and rarely more than in three or four, dioceses. Their institutional or organizational careers within the church bureaucracy, therefore, occur among regional dioceses. The dominant organization setting which provides potential networking linkages before priests become bishops are the seminaries. Members of the clergy, like politicians and intellectuals, establish life-long friendships with each other as well as with professors, administrators, and even their bishop, as young students in their local seminaries.

The seminary becomes the locus of important networking among future bishops because careers which are concentrated inside the Catholic educational structure dominate the career backgrounds of bishops generally. More than half of all Mexican bishops born after 1920 concentrated their priestly endeavors in education. For example, José Salazar López, cardinal archbishop of Guadalajara from 1973 to 1987 and president of the Conference of Mexican Bishops from 1973 to 1982, attended the seminary of Guadalajara in the 1920s and then served as a professor and administrator from 1934 to 1960, when he was appointed bishop.[36]

The Catholic clergy is at a disadvantage in facilitating these ties in comparison to its peers in the military, politics, and intellectual life, because their early education is so geographically dispersed among numerous diocesan seminaries. However, this dispersion is balanced by the fact that many leading religious figures represented in the power elite were educated or taught at several regional seminaries, notably Guadalajara, Morelia, and Puebla. Prominent clergy also attended the interdiocesan seminary at Montezuma, New Mexico, and the prestigious Gregorian University in Rome, both unifying mechanisms for drawing together priests across the republic.[37] A similar pattern can be found among North American archbishops and cardinals, the vast majority of whom were graduates of the Gregorian University.[38]

The clergy at Montezuma, because of its geographic isolation from any American community, did not absorb experiences from the United States

36. *Diccionario Porrúa: Historia, biografía y geografía de México* (Mexico City: Porrúa, 1995), 3062.

37. For evidence of these ties at Montezuma, see Luis Medina Ascencio, *Historia del Seminario de Montezuma: Sus precedentes, fundación y consolidación, 1910–1953* (Mexico City: Editorial Jus, 1962), and José Macías, *Montezuma en sus exalumnos: 1937–1962* (Mexico City, 1962).

38. Thomas Reese, *Archbishop: Inside the Power Structure of the American Catholic Church* (New York: Harper and Row, 1989), 78.

culture. As the bishop of Aguascalientes recalled, "to be a long way from your country and family does engender a fraternal relationship and unity among companions from other dioceses of the republic, but we didn't have many ties to the United States or other countries. Our values about society were not affected by the social context; our professors did impart clear and firm principles which allowed us to have a clear vision of our mission and our role within society."[39]

The students attending the Gregorian University were able to extend their networking ties to priests from other theological colleges, including those operated by various religious orders, as well as to priests from other countries, contributing to extensive collaboration in Latin American episcopal organizations. A bishop who attended the Brothers of Mary college in Rome describes a typical contact with the Gregorian students: "Occasionally I participated in one of the cultural or academic events. In those years I had strong contacts with students from the Colegio Pío Latino Americano, all students at the Greg. All of Latin America was represented except Brazil which had its own Colegio. My strongest contact was with the Mexican seminary students. Many today are bishops. . . . I continue to be in contact with the Mexicans."[40]

Among the fifty bishops in the power elite sample, one out of five spent a number of years in association with the Palafoxian Seminary in the archdiocese of Puebla. As my analysis of their backgrounds illustrates, these influential bishops overlapped with each other as students, professors, administrators, or bishops at this seminary, where they typically established very close relationships. The same is true at the Gregorian University, where more than half of the elite clergy attended, and Montezuma, which graduated one out of four leading bishops.

The range of networking is narrower in these latter two institutions because it is confined essentially to students, since most of the instructors were foreign Jesuits and clergy. One bishop who spent six years in the late 1930s and early 1940s at the Gregorian University and the residence hall of Mexican priests, the Colegio Pío Latino Americano, recalled a universal experience there: ". . . it can be said that in Rome deep friendships began and matured among those who lived in the Pío Latino and the Gregorian which, on returning to our countries or traveling to other nations, were

39. Letter to the author from Bishop Rafael Muñoz Núñez, Aguascalientes Diocese, Aguascalientes, Mexico, December 15, 1997.

40. Letter to the author from Bishop José Rovalo Azcué, Mexico City Diocese, Mexico, May 13, 1997.

very helpful. . . . And of course, the confluence of experiences united those of us who experienced it more closely."[41]

FORMAL NETWORKING WITHIN POWER ELITE GROUPS: THE CASE OF THE INTERLOCKING DIRECTORATE

The fundamental argument of this chapter is that Mexican power elites form networks most typically through informal means. This does not mean, however, that organizational sources of networking are unimportant. They play a crucial but not dominant role.

The most developed literature on formal networking *within* elites is that focused on prominent businesspeople and capitalists in the United States. The most common theoretical approach to testing assumptions about their connections lies with an analysis of corporate board membership. A large literature exists on this "revolving door" quality for the United States, and some of the conclusions are contradictory. Most of the contradictions stem from definitional differences from one study to another.

The findings in this literature suggest three central questions. First, is the ownership of leading firms in the hands of a small capitalist class, or has public ownership (through sales of stock) led to the pluralization of control over economic resources? Second, what constitutes control over corporate decision making? Specifically, what proportion of stock would one need to exercise influence over corporate policies, and who actually owns the stock? Third, what is the composition of corporate boards which determine the broad scope of company policy? Specifically, who are their members, what is their background, whom do they represent, and to what degree do the same individuals control multiple boards?

Why do overlapping board directorships matter? According to Michael Useem, who has explored this issue carefully among American business elites, "few experiences, according to corporate executives, are more useful for current intelligence on the business environment than service on the board of directors of another major corporation," and interlocking directorates "maximizes the flow of information throughout the network."[42] Mexican capitalists are equally beneficiaries of this pattern. The second major consequence, according to analysts, is that the "enormous over-

41. Letter to the author from Bishop Emeritus Manuel Talamás Camandari, Chihuahua, Chihuahua, January 4, 1997.
42. Michael Useem, "The Inner Circle and the Political Voice of Business," 146–47.

representation of financial companies, especially banks, among the most central firms is indicative of the preeminence of financial capital in determining and shaping intercorporate affairs."[43]

Implied in the overrepresentation of banks is a third consequence, that the interlock insures the availability of necessary capital to the firm. This pattern occurred historically because without well-established stock exchanges, family-controlled firms were forced to align themselves with a bank or holding company that could guarantee them the necessary capital.[44] Mexico's stock market did not generate significant sources of capital for major firms until the late 1980s.

A fourth consequence of interlocks is that they produce a significant effect on corporate strategies.[45] For example, a study of interlocking corporations and banks in St. Louis, Missouri reported that interlocking banks were more likely to make loans to corporations and less likely to engage in mortgage lending than unconnected banks.[46] According to a U.S. Federal Trade Commission report, a fifth consequence is that "the existing law on interlocking directorates is inadequate and that interlocks among our great corporations are especially inimical to competition because the economy has become increasingly concentrated among a few hundred corporations."[47]

In the United States, scholars long have assumed that the need for capital gradually led to a dispersion of control away from capitalist families to that of outside investors, both individual and corporate. Analysts agree

43. Beth Mintz and Michael Schwartz, "Corporate Interlocks, Financial Hegemony, and Intercorporate Coordination," in *The Structure of Power in America: The Corporate Elite as a Ruling Class* (New York: Holmes and Meier, 1987), 36, 40.

44. John Scott, "Networks of Corporate Power," *Annual Review of Sociology,* 17 (1991), 191.

45. Joseph Galaskiewicz and Stanley Wasserman, "Social Network Analysis: Concepts, Methodology, and Directions for the 1990s," *Sociological Methods and Research,* 22, no. 1 (August 1993), 16. G. Lowell Field, John Higley, and Michael G. Burton conclude that "firms tend to interlock with firms in sectors *constraining the firm's profits*" [emphasis mine], and "market structure patterns interlock structure and interlocking structures repattern market structure." "In Defense of Elite Theory: A Reply to Cammack," *American Sociological Review,* 55 (June 1990), 433.

46. Mark S. Mizruchi and Joseph Galaskiewicz, "Networks of Interorganizational Relations," *Sociological Methods and Research,* 22, no. 1 (August 1993), 58.

47. United States Senate, Committee on the Judiciary, Subcommittee on Antitrust and Monopoly, *Economic Report on Corporate Mergers* (Washington, D.C.: GPO, 1969), 270.

that any individual or family with 4 to 5 percent of all stock and representation on the board would exert control.[48] As late as the mid-1960s, according to the most comprehensive studies of the United States, of the top 300 industrial corporations, 40 percent, and possibly another 15 percent, were family controlled.[49] In a more recent analysis by *Fortune* magazine, its researchers discovered that of the 500 leading U.S. industrial corporations, 150 were controlled by one or more members of a single family, leading Thomas Dye to conclude that the "disappearance of the traditional American capitalist may have been exaggerated."[50]

In Mexico, we begin with an entirely different set of assumptions about family ownership. In the mid-1980s, of the leading sixty firms and banks, with the exception of publicly and foreign-owned corporations, all (accounting for 65 percent) were controlled by leading capitalist families, all of whom are represented in the present power elite sample.[51] In the last decade and a half, as Mexico's stock market grew rapidly and foreign individuals and firms began to invest heavily in Mexican firms, one would have expected this pattern to decline. This is not the case.

Financial institutions also have played a critical role in Mexican corporate development, but in most cases, banks were founded and controlled by large holding companies or *grupos* controlled by leading capitalist families, a pattern occurring elsewhere in Latin America. Banks were not the source of control. As Francisco Durand points out in Peru, "the more powerful *grupos* exist as highly articulated units administered through entrepreneurial holdings and family ties rather than through banks. Commercial banks, in most cases, are one of the *grupos'* important firms, however, the direction of the *grupo* is not necessarily located in the bank."[52]

There is no question that a small number of individuals and families, fewer than 500 individuals, control an overwhelming percentage of the

48. According to Maurice A. Zeitlin, "the Patman Committee [government appointed] concluded that effective control could be assured with even *less* than a 5 percent holding, 'especially in very large corporations whose stock is widely held.'" Stock which is widely held would rarely be the case in Mexico. "Corporate Ownership and Control: The Large Corporation and the Capitalist Class," *American Journal of Sociology*, 79 (1974), 1087.

49. G. William Domhoff, *Power Structure Research*, 64, citing the work of Philip Burch.

50. *Who's Running America? The Bush Era*, 5th ed. (Englewood Cliffs: Prentice-Hall, 1990), 45.

51. Roderic Ai Camp, *Entrepreneurs and Politics in Twentieth Century Mexico* (New York: Oxford University Press, 1989), 192.

52. Francisco Durand, *Business and Politics in Peru: The State and the National Bourgeoisie* (Boulder: Westview, 1994), 61–62.

GDP in Mexico. For example, in 1998 just ten of the capitalists included in the power elite sample controlled 15 percent of Mexico's GDP and accounted for 25 percent of the net sales of all companies traded on the Mexican stock exchange.[53] In 1989, thirty-seven members of the exclusive capitalist organization the Council of Mexican Businessmen, all but three of whom are included among the power elite, controlled seventy major holding groups representing 22 percent of the GDP and employing 450,000 workers.[54] The concentration of large holding companies increased in the 1990s. Six of the largest 98 firms accounted for 40 percent of total assets, and 50 percent of sales were concentrated in only ten of these firms.[55]

The question of who actually controls the stock is difficult to answer even in the United States, where a lot of information is accessible by law. But as Zeitlin correctly points out, the difficulty lies in discovering the "beneficial owners," not just the "shareholders of record," which are often trusts, holding companies, or foundations controlled by capitalist families.[56] As an illustration of this very problem, Domhoff cites a careful study of the Weyerhauser family in which the investigator discovered many individuals on boards who were not previously known to be family members. He concluded that the family retained control over several other firms previously thought to be publicly owned.[57]

Knowledge of the precise ownership of shares is extremely difficult to come by in Mexico, but sufficient information is available in business magazines and important newspapers to determine that family control of the leading seventy-five firms and banks examined far exceeds the 5 percent figure, and often Mexican family members or individual capitalists retain

53. Araceli Muñoz, "The Men Who Move Mexico: Mexican Wealth is Highly Concentrated," *El Financiero* (international edition), January 5, 1998, 1, 8. They were Carlos Slim Helú, Alfonso Romo Garza, Ricardo Salinas Pliego, Roberto González Barrera, Emilio Azcárraga Jean, Lorenzo Zambrano Treviño, Claudio X. González, Eugenio Garza Laguera, Jerónimo Arango, and Dionisio Garza Sada.

54. Rafael Montesinos Carrera, "Empresarios en el nuevo orden estatal," *El Cotidiano*, 8, no. 50 (September/October 1992), 114.

55. Matilde Luna, "Entrepreneurial Interests and Political Action in Mexico: Facing the Demands of Modernization," in Riordan Roett, ed., *The Challenges of Institutional Reform* (Boulder: Lynne Rienner, 1995), 84–85.

56. Maurice A. Zeitlin, "Corporate Ownership and Control," 1086.

57. G. William Domhoff, *Power Structure Research*, 62. This is reported in the work of Marvin G. Dunn, "The Family Office: Coordinating Mechanism of the Ruling Class," in G. William Domhoff, ed., *Power Structure Research* (Beverly Hills: Sage, 1980), 17–46.

50 percent or more of a firm's stock. For some of these firms, no public stock has ever been issued.[58]

Who makes up these boards of directors and to what degree are they interlocked? The simplest way of defining an interlocking directorship is when "a particular individual sits on two or more corporate boards. The boards of large enterprises include both internal executives and outside non-executives among their members."[59] But firms may be interlocked in other, often indirect, ways. As Ronald Burt suggests, firms may be linked directly through powerful subsidiaries which they control, or indirectly through financial institutions, which often serve as intermediaries between two firms.[60] In fact, financial institutions play a central role in interlocks, typically have the highest number of interlocks among various corporations, and have become more rather than less influential in this networking process.[61]

United States firms have always been interlocked. For example, in 1905, the directors and managers of the twenty most interlocked companies held 1,221 positions in other firms, an average of sixty-one interlocks per company. By 1964, this average fell to twenty-four. Of the leading firms examined, more than 80 percent shared interlocking board members.[62] In a study by Salzman and Domhoff, 95 percent of 201 corporations examined were linked at least once, and 82 percent were linked to at least five other companies in their sample.[63]

---

58. Based on a detailed analysis of official annual reports, including board membership, and published accounts of individual ownership.

59. John Scott, "Networks of Corporate Power," *Annual Review of Sociology,* 17 (1991), 182.

60. Ronald S. Burt, "A Structural Theory of Interlocking Corporate Directorates," *Social Networks,* 1 (1979), 433.

61. Michael P. Allen, "The Structure of Interorganizational Elite Cooptation: Interlocking Corporate Directorates," *American Sociological Review* 39 (June 1974), 403; Beth Mintz and Michael Schwartz, "Corporate Interlocks, Financial Hegemony, and Intercorporate Coordination"; and John A. Sonquist and Thomas Koenig, "Interlocking Directorates in the Top U.S. Corporations: A Graph Theory Approach," *The Insurgent Sociologist,* 5, no. 3 (spring 1975), 223.

62. David Bunting and Jeffrey Barbour also found that "the percentage of individuals holding multiple positions and the percentage of multiple positions held by single individuals has decreased from 1905 to 1964. We found that the *absolute number of individuals holding multiple positions has remained nearly constant since 1905* [emphasis mine]." The figure they referred to translated into 89 percent of the firms. "Interlocking Directorates in Large American Corporations, 1896–1964," *Business History Review,* 45 (autumn 1971), 323, 335.

63. Harold Salzman and G. William Domhoff, "The Corporate Community

The interlocking directorate patterns found in the United States exist in other countries, both pre- and post-industrial. For example, in Germany, because of specific historic economic conditions, large banks and commercial firms are allied through stockholding, director interlocks, and shared loan consortia.[64] In Japan, numerous coalitions among major corporations also exist. And in Taiwan, extensive business networks are based on intermarried business groups.[65]

To what extent are Mexican firms linked through the same techniques which exist in other countries, and how extensive are these linkages? In my analysis of seventy-five firms which have consistently ranked among Mexico's top 100 from 1970 through 2000, all remained in the hands of prominent capitalists (except for the banking chains, which for a brief period were government owned and operated). Membership on these boards documents extensive ties among that power elite.

Eight of these seventy-five firms were solely owned by a capitalist member of the power elite or had no non-family board members. The remaining 90 percent were controlled by multiple leading capitalist families. Some of Mexico's top capitalists have served on at least eight of these boards, illustrated by banker Agustín F. Legorreta Chauvet, whose grandfather, great-uncle, and father were presidents of Banamex, Mexico's leading private banking chain, and whose brother owns and directs several other of those top companies. Influential bankers are very well represented on most of these boards. These firms would be linked even more strongly through their boards of directors if lists of board members were expanded to include individuals outside the power elite.

Boards of directors obviously function as a significant vehicle for networking among leading Mexican capitalists. Because boards are visible, organizational entities, it is easier to identify relationships represented among those directorships. That is true in the United States as well as in Mexico. Membership on a board, however, especially when the board is controlled by a single capitalist CEO or his immediate family, is not the

---

and Government: Do They Interlock?" in G. William Domhoff, ed., *Power Structure Research* (Beverly Hills: Sage, 1980), 233.

64. Mark S. Mizruchi and Joseph Galaskiewicz, "Networks of Interorganizational Relations," 55.

65. John Scott, "Networks of Corporate Power," 192–93. Generally such groups are more suited to the economically developing world than to the more developed capitalist economies. Harry W. Strachan, *Family and Other Business Groups in Economic Development: The Case of Nicaragua* (New York: Praeger, 1976), 53.

primary source of a personal linkage between the firm owner and board member. Some other connection typically determined initially whether or not a specific individual was selected to serve on that capitalist's board. Serving on the board with other "third party," non-family board members provides a significant channel through which family and non-family board members alike could link up with each other.

The 299 sources of networking among Mexico's capitalist power elite presented in table 5 can be categorized into seven types of contacts: educational (typically school friends), partners (invested together in establishing a firm), board members (serving on a co-elite's board), family (related to or relative connected to another elite member), civic (involved together in a civic task or organization, such as founding a university), social (friendship through other settings), and career (superior-subordinate relationship between employer and employee). These categories were developed to suggest the importance of distinct types of networking linkages and to provide useful comparisons across elite groups.

Service on a board of directors accounts for a third of the known ties occurring among Mexican capitalists. Family ties, including spouses and in-laws, first cousins, uncles and aunts, parents, and grandparents, account for 45 percent of all capitalists' ties. Pure business relationships, either between partners or among individuals who work together in the same firm, explain only a small portion of the networking sources, and friendship, developed most commonly through early years in preparatory school and college or on civic boards, is responsible for the remaining contacts.

Sometimes these networking sources are combined. For example, the long-time CEO of Grupo Condumex, a major holding company in the 1970s, is the brother-in-law of a significant stockholder in Grupo Modelo, a leading beer manufacturer. But the CEO met his future spouse while he and his future brother-in-law were students at the National University in the 1930s. Both also studied under a prominent mentor to numerous influential politicians, intellectuals, and capitalists.[66] Thus, their student friendship was the original source of the personal contact, and the CEO cemented the closeness of this tie by marrying his friend's sister. A number

---

66. The two in-laws were Eduardo Prieto López and Juan Sánchez Navarro. The mentor was Manuel Gómez Morín. Gómez Morín and Sánchez Navarro later founded a business together, and Prieto López and Sánchez Navarro founded the Industrialists Club in Mexico City, one of the most influential sources of social contacts among capitalists. See *Proceso*, August 10, 1997, and Elvira Conchiero, *El gran acuerdo: Gobierno y empresarios en la modernización salinista* (Mexico City: ERA, 1996), 105.

of prominent figures also established ties to other figures through their parents, and even in one case, a grandparent. The CEO of Industrias Peñoles, one of the top thirty companies in Mexico in the 1990s, was connected to the late CEO of Banco Comermex, through his mentor and father, the Comermex CEO's business partner in the 1950s.[67]

As numerous examples illustrate, networking contacts within Mexico's power elite occur both formally and informally. A critical actor in establishing these relationships is the mentor. The emphasis of American theorists on organizational networking in studies of the United States and postindustrial Europe, while significant, overlooks a huge portion of networking sources in other societies, and perhaps even in the United States.

Studies of American elites cannot tell us with any certainty that organizations, specifically positions within institutions in the private, public, and civic sectors, are the most important sources of networking contacts. They can only suggest that in the measurement of institutional sources, typically positions held in formal organizations, the frequency of elite contacts within and between leadership groups transpires at a specific rate.

Given the fact that nearly all major studies rely on organizations as their only means of measuring networking contacts, they convey the impression in the literature that these are without question the most important networking sources, reinforcing an emphasis on institutional studies. It is apparent that scholarship has pursued this institutional channel because it is the easiest approach, although it too requires substantial, time-consuming research to support its conclusions. This research strategy, while understandable, is quite unfortunate because it has led to erroneous assumptions when applied to other cultures, and as Burch suggests, may well be equally misleading in American elite studies.

The analysis of networking sources within leading Mexican power elite groups suggests several significant findings. First, as we have seen from the Mexican power elite sample, organizational positions do not account for the majority of identifiable networking sources among elites. Networking sources are quite varied, and formal positional linkages, while influential, are not dominant. Indeed, while numerous networking connections within organizations can be established among power elites, those linkages may not be the original source of the networking contact.

67. Alberto Bailleres Gonzalez, CEO of Industrias Peñoles, and Carlos Trouyet, a major stockholder in Banco Comermex. *Expansión*, April 13, 1994, 34.

Second, by ignoring the more subjective, informal ties, organizational networking theorists imply that formal positions are the only source of personal networks. These theorists have not assumed the existence of other sources of networking, and therefore have not pursued a substantive strategy of eliminating various networking settings and actors.

It follows that extensive efforts to illustrate formal networking ties and economic interlocks through an analysis of boards of directors, while proving the potential influence of the interlock, *do not necessarily explain the network source.* The assumption is that two individuals serving on the same board are linked or potentially linked in a shared organizational network. The actual determinant of their network tie may not have been the board membership but a prior contact, informal or formal, often facilitated by a mentor, which led to their being appointed to a particular board. Specific individuals are not appointed to influential boards just because they have identifiable economic credentials, but because they are known to someone on that board through another means of contact.

A position on the same board does not preclude contact stemming from some other board or corporate position, but the actual source of the contact also could be a social friendship, one which occurred through a shared mentor, a mutual friend, a family member, an educational experience, or even a specific event shared by any two individuals (military service, political activity, etc.).

Third, a comparative analysis of corporate board membership, as an illustration of formal networking ties within a power elite, does reveal significant similarities among Mexican, North American, and other countries' corporate leaders. In fact, it suggests that in countries similar to Mexico, where corporate financial control is not as widely dispersed as in the United States, board positions facilitate extensive contacts among capitalist elites. Those contacts are more extensive in Mexico than in the United States.

Fourth, the key actor in facilitating informal and formal networking ties in Mexico is the mentor. As we have seen, a mentor may be a successful professional in the same career field, may be an influential leader who comes directly from an individual's family, or even a future elite's teacher. Because mentors have been ignored in the examination of elites, especially from a theoretical perspective, almost no evidence exists to assess their comparative role and their importance in other societal settings. This theoretical gap is even greater than the theoretical blindness to informal networking sources.

The argument can be made that the reasons for this theoretical lacunae in mentorship and informal networking sources are complementary. Mentors are self-appointed, and therefore are informal actors. Because they often come into contact with their disciples through less formal settings than holding peer positions in an institution, they are difficult to identify without examining personal memoirs, perusing published interviews, or establishing direct contact with the elite subject.

The fourth broad conclusion from the examination of power elite networking *within* each of the Mexican groups is that the peculiar structures of each group strongly flavor the nature of the networking source. As we have seen, the wealthy family backgrounds of capitalists, and the degree of family control over the most powerful corporations, change the mix of networking sources and mentors to favor kinship ties and family mentors within this group, just as it does elsewhere in Latin America and the Third World. But elite Mexican clergy, who form a group smaller even than capitalists, typically establish their initial networks through their own formal institution's educational experiences as students, professors, and administrators. Thus, the formal and informal sources of networking, within separate Mexican leadership groups, reinforce one another.

The networking characteristics of different groups can be described, to a certain degree, as open or closed, depending on the organizational coherence of the power elite. The strongest example of a *closed network* is the Mexican armed forces. The armed forces provide an organizational umbrella which narrows the settings in which networking connections are established. Although mentors remain crucial to networking ties within the military, the mentor, almost exclusively, will be a military officer. For example, as we have seen, education is the setting for numerous military networking contacts. But in the case of the military, the mentor is a career officer teaching in a military school.

The opposing organizational setting, the *open network*, is best represented by leading Mexican intellectuals. Intellectuals are only loosely connected, as in most cultures, whether one describes their workplace or their formative institutions. Because Mexico's leading intellectuals come from a variety of public institutions, their mentors may be educators or teaching politicians, not just other intellectuals.

These findings reinforce the importance of understanding the organizational structure of individual elite groups. Theorists have correctly recognized the influence of the larger societal structures on elite formation and networking, but rarely have provided substantive observations from which to assess differences among organizations which are fundamental to explaining the formation, credentialing process, and decision-making power of elite groups.

The fifth major finding is that Mexicans who exercised the most influence within their respective areas of responsibility in the last third of the twentieth century have close ties to one another, ties which affect their personal and professional relationships. Such friendships are potentially important for the decision-making process since they affect access to information about policy decisions, allow individuals to express opinions on policy issues directly to decision makers, and provide a long-term ideological thread encompassing mentors and disciples in their careers and educational experiences.

The strength of these friendships, especially between mentors and disciples, surely influenced incremental policy strategies pursued by various elite groups over the last half of the twentieth century. In other words, the more tightly woven the networking relationships *within* each elite group, the more easily ideological continuity can be sustained. However, and this is a critical point, because the mentors themselves are drawn from their ranks, once a core group of disciples has fashioned an ideological shift, a dramatic shift in ideology or direction could also be accomplished.

These findings about the relationship and sources of networking in the creation of power elite circles are confined only to linkages *within* each group. The impact which Mexican elites, or any other power elite, might exercise would be magnified many times if each individual group were connected, through networking ties, to influential leaders outside their sphere of influence. In order to understand the potential which power elites and mentors might exercise beyond their own sphere of responsibility, it is essential to examine their networking *across* categories. That is the difficult task of the following chapter.

4   Networking across Power Elite Circles

I have argued that a power elite, in the narrow sense, exists in Mexico. A small number of influential figures have influenced many of the decisions *within* their respective policy arenas, whether they are cultural, political, economic, military, or religious. The applicability of power elite theory breaks down dramatically if it is conceptualized as a small group of elites who directly exercise influence over policies and attitudes in two or more policy arenas. Therefore, scholars have attempted to demonstrate the breadth of this influence by identifying the extent to which any individual holds a position in two or more power elite circles. As the data in chapter 1 make clear, no evidence exists to support this type of influence *across* Mexican policy circles, which is equally true in the United States. In Venezuela and Japan, however, such linkages are the norm.[1]

The primary assumption of prior research on the exchange of influential leaders across policy boundaries is that such individuals can be identified and measured on the basis of high-level positions held in significant organizations. For example, a person who sits on the boards of several Fortune 500 companies and also has served in a cabinet post is viewed as having exercised influence in both the economic and political arenas. This analysis, as I have suggested previously, relies solely on measuring the number of positions individuals hold in select organizations.

The data in this chapter suggest that in Mexico, the organizational networking approach grossly undermeasures the extent to which power elite

1. For example, Allen Barton found that only a minuscule .7 percent of his sample of American elites were linked to one another. "Background, Attitudes and Activities of American Elites," in Gwen Moore, ed., *Studies of the Structure of National Elite Groups,* 1 (Greenwich: JAI, 1985), 205. In sharp contrast to this figure, 61 percent of Venezuelan elites reported direct links *across* elite groups.

circles are linked *across* policy arenas. This chapter proposes to explore an alternative argument which suggests that influential individuals potentially have the ability to influence attitudes and decisions in policy arenas through extensive personal contacts which are not dependent on formally held organizational positions. These informal or indirect contacts are the most difficult to identify because they are not typically available in standard biographical directories or published organizational flow charts. Mentors often serve as the informal connecting link in these personal network relationships.

The analysis of networking ties *within* each of the power elite groups revealed major differences in emphasis among networking sources from one group to another. Among the most important were *career positions, family, educational institutions, corporate boards,* and *journal staffs.* It is likely that such differences also exist in how power elites network with their peers *outside* their circles.

To measure the extent to which power elites network *across* their respective circles, it is necessary to collapse many networking sources specific to a particular power elite into broader categories. Three broad networking sources are significant to establishing influential personal relationships *across* all Mexican power elite boundaries:

Educational—friendships developed through an education setting
Career—friendships initiated through a career contact, typically in an
   organizational setting
Family—friendships established through extended kinship ties

I was able to identify 502 known sources of friendships across power elite groups.[2] In order of importance, those sources are educational, career, and family. (See table 8.)

One indirect variable, adult residence, dramatically affects the extent of networking contacts across power elite groups. It provides a crucial setting for generating important networks through all three of the sources, and especially for educational and career sources. All networking sources occur within a geographic setting where power elites reside and work. The smaller the residential setting, the more likely it is that power elites know each other long before they achieve their vaunted status. In a larger society

2. Although it is difficult to calculate with certainty, if we assume that each member of the power elite has *strong* personal ties to between ten and twenty other members, the possible unidirectional linkages might range from 2,000 to 4,000 different friendships.

Table 8. Sources of Networking Ties across All Mexican Power Elites

Type of Power Elite	Source of Cross-Category Friendship		
	Education (%)	Career (%)	Family (%)
All Power Elites	41	37	22
Politicians Only	51	22	27
Intellectuals Only	45	23	32
Capitalists Only	48	14	38
Military Only	22	72	6
Clergy Only	7	87	6

NOTE: Based on 502 known sources of friendship with a power elite member from a different power elite category. (*N*= 398)

with more dispersed institutional resources, place is less likely to function as a basis for networking. In the United States, for example, residing in Washington, D.C., would be conducive to networking between politicians and military officers, but a leading intellectual living in Washington, D.C., would be far removed from the New York–Boston locus of America's largest and most influential group of cultural leaders.[3]

By international standards, Mexico is a populous country, with nearly 100 million people, but its institutional resources are not well distributed. Three major cities exert an overwhelming influence on power elite leadership in all circles except that of higher clergy, whose origin and residence is widely dispersed throughout the republic. Their dispersion makes it more difficult for priests to network with other power elite members because they are not concentrated in the three urban locales where most power elites reside: Mexico City, Monterrey, and Guadalajara. However, the dioceses for these three cities are the most influential in Mexico, and each has been recognized as an important religious center by the Pope, who has converted their sitting archbishops into cardinals.

It might be expected that bishops' geographic dispersion would limit their networking. This is not the case, however; bishops are connected through regional associations and through the Mexican Council of Bishops (episcopate). The small number of active bishops during the years examined, representing approximately 60 to 100 dioceses, easily facilitates strong personal connections.

3. Charles Kadushin, *American Intellectual Elite* (Boston: Little, Brown, 1974), 23–24.

Geographic setting has a bearing on interpersonal networking among power elites in two main ways: place of birth and city of residence in adulthood. A power elite's birthplace becomes advantageous to networking possibilities in two ways. First, for those power elites born in centers where older, established power elites reside, the potential for their families to make contact is increased. Second, power elites born in the three primary cities where power elites reside as adults rarely leave those cities, and therefore they spend their entire childhood in a setting populated by older, established power elites and future power elites their own age.

An elite's birthplace gives him the added opportunity to make contacts through educational institutions and through social activities in those locales. For example, a leading member of the political opposition in Mexico and former president of the National Action Party from 1984 to 1986, who became director general of Vidrios y Cristales of Monterrey, a major glass manufacturing firm, moved to this northern industrial center when he was seven, joining the Boy Scouts in 1933 at age eleven. He considers his experiences in the scouts to have been formative, and a fellow member of his scout den who later became president of Vidrios y Cristales recruited him to the company, becoming his professional mentor.[4]

The most common geographic variable in terms of birthplace is whether or not the individual comes from an urban setting. Four out of five power elites were born in urban locales at a time when the majority of Mexicans lived in rural communities. This has been true of Mexican elites for generations.[5] The only group within the power elite which is remotely representative of the rural population are the top bishops, of whom two-fifths were born in small towns and villages. Given their rural origins, clergy are the least likely to have established ties with other power elites as a consequence of their place of birth.

Nevertheless, there are some fascinating exceptions to urban backgrounds. Federico Reyes Heroles and Miguel Basáñez, both influential members of the cultural elite, became childhood friends in the small gulf community of Tuxpan, Veracruz because their fathers were friends. Reyes Heroles's father, who served as mayor of Tuxpan, rose to become one of the most influential political voices of his generation, and a mentor to

---

4. That power elite was Pablo Emilio Madero Belden. See *Líderes*, 6 (1994), 98–99.

5. For example, see Peter H. Smith's early findings for Mexican political leaders. *Labyrinths of Power: Political Recruitment in Twentieth-Century Mexico* (Princeton: Princeton University Press, 1979), 71–72.

President Miguel de la Madrid.[6] Miguel Basáñez's father, a businessman, came to know another mayor of Tuxpan, who was the father of one of Mexico's most influential capitalists, Roberto Hernández Ramírez, who was born there.[7] Reyes Heroles and Basáñez also have the potential for establishing ties to President Vicente Fox, because Fox and Hernández Ramírez are close friends from their college days in the business administration program at Ibero-American University.[8]

Another way of exploring urban birthplaces is to examine the proportion of power elites who were born in thirty-one state capitals or Mexico City, typically the most influential cities. This pattern is overwhelmingly present among intellectual and capitalist power elites, most of whom were born and generally raised in capital cities—a nearly universal bias among First and Third World countries.[9] These intellectuals and capitalists were more likely to share a certain cosmopolitan culture and to meet their own elite peers or other peers in these settings. An intimate American observer of leading capitalists in Monterrey, capital of Nuevo León, concluded: "There is obvious overrepresentation of local born men in the sample, suggesting that local birth, with the attendant social and family connections it would provide, is of considerable importance in determining whether an individual wins elite status in the city."[10] Again, clergy are the most disadvantaged in this regard since only one out of three came from a Mexican capital.

If the primary source used by a power elite to network outside his own group is not education or family, then place of adult residence becomes a critical geographic agent for promoting career, civic, and social contacts among elites, future elites, and their mentors. Just how centralized is Mexico's power elite? If we classify the five elite groups according to their place

6. Reyes Heroles did not view his father as a mentor, but it is possible that his brother Jesús, a prominent political figure who became ambassador to the United States, did. See Pilar Jiménez Trejo and Alejandro Toledo, *Creación y poder: Nueve retratos de intelectuales* (Mexico City: Contrapuntos, 1994), 169.

7. His great-uncle Tirso Hernández García, his paternal grandfather's brother, was a division general and prominent figure in the military, having directed several of the most important departments in the secretariat of national defense.

8. *Diario de Yucatán,* July 25, 2000.

9. Robert D. Putnam, *The Comparative Study of Political Elites* (Englewood Cliffs: Prentice-Hall, 1976), 32.

10. George R. Andrews, "Toward a Reevaluation of the Latin American Family Firm: The Industry Executives of Monterrey," *Inter-American Economic Affairs,* 30 (winter 1976), 32.

of adult residence, the distribution is revealing, demonstrating the overwhelming importance of just three Mexican cities. Mentors are also found in equally high numbers in these locales. (See table 9.)

The residential data suggest that seven out of ten Mexican power elites spend most of their adult lives in these three cities. Three of the elite groups, politicians, intellectuals, and capitalists, share a particularly strong affinity for just one city, Mexico's capital. In a political system which has been dominated by a single party for most of the century, and a governmental system dominated by the federal, executive branch, it is not surprising that 91 percent of the political power elite would have resided in Mexico City. What makes Mexico City a particularly favorable environment for inter-elite networking is that this city is also the most common residence for both intellectual (92 percent) and capitalist elites (66 percent).

Adult residence goes a long way in explaining potential patterns among power elites. Three influential patterns are apparent. First, clergy on the basis of residence are completely isolated from the other four groups, although a small but influential portion of its members are connected to a third of Mexico's prominent capitalists in Monterrey and Guadalajara. The cardinal archbishop of Monterrey, for example, who has led this important diocese since 1984, is well connected to many prominent power elites from business and politics who have resided in Monterrey, including the former state governor, who presided over the PRI, top capitalists who were members of the Catholic lay organization the Knights of Columbus, and a local National Action Party leader in Monterrey who reached national prominence.[11]

On the surface, a potential for some increased contact appears possible between top-ranking officers and bishops since the military is the only group other than clergy where the majority have resided *outside* of the three major cities. But military officers and clergy normally do not socialize, and for historic reasons, they have not been closely associated. Finally, no institutional links exist on the regional level which might bring them together. A zone commander and the bishop of the local diocese would be known to each other, but zone commanders generally serve for

11. The cardinal was Adolfo Suárez Rivera, the PRI president was Alfonso Martínez Domínguez, the PAN leader was Pablo Emilio Madero Belden, and the capitalists were Eugenio Clariond Garza and Alejandro Garza Laguera. *La Jornada,* November 17, 1988, 1, 4; *Punto,* September 8, 1986, 17; and *Cambio,* May 15, 1989, 38.

Table 9. Adult Residence of Mexican Power Elites

	Place of Residence as Adult			
Type of Power Elite	Mexico City (%)	Guadalajara (%)	Monterrey (%)	Other (%)
Political	91	0	0	9
Intellectual	92	0	6	2
Capitalist	66	4	27	3
Military	39	1	0	60
Clergy	8	5	5	82

NOTE: $N = 398$.

short periods of time, while bishops typically are in place for many years, often decades. An analysis of networking linkages between religious and military power elites provided no evidence of important contacts.

Top clergy, in spite of the fact that most have resided outside of these three cities, have established extensive contacts with an influential portion of Mexico's leading politicians. Place of residence, combined with the politician's position, determined the nature of their contact. Every state capital is represented by a diocese, and therefore any member of the political power elite who was a governor typically would have developed some ties to the local bishop.

Local ties are a particularly influential source of networking between members of the clergy and prominent members of the National Action Party (PAN) since capital city mayors and state governors provide the primary career trajectories among PAN heavyweights, and PAN has historic ideological ties with social Catholicism.[12] The archbishop of Chihuahua from 1969 to 1991, for example, who exerted a major influence on church pastoral policies, knew one of the party's most influential leaders and a presidential candidate, both as mayor of Chihuahua in 1983–85 and as a local Catholic lay leader.[13] The same is true of Vicente Fox, whose presidential victory is likely to favorably impact the importance of urban, regional origins other than Monterrey and Guadalajara.[14]

12. Donald A. Mabry, *Mexico's Acción Nacional: A Catholic Alternative to Revolution* (Syracuse: Syracuse University Press, 1973).

13. Adalberto Almeida Merino was the bishop, and the PAN figure, Luis H. Alvarez, represented President Fox as his official negotiator with the Zapatistas. Enrique Krauze, "Chihuahua: Ida y Vuelta," *Vuelta*, no. 115 (June 1986), 38–39.

14. The Mexican press has reported that his closest ties in the officer corps and

Contrary to popular belief, politicians from the Institutional Revolutionary Party (PRI) often establish equally close ties to clergy on the local level. The archbishop of Puebla is a good friend of Manuel Bartlett, the former governor and a leading national politician in the last three decades.[15] The bishop of Mexicali, who twice served as secretary general of the Mexican episcopate, knew President Ernesto Zedillo as a child because Zedillo helped his parents build the San Antonio chapel in his diocese.[16] An outspoken conservative bishop who initially was a disciple of progressive bishop Sergio Méndez Arceo, he plays golf and attends soccer matches with numerous PRI officials.[17]

This local networking pattern has become far more significant in the 1990s. When one considers the fact that nearly all of the leading presidential contenders from the three major parties in 1999 were governors, the importance of residing in state capitals becomes apparent.[18] This regional experience has contributed to a different, younger political prototype, the *hybrid politico*. This hybrid combines qualities found among an older generation of politicians with those of a younger group of leaders. Regional background is among the most notable of these newer qualities, discussed at length in chapter 10.

Certain states have produced a disproportionate percentage of the national political leadership. For example, the state of México, which surrounds most of the Federal District, including highly industrialized sections, is the country's most populous. Four of its former governors are

---

in the higher clergy are to the former regional commander in Guanajuato and to the local bishop.

15. Personal interview with Archbishop Rosendo Huesca Pacheco, Puebla, Puebla, December 5, 1998.

16. Gabriel Ibarrola Arriaga, *Familias y casas de la vieja Valladolid* (Morelia: Fimax, 1969), 387; personal interview with Archbishop Manuel Pérez Gil González, Tlalnepantla, México, February 18, 1991; Luis del Villar, *Los que mandan* (Mexico City: Editorial Quehacer Político, 1990); and *FBIS*, April 6, 1994, 12.

17. The bishop, Onésimo Cepeda, boasts one of the most off-beat careers of any sitting bishop in Mexico, having been a night club entertainer, bullfighter, and banker. He was also at one time a business partner of Carlos Slim, one of Mexico's most influential capitalists, who he probably met while both were attending the National University in the late 1950s. Slim was educated by the Augustinian order in Veracruz, and Cepeda did not join a seminary until he was twenty-four years old. *Reforma*, July 6, 2000, 10A, and *Mexico Business*, April, 1999, 9.

18. These would include Francisco Labastida Ochoa (Culiacán, Sinaloa); Manuel Bartlett Díaz (Puebla, Puebla); Roberto Madrazo (Villahermosa, Tabasco); Cuauhtémoc Cárdenas (Morelia, Michoacán); and Vicente Fox (Guanajuato, Guanajuato).

members of the power elite, all of whom worked closely with the archbishop, who headed the diocese during all of their gubernatorial terms.[19]

The second geographically supported networking pattern which emerges is that capitalists, on the basis of adult residence, are a bipolar group. A tiny percentage of leading capitalists live in Guadalajara, Mexico's third largest city, but compared to Monterrey and Mexico City, their representation is minuscule.[20] Monterrey, on the other hand, is the favored residence of a fourth of the capitalist power elite.

Monterrey, which is viewed by many Mexicans, residents and nonresidents alike, as a vibrant industrial center, as a cultural setting actively promoting private enterprise, and as an ideological counterpart to the capital city and the governmental influence it represents, encourages ties among political, capitalist, and religious figures from the North. As the National Action Party increases its foothold in national politics, given its presence in the North, Monterrey will serve increasingly as a point of contact among these power elites.

Monterrey's influence was evident early in the Fox presidency. Fox came to know influential businessmen in Monterrey because that city dominates the manufacturing of glass bottles, a product Fox needed to expand Coca-Cola of Mexico when he was CEO. One individual, a capitalist power elite family member, was then director of planning for the bottling division of Vitro, the largest glass producer; another power elite member met Fox when he worked for the Monterrey-based beer industry group which eventually purchased Coca Cola. Both men contributed financially to Fox's campaign.[21]

19. They are Carlos Hank González, Mario Ramón Beteta, Alfredo del Mazo, and Emilio Chuayffet. Former governor Alfredo del Mazo commented on his relationship to the archbishop. Personal interview, Mexico City, February 15, 1991.

20. According to Alicia Gómez López, five families control the leading companies in Jalisco: Aranguren, Martínez Guitrón, López Chávez, Gutiérrez Nieto, and Gómez Flores. Three are represented among the capitalist power elite, and two of them, Jorge Martínez Guitrón, founder of Grupo Sidek, and Ignacio Aranguren Castiello, CEO of Grupo Aranguren, are recognized by their capitalist peers as nationally influential, having been invited to join the exclusive Mexican Council of Businessmen. See *Crisis y transición en Jalisco* (Guadalajara: University of Guadalajara, 1997), 107.

21. Carlos Acosta Córdova and Antonio Jácquez, "Los magnates regiomontanos empiezan a obtener su recompensa," *Proceso*, August 6, 2000, www.proceso. com.mx. Federico Sada González held the position in the bottling division, and is the brother of a capitalist power elite, and Alfonso Romo Garza was the beer industry official. He is CEO of Grupo Pulsar International, which produced a fifth of the world's seeds in the 1990s.

The third geographic pattern revealed in the data is that four of the elite groups—the political, intellectual, capitalist, and military—are prominently represented in the capital. Indeed, nearly two-thirds of the power elite from these four groups have spent most of their adult lives, and in many cases their childhoods, in Mexico City. Even clergy establish important connections here. For example, one of the most influential capitalists supported the founding of the Jesuit-run Ibero-American University and presided over its board from 1966 to 1969. More importantly, he supported the creation of the Colegio México for Mexican seminary students in Rome, a residence hall most bishops resided in after the 1960s.[22]

Mexico's geographic pattern is typical of most countries other than the United States: a centralized capital city where most of the intellectual, political, and economic resources are concentrated. These residential concentrations mean that networking possibilities are especially high within intellectual, political, and capitalist groups, and between intellectuals and politicians.

Mexico City shares strong parallels with Paris and London, not with Washington, D.C. Even New York City, which could claim in a fifty-mile radius from the Empire State Building half of the United States leading intellectuals in the early 1970s, pales in comparison with Mexico City in its concentration of elites.[23] As Irving Howe concludes, New York intellectuals have few if any connections with a stable of high-ranking politicians or significant representatives of the rich.[24] By contrast, in London "it is quite common to find writers, journalists, Oxford dons and Members of Parliament mingling at cocktail parties or similar occasions."[25]

Lewis Coser argues that physical proximity among intellectuals allows for a shortened line of communication and an increased transmission of their ideas. Guadalajara and Monterrey cannot compete with Mexico City in this regard. Just as Guadalajara draws potential intellectuals from smaller, outlying communities in the West, Mexico City draws intellec-

22. Carlos Trouyet was a major figure in founding numerous antecedents to major holding companies. *Diccionario Porrúa: Historia, biografía y geografía de México* (Mexico City: Porrúa, 1995), 3588–89.
23. Charles Kadushin, *American Intellectual Elite*, 23. Only 11 percent resided in Washington, D.C.
24. Irving Howe, "The New York Intellectuals: A Chronicle and a Critique," *Commentary*, 4 (October 1968), 44.
25. Lewis Coser, "The Differing Roles of Intellectuals in Contemporary France, England and America," paper presented at the Symposium on Sociology of the Intellectual, Buenos Aires, July 3–5, 1967, 6.

tuals from Guadalajara, who move to the capital to obtain recognition and establish contacts with other leading intellectuals.[26]

FAMILIAL NETWORKING SOURCES

It is possible to analyze the impact of each networking source among the five power elite groups. Familial sources are easily described as a form of networking, but information on family background often is difficult to come by. Familial sources describe ties which are formed through the immediate extended family, including parents, grandparents, siblings, in-laws, and aunts and uncles. However, families are not equal in their ability to contribute to networking relationships.

Having an elite parent whose occupation is the same as the chosen occupation of the child increases the potential for that person to use his parents or another close relative to make personal contacts with other potential or actual power elites. In fact, in the case of the Japanese elites, children actually inherit a successful parent's *koenkai*, or network.[27] Studies have shown that for some types of elite leadership (e.g., in Turkey), when a parent's occupation corresponds to the child's profession, the probability of the child's success is greatly enhanced.[28] This is explained, in part, by the fact that most mentors who are from an elite's own family, such as the late president Miguel Alemán and his son, Miguel Alemán Jr., are themselves highly successful.

An occupationally based relationship between a father's occupation and an elite's is clearly present among some leadership groups. Table 10 examines the distribution of occupations among all power elite fathers. It reveals that three of the five power elite groups—politicians, military officers, and capitalists—come from families where their father is more likely

26. Roderic Ai Camp, *Intellectuals and the State in Twentieth Century Mexico* (Austin: University of Texas Press, 1985), 76–80, based on interviews with prominent Guadalajaran cultural elites.

27. Donn M. Kurtz II, "First Families in Japan, Mexico, and the United States," paper presented at the Southern Political Science Association meeting, Atlanta, November 2000.

28. Joseph S. Szyliowicz detailed exploration of Turkey's political leadership concluded that familial ties played a crucial role, and that 62 percent of the most successful public figures could claim fathers who were elites, while those with the least successful careers were the children of elite fathers only 38 percent of the time. "Elite Recruitment in Turkey: The Role of the Mulkiye," *World Politics*, 23 (April 1971), 396.

Table 10. Father's Occupation among Mexican Power Elites

| | Power Elite Group | | | | |
| | Politician (%) | Intellectual (%) | Capitalist (%) | Military (%) | Clergy (%) |
Father's Occupation					
Professional	22	29	7	13	25
White Collar	11	12	1	23	0
Laborer/Peasant	20	6	3	13	33
Politician	17	15	5	0	0
Military Officer	7	3	3	36	0
Business Manager	7	26	24	5	33
Capitalist	4	6	56	0	0
Small Businessman	5	3	1	10	9
Small Farmer	7	0	0	0	0

NOTE: *Professional* refers collectively to all other professions not specified in the figure. *White collar* refers to non-manual occupations, such as bank teller or salesperson, which typically do not require a college or professional degree in Mexico. (N = 398)

to practice the same profession as the child, and consequently to also serve as the child's mentor.[29]

To illustrate this pattern, let us examine figures for these three groups. Fifty-six percent of capitalists were the children of capitalists, not just ordinary upper-class businessmen, but extremely wealthy Mexicans. Another fourth of capitalists' fathers held management positions in the private sector.

Capitalist was the single largest occupational category among the fathers of Mexican power elites. Furthermore, the overwhelming majority of capitalist fathers were parents of power elite capitalists. The self-perpetuating family quality of Mexican business leaders is characteristic of the business leadership culture in many societies. In the United States, which offers one of the most supportive and open environments for achieving prominence in business, leading business figures are typically children and grandchildren of businessmen.[30]

29. Although we can only identify one parent's occupation in this table, and information is typically available for fathers, mothers who pursue professional occupations, increasingly the case in Mexico, produce equally important linkages.

30. Suzanne Infield Keller, *The Social Origins and Career Lines of Three Generations of American Business Leaders* (New York: Arno Press, 1980), 61. For example, in 1900, when 8 percent of the general population were businessmen, 50

This multigenerational occupational pattern is illustrated in the ancestors of a member of our capitalist power elite, Cresencio Ballesteros Ibarra, who retired in 1996 as CEO of Grupo Mexicano de Desarrollo, one of Mexico's largest holding companies:

> My father was a civil engineer who at one time had the largest civil engineering practice in Mexico. He did business with North American, European, and even Russian companies, and strongly supported the 1910 Revolution. He knew Lázaro Cárdenas, Francisco José Mújica, and Manuel Avila Camacho during this period. He was founder of the National Irrigation Commission, which as you know later became the basis for the ministry of hydraulic resources. Like my grandfather, he too died young, in 1932, when Cárdenas was still governor of Michoacán. I think my father was one of the most notable civil engineers in Mexico during this period of our history. General Cárdenas once told me that without my father's efforts, the National Irrigation Commission would never have been born.[31]

Ballesteros, who considered his father a mentor, not only followed in his father's footsteps, graduating with a civil engineer degree and initially working for the National Irrigation Commission, but founded Constructora Ballesteros, a construction firm like his father's, which became the heart of his business enterprises. His son, CEO of Grupo Synkro and Mexicana Airlines, as well as the managing director of Constructora Ballesteros for many years and a civil engineer, is also a member of the capitalist power elite.[32]

Only top Mexican military officers come close to capitalists in terms of the proportion of sons who pursued the same careers as their fathers. More than a third of top military officials were children of military officers. The military power elite accounted for most of the fathers in the military. The

---

percent of the business leaders were the children of businessmen. In 1950, that figure was 57 percent. Reinhard Bendix and Seymour Martin Lipset examined a different sample of American businessmen from Keller. Those born in 1771 or 1891 came from parents who were businessmen in proportions that were never lower than 63 percent and reached 74 percent by the 1920 generation. *Social Mobility in Industrial Society* (Berkeley: University of California Press, 1959), 122.

31. Personal interview with Cresencio Ballesteros, Mexico City, July 26, 1984.

32. Ballesteros bought Mexicana Airlines when it went bankrupt and was president of the board of Union Carbide and John Deere of Mexico, two of the leading foreign companies. For background on his career, see *Expansión*, April 26, 1995, 18, 20. For his son, José Luis, see *Mexico Business*, July 1996, 55. Cresencio's brother Guillermo, co-founder of the family construction firm, became CEO of Grupo Visa. Ballesteros's grandfather was a career, military officer and aide to Benito Juárez during the French Intervention and Liberal-Conservative conflict.

military as a "family" profession holds in other cultures as well, including Brazil, the United States, and England.[33]

Among the most carefully examined leadership group in public life are judicial officials. Donn Kurtz has explored family backgrounds of United States supreme court justices over multiple generations. He discovered that over a third had a parent in public office, and two-thirds were members of political families. Even among recent Supreme Court appointees, a sizeable number of the justices are related to public figures.

On the basis of his detailed empirical analysis, Kurtz developed a generational theory which suggests that 30 percent of any group of public leaders are descended from 1 percent of the population.[34] He tested that theory on United States presidents and among other chief executives world wide, including Japan, and demonstrated that these figures accurately predict the current distribution of parental occupations among top politicians.[35]

The percentage of politicians in Mexico's power elite whose parents were politicians is small. Power elite politicians account for nearly two-thirds of all power elite fathers who also were public figures. These prominent public figures often mentored their child as well as other political

33. In Lloyd Warner's comprehensive study of civilian and military leaders in the United States, which considered the parental background of officers from the rank of colonel through four-star general, he concluded that the sons of military officers are represented five times greater than would be expected from military occupations in the general population. *The American Federal Executive: A Study of the Social and Personal Characteristics of the Civilian and Military Leaders of the United States* (New Haven: Yale University Press, 1963), 33. R. F. Schloemer and G. E. Myers's examination of U.S. Air Force officers found the same pattern: 2 percent of their grandfathers, 23 percent of their fathers, and 4 percent of both were career military. Forty-seven percent had also served in the military in a noncareer capacity. "Making It at the Air Force Academy: Who Stays? Who Succeeds?" in Franklin D. Margiotta, ed., *Changing World of the American Military* (Boulder: Westview, 1978), 338. For the U.S. Navy, John F. Fitzgerald found among naval cadets at Annapolis that one-fourth were the children of career military fathers. See John F. Fitzgerald and Charles L. Cochran, "Who Goes to the United States Naval Academy," in *Changing World of the American Military*, 362. In Brazil, Alfred Stepan found approximately the same percentage of entering cadets were the children of a career military father. *The Military in Politics: Changing Patterns in Brazil* (Princeton: Princeton University Press, 1971), 33.

34. Donn M. Kurtz II, *Kinship and Politics: The Justices of the United States and Louisiana Supreme Courts* (Baton Rouge: Louisiana State University Press, 1997), 93.

35. Donn M. Kurtz II, "Testing a Model of American Elite: Generational Continuity with Cross Generational National Data," *Social Thought and Research*, 22, no. 1–2 (1999), 218–19.

power elites. Figures for the percentage of power elite politicians who are politicians' children are comparable to those for Mexican national politicians generally.[36] Political families disproportionately produce national politicians in most Third World countries. V. B. Singh's study of elites in India found that approximately two-thirds of Indian politicians came from families who were active or interested in politics, and an equal amount had relatives in politics.[37]

Roman Catholic clergy often have relatives among their extended kin who had careers as nuns or priests, but the rule of celibacy prevents them from relying on a parent to give them the level of personal access to other religious individuals that might prove important in establishing an effective personal network. Nevertheless, many successful clergy have indicated that a close relative assisted their careers. Such is the case of the late progressive bishop Sergio Méndez Arceo, whose father was a successful lawyer but whose uncle was a prominent archbishop whose public declarations were used as a pretext for the church-state conflict in the 1920s.[38]

Power elites whose parents spent their lives in manual labor, such as peasants and blue-collar workers, offer the least potential for family-initiated networking ties. This background is most likely to be found among politicians and clergy: a fifth and a third, respectively, of power elite politicians and clergy had parents with backgrounds in manual labor.

A parent's occupational background contributes to the importance of family as a networking agent; but a parent's level of achievement within a specific occupation pushes the importance of family ties to an even higher plane. In other words, the son of a three-star general in the Mexican army who hoped to pursue a successful career in the armed forces would have personal ties with influential members of the officer corps from the beginning, and would be in a much better position than an aspiring officer whose father was a staff sergeant or even a colonel.

To what degree are Mexican power elites actually connected to prior

36. Roderic Ai Camp, *Political Recruitment across Two Centuries: Mexico, 1884–1991* (Austin: University of Texas Press, 1995), 180–81.

37. V. B. Singh, *Profiles of Political Elites in India* (Delhi: Ritu, 1984), 52.

38. Like his nephew, Archbishop José Mora y del Río obtained a Ph.D. from the Gregorian University and was known for his social activism. He served as archbishop of Mexico from 1908 to 1928, and died in exile. *Excélsior*, February 10, 1997, A1, and *Diccionario Porrúa: Historia, biografía y geografía de México* (Mexico City: Porrúa, 1995), 2350. Octaviano Márquez y Toriz, archbishop of Puebla, was preceded as bishop by his older brother, and had two aunts who were nuns. See Luis Nava Rodríguez, *Octaviano Márquez y Toriz* (Mexico City: Editorial Jus, 1978).

elites through their parents? Three-quarters of all power elite members do not have notable parents, regardless of their occupation. However, the fact that a fourth of our sample come from family backgrounds where the father, and in some cases the mother, has a national reputation, is noteworthy.

Influential Mexican clergy and military officers are least likely to have grown up in an influential family environment, while power elite capitalists and politicians are most likely. Politicians are the most eclectic in terms of notable parent backgrounds, having prominent parents from each of the other four power elite categories, the only leadership group where that is the case. This finding suggests that politicians, through kinship networking ties, would have the broadest access to influential elite families.

An excellent illustration of kinship networking across power elites can be found in the family of the late Hugo B. Margáin Gleason, whose father was a distinguished physician and professor at the National School of Medicine. His aunt married the treasurer of the National Action Party, who was also a relative of one of Mexico's formerly wealthiest families and a member of the capitalist power elite.[39] Another one of Hugo Margáin's aunts married a top scientist. A third aunt married an industrialist whose mother was one of Mexico's most successful female entrepreneurs, the intimate friend of presidents and the mistress of a major painter in the art world, muralist Diego Rivera. Margáin himself married a woman who tied him through kinship to another leading capitalist family and member of the power elite.[40] Margáin considered his father, as well as Antonio Carrillo Flores, who was a major politician prior to 1970, his most important mentors.[41]

Family networking might help an individual Mexican officer in his military career, but generally would not be useful in establishing personal networks *across* elite groups. Although only one-tenth of leading Mexican military officers' fathers were as influential as Margáin's father, all came from influential military families. An exception to this is the family of a

39. This refers to the Creel Terrazas family, two of the most influential capitalist families during the Porfiriato.

40. Personal interview Hugo B. Margáin, Mexico City, March 14, 1977; *Enciclopedia de México*, 8, 271–72; *Reforma*, September 12, 1997; *Líderes*, 7 (1995), 137–43.

41. Personal letter to the author. As Margáin noted, "During my entire career, Carrillo Flores was most important. We became very good friends and I was part of his group." They met at the National University, in Carrillo Flores's philosophy of law class.

former defense secretary whose father, a division general, served on Manuel Avila Camacho's staff in the defense secretariat in 1933–34, prior to Avila Camacho becoming president in 1940, thus giving him access to influential politicians.[42]

The data also reinforce, once again, the importance of prominent capitalist families in the backgrounds of elite capitalists: one out of two members of the capitalist power elite can claim a notable parent, and nearly all of those influential parents were prominent capitalists. For example, a former president of the Mexican Council of Businessmen and principal stockholder, with his brother, of the Grupo San Luis in the 1990s is the son of a prominent industrialist who is also a cousin of revolutionary president Francisco I. Madero. He is in addition the grandson of a landowner who served as secretary of the treasury from 1911 to 1913.[43]

Parents are not the only vehicle through which family serves as a networking source and mentor. The personal stories of power elites suggest that relatives in the immediate family (siblings, in-laws, aunts and uncles, and grandparents) might be equally important to establishing personal ties among other Mexican power elites, and as mentors, even when those relatives are not among the most prominent figures in their profession.

Relatives expand the breadth of family-initiated networking ties. For example, through relatives, elite capitalists double their already-high level of parental ties to ordinary capitalists. Intellectuals, whose parents are not strongly represented in any of the occupational categories, nevertheless are potentially the most well connected of the five elite groups through their immediate family, having some family members in all occupations. Enrique Florescano Mayet, a distinguished historian and author, is married to a prominent historian who is the daughter of an independent party candidate for president who was senate majority leader from 1958 to 1964. His wife pursued a political career in the 1990s and was an important collaborator of a recently arrived member of the political power elite.

Both military officers and clergy increase their personal connections

---

42. Father and son are Gustavo Arévalo Vera and Juan Arévalo Gardoqui. Arévalo Gardoqui's brother, a colonel in the medical corps, served as a congressman from Baja California in the 1960s. *Cien biografías,* 279–81; *Revista de Ejército y Fuerza Aéreo,* January 1987, xii–xiii.

43. This was Antonio Madero Bracho. His cousin, Pablo E. Madero Belden, another member of the power elite, is a leading figure in the political opposition, having served as president of the National Action Party in the 1980s. His grandfather was Evaristo Madero Farías. *Expansión,* April 9, 1997, 48; *Excélsior,* July 31, 1997; *Excélsior,* June 22, 1996.

through relatives. Extended kinship ties are especially important for clergy, who rely on uncles and aunts to provide them with significant contacts to leaders in the Catholic Church. The long-time secretary general of the Mexican Catholic Episcopate and archbishop of Tlalnepantla, for example, came from a wealthy landholding family with roots in Morelia, Michoacán extending back to the sixteenth century. His grandfather, a prominent lawyer, was president of the state supreme court and rector of the most prestigious university. His grandfather, already connected professionally to the state's leading politicians and intellectuals, was a good friend of the bishop. His father's cousin was also a bishop.[44]

Family networking is characterized by a distinctive quality not found among typical networking sources: loyalty generated by blood. In societies where political and economic conditions are unpredictable, family networks increase their importance in performing many functions, a pattern typical in China and the Middle East for generations.[45] Even when a country is fractured by profound political and ideological cleavages, such as Nicaragua in the 1980s, "the burden of traditional family networks is still heavy . . . ," and these networks "survive for a long time after revolutionary political change and contribute to molding its development."[46] Mexican power elites and their peers in many Third World countries rely heavily on family to achieve professional and personal goals.

Socioeconomic class as a contributor to personal networking is inextricably linked to familial networking sources, yet we know little about its role once an elite position has been attained.[47] It differs from parental

44. Personal interview with Manuel Pérez Gil González, Tlanepantla, February 18, 1991. One of those important generational connections was to the family of Manuel Martínez Solórzano, a physician and professor at the Colegio de San Nicolás de Hidalgo (which Pérez Gil González's grandfather directed), mayor of Morelia, and a constitutional deputy. Martínez Solórzano's son, Antonio Martínez Báez, was a mentor to many public figures in the political power elite, including Miguel de la Madrid. See Gabriel Ibarrola Arriaga, *Familias y casas de la vieja Valladolid* (Morelia: Fimax, 1969), 387.

45. See for example the work of Lucian W. Pye, *The Spirit of Chinese Politics* (Cambridge: Harvard University Press, 1992), and James Bill, *Politics in the Middle East* (New York: Harper, Row, 1993).

46. Carlos M. Vilas, "Family Affairs: Class, Lineage and Politics in Contemporary Nicaragua," *Journal of Latin American Studies*, 24 (1992), 338.

47. As Gwen Moore and Richard D. Alba argue, "one would expect upper class origins to be advantageous even within elite groups. This would result in differentiation *within* elite groups according to social origins, with key positions and network centrality being disproportionately held by those from the upper class." "Class and Prestige Origins in the American Elite," in Peter Marsden and Nan Lin, eds., *Social Structure and Network Analysis* (Beverly Hills: Sage, 1982), 40.

occupation in that a parent's occupation may provide knowledge, interest, and connections within his or her profession that are distinct from the advantages associated with wealth.

Middle- and upper-class backgrounds are overrepresented among most successful people in nearly all influential professions in all societies. Thomas Dye's "systematic mappings of positional connections among 400 national organizations spanning a dozen institutional sectors [in the United States] uncovered a core leadership that was heavily over-represented by upper social class origins."[48] Higley's survey of democracies found that upper-class origins remain advantageous for achieving membership in the elite; however, their importance fades once membership has been achieved.[49]

Upper-class origins are not important in distinguishing the most influential circles of elites, however.[50] This would be true of most groups within the Mexican power elite, such as clergy, politicians, military officers, and intellectuals, but is not the case of leading capitalists, where wealthy family connections have been shown to be the norm. The acquisition of capital, when jump-started by family inheritance and insider company status, especially when the business is family owned, proves to be an extraordinarily influential means of establishing personal ties among wealthy capitalist families.[51]

Wealth is an important variable in the family networking process. Since

48. David Knoke, "Networks of Elite Structure and Decision Making," in Stanley Wasserman and Joseph Galaskiewicz, eds., *Advances in Social Network Analysis* (Thousand Oaks: Sage, 1994), 277. Thomas R. Dye admits, however, that U.S. military elites "were distinctly not upper-class" in origin. Indeed, if in the present case I dropped the criterion of including fathers who were generals, none of the military elites in the sample would be "upper class." *Who's Running America? Institutional Leadership in the United States* (Englewood Cliffs: Prentice-Hall, 1976), 152.

49. John Higley et al., "Elite Integration in Stable Democracies: A Reconsideration," *European Sociological Review*, 7, no. 1 (May 1991), 43.

50. Peter Smith examined this question statistically for pre-1970 Mexican political elites, but unfortunately, he lacked family background data on sufficient numbers of cases to suggest there was a statistical relationship between class and level of attainment. See *Labyrinths of Power*, 108–9.

51. Larissa Lomnitz and Marisol Pérez Lizaur, the only authors who have explored an upper-class family in extensive detail, go even further. "Members who conform to the requirements of the Family ideology have access to Family resources in terms of personal, economic, political, and social advancement; those who fail to conform are penalized by withdrawal of kinship recognition." "The History of an Urban Upper-Class Family in Mexico," *Journal of Family History*, 2 (winter 1978), 408.

family is a central vehicle through which Mexicans achieve and maintain power elite status, levels of family income may determine the extent of networking ties among certain categories of power elites. Information presented in table 11 suggests that the parents of Mexico's power elite, like power elite parents worldwide, are overrepresented among the rich.[52] Wealthy parents account for nearly a fourth of all parents among Mexico's power elite. This figure is eleven times that of the general Mexican population (2.0 percent) in 1950, an average date of birth close to the birth dates of many elites in the present sample.[53]

The one-fourth figure is far from an accurate representation of Mexico's power elite collectively because three-quarters of those rich parents are found *only among capitalist power elites.* If we exclude capitalists from our calculations, wealthy parents account for only 8 percent of all power elite parents—still a disproportionate percentage, four times the general population, but not nearly as exaggerated as when capitalists' parents are included.

The socioeconomic data reported in table 11 also suggest wide divergences among the five power elite groups. Again, as is apparent worldwide, the middle class dominates in Mexican power elite groups. Middle-class origin is disproportionately represented among power elite parents collectively, and among political, intellectual, and military elite parents individually. This is fairly close to general population distributions (25 percent in 1950) for religious and capitalist groups. The military and influential clergy have the most representative share of working-class parents, about half the normal distribution found within the general Mexican population.

High socioeconomic status, by contributing to career success, enhances the ability of an individual to make contacts, to serve as a mentor, and to expand his personal network. It does so in three ways. First, socioeconomic class is one way of measuring the success of a parent's professional achievement. A wealthy lawyer, for example, is likely to have much more access

---

52. I have made these judgments on family wealth, where information is available, on the basis of parents' occupations, and in the case of many capitalists, on actual figures of stock holdings in major corporations.

53. The figures for the class distribution among the general population are from Roger D. Hansen, *The Politics of Mexican Development* (Baltimore: Johns Hopkins University Press, 1971), 180. Hansen's figures are speculative, and are based on income data from the Mexican census. The most detailed analysis of the class structure in Mexico can be found in Stephanie Granato and Aida Mostkoff, "The Class Structure of Mexico, 1895–1980," in James W. Wilkie, ed., *Society and Economy in Mexico*, vol. 10 of *Statistical Abstract of Latin America Supplement Series* (Los Angeles: UCLA Latin American Center, 1990), 103–15.

Table 11. Socioeconomic Origins of Mexican Power Elites

	Socioeconomic Status of Parents		
Type of Power Elite	Working Class (%)	Middle Class (%)	Wealthy (%)
Political	24	70	6
Intellectual	14	70	16
Capitalist	9	31	60
Military	36	62	2
Clergy	31	31	38

NOTE: Classification based on self-identification, if parents were employed in manual occupations, and published economic wealth. ($N = 398$)

to other equally successful lawyers than a lawyer who has worked as a public defender most of his career.

Second, a parent's wealth, as distinct from his or her profession, provides children with access to other means of networking unavailable to a child from a typical middle-class professional family, including private grammar and secondary school education and social clubs. Only in the case of capitalists, who by definition have extreme wealth, and blue-collar employees and small farmers, who would have few financial resources, would occupational and socioeconomic networking sources duplicate each other.

Third, if we look specifically at parental occupation, which is one aspect of socioeconomic status, we can see that type of occupation matters. For example, a parent who was a successful botanist would not likely have the same networking potential as an equally successful lawyer, because few Mexican power elites become botanists.

Class backgrounds may help to explain successful networking behavior for psychological reasons, too. Studies show that social background plays an important role in determining children's level of participation in social activities. Students with college-educated fathers are more than three times as likely as students whose fathers have never gone beyond the eighth grade to be involved in any social or political activity.[54]

Friendships develop in numerous situations. Many leading figures met each other at dinner parties or social hours organized by mutual friends. A humorous illustration of the initiation of such a long-term friendship is that between two of Mexico's most influential writers, Elena Ponia-

54. David Abbott Ziblatt, "Teenagers: Their Concept of Politics," Ph.D. dissertation, University of Oregon, 1965, 27.

towska and Carlos Fuentes, who met while dancing at a party in Mexico City. As Poniatowska recalls, Fuentes didn't dance very well, but they talked continuously while dancing.[55]

Other power elites have cemented or established friendships while participating in unique activities in their city of residence. Mexico's notable muralist David Alfaro Siqueiros was imprisoned numerous times by the Mexican government for political reasons. He went on a hunger strike in 1960, and four additional members of the intellectual power elite in this study participated in a sympathy hunger strike at the San Carlos Academy, the capital's leading art school.[56]

Interviews with various members of the power elite confirm the notion that these "unique" experiences, sometimes under tense circumstances, push new and old friendships to a higher plane. These types of circumstances cross elite groups as well. For example, a major figure of the Mexican left and long-time leader of the Mexican Workers Party told the author shortly before his death that he and another leading politician of the left came to know Sergio Méndez Arceo, the progressive and controversial bishop of Cuernavaca, when both were political prisoners from 1968 to 1970 following the student massacre in Tlatelolco Plaza. Méndez Arceo visited them and other prisoners on a regular basis during their incarceration.[57]

EDUCATIONAL NETWORKING SOURCES

These examples refer to unusual circumstances, and in some cases the individual responsible for initiating the friendship established his initial

---

55. *Líderes*, 7 (1995), 131. An outstanding illustration of the "cross-fertilization" which occurs socially among Mexican intellectuals, politicians, and capitalists is illustrated in the television heir Emilio Azcárraga Jean's wedding to Alejandra de Cima Aldrete in the fall of 1999. Among the guests were Vicente Fox Quesada, PAN presidential candidate; Porfirio Muñoz Ledo and Manuel López Obrador, PRD leaders; Ricardo Salinas Pliego, a major capitalist; Francisco Labastida Ochoa, PRI presidential candidate; Esteban Moctezuma Barragán, secretary general of PRI; José Antonio González Fernández, PRI president; General Enrique Cervantes Aguirre, secretary of national defense; six other cabinet members, including treasury and government; Miguel Alemán Velasco and Carlos Slim, leading capitalists; and Enrique Krauze and Héctor Aguilar Camin, influential intellectuals. *Diario de Yucatán*, October 24, 1999, www:diariodeyucatan.com.

56. They were José Revueltas, Emmanuel Carballo, José Emilio Pacheco, and Carlos Monsiváis. *Excélsior*, December 28, 1996.

57. The other leftist leader was Pablo Gómez Alvarez. Personal interview with Heberto Castillo Martínez, Mexico City, July 12, 1993.

ties through some other means. The most common source of networking ties to power elites outside another power elite's circle, and especially among politicians, intellectuals, and capitalists, is education. Education is somewhat important for military networking, given some contact at the National Preparatory School and the National University, as well as at the Heroico Colegio Militar, between future prominent military officers and politicians.

For example, President José López Portillo and the man he appointed as head of the air force attended elementary and preparatory school together in Mexico City. Another general in this study, a zone commander and president of the Higher Military Court, received his law degree with the influential 1950 generation at UNAM, which included three prominent cabinet figures and author Carlos Fuentes.[58] Some of Mexico's younger leading intellectuals have taught at the Colegio de Defense Nacional, from which seven of the top military elites in the sample graduated.[59]

Mexican clergy establish the fewest networking ties through education at any level. Unlike any of the other power elites, they enroll at an early age in lower seminaries, which excludes them from contact with most other potential power elite members. Since most of these seminaries are located in the provinces, away from Guadalajara, Monterrey, and Mexico City, priests are not likely to meet other elites in their adolescent years. And, unlike the officer corps, many of whom attend public schools in Mexico City prior to enrolling in the military academies at sixteen or seventeen, clergy typically have gone abroad to complete their studies at clerical institutions in Montezuma, New Mexico, or at the Gregorian University.

There are occasional instances of influential non-clerical power elites attending such facilities, such as a prominent PAN leader who initially trained as a Jesuit in Guadalajara, attending seminary from 1936 to 1948, or internationally recognized novelist Juan Rulfo, who attended the Guadalajara Seminary with the future bishop of Hermosillo in the 1930s.[60] The late PAN president attended the Gregorian University in 1971, but his student days occurred later than the years of study for all of the bishops in the power elite sample. However, he completed a degree in Greek phi-

---

58. Air force general Miguel Mendoza Marquez and army general José María Rios de Hoyos.

59. These include Sergio Aguayo and Luis Rubio.

60. Eraín González Morfín is the notable example. The long-time bishop of Hermosillo was Carlos Quintero Arce. Donald J. Mabry, *Mexico's Acción Nacional*, 88.

losophy at Freiburg Pontifical University in Switzerland with a bishop from the power elite, and taught at the Conciliar Seminary of San Ildefonso in the 1980s.[61]

The range of educational contacts among Mexico's five power elite groups can be illustrated in greater detail by looking at the schools they have attended. These data reveal important characteristics about the nature of networking within an educational setting. Of the Mexican universities listed in this compilation, only sixteen institutions account for three or more graduates who are power elite members. Of these sixteen universities, thirteen are essentially institutions which *exclusively* educated one elite group (no more than one other member of the power elite studied there).

Only three Mexican universities can reasonably be described as providing a setting where power elites and mentors from multiple groups might meet: the Jesuit-operated Ibero-American University (capitalists, politicians, and intellectuals), the Technological Institute of Higher Studies in Monterrey (capitalists, politicians, and intellectuals), and UNAM (all groups except the clergy). Military and religious power elites are largely excluded from these three institutions. Two military officers attended UNAM, but none of the three universities provides a setting for significant contacts among more than three of the five groups.

If any Mexican educational institution could be said to facilitate networking across power elite groups, it would be the National University, which educated a sizeable portion of Mexico's top intellectuals, capitalists, and politicians, as well as their mentors. A notable example of networking ties established there can be found in the class of 1939–44, which included eight power elites, five politicians, one intellectual, and two capitalists. One of those politicians was President José López Portillo.[62] Sixteen capitalists

61. The two figures were Carlos Castillo Peraza, the PAN leader, and Onésimo Cepeda, the bishop. *Who's Who in Mexico* (Washington, D.C.: Worldwide Reference Publications, 1987), 105; and *Diario de Yucatán*, September 14, 2000.

62. Those students included Carlos Abedrop Dávila, an economics major who became president of the Mexican Bankers Association during the López Portillo administration; Bernardo Quintana Arrioja, an engineering student who founded Ingenieros Civiles Asociados (ICA), one the largest construction firms in Latin America, and who served on Abedrop's board; Alonso Aguilar Monteverde, capitalist critic and disciple of leading mentor Narciso Bassols; Joaquín Gamboa Pascoe, major labor leader and son-in-law of Fidel Velázquez, the most important labor figure in the second half of the century; Jesús Reyes Heroles, secretary of government under López Portillo, whose intellectual mentors included Jesús Silva Herzog (who produced numerous disciples and who was father of Treasury Secretary Jesús Silva Herzog Flores); Emilio Martínez Manatou, López Portillo's secretary of

attended the National University, but none have graduated from the university since 1968, which suggests that UNAM's role in bringing together future capitalists with politicians and intellectuals has declined.

Foreign universities have made important contributions to networking ties among Mexico's power elites. Among the twenty foreign institutions attended by two or more power elites, nine essentially catered exclusively to one group, leaving thirteen universities where friendships could be established across power elite groups. Contrary to what one might expect, the Oxbridge schools are not a major influence on Mexico's power elite. Only four important political figures attended those universities in the 1960s and 1970s, and the London School of Economics was more important than Oxford or Cambridge to cultural figures.

Given Mexico's natural cultural ties to and intellectual influences from France, it is not surprising that France was more important than England in educating future power elites. French institutions have primarily graduated cultural elites, and to a lesser extent prominent politicians. The United States, however, offered the greatest possibilities for inter-elite networking, especially at Harvard University. An important reason for Harvard's impact is the fact that two Mexican presidents, Miguel de la Madrid and Carlos Salinas de Gortari, are alumni. Yale also exerted an important networking role, and also is the alma mater of a recent president, Ernesto Zedillo.

Educational settings are the most important source for networking among Mexican power elites, but only politicians and intellectuals establish extensive friendships with one another through education. Educational networking tends to separate most of the power elite groups, such as clergy, military officers, and even capitalists, rather than promote contacts with members of other groups. For example, a leading politician who served as secretary of government from 1988 to 1992 is the only non-military member of the entire power elite whose educational background was military (he graduated from the Heroico Colegio Militar).[63]

As the Mexican political arena becomes more plural after the Fox vic-

---

health and a strong pre-candidate for the presidency; and José Campillo Sáinz, director of legal affairs for the Monterrey Steel Foundry, one of the Monterrey group's most important firms, and professor of Miguel de la Madrid at UNAM.

63. The military education of the politician Fernando Gutiérrez Barrios overlapped with that of General Raúl Juárez Carreño, who served as *oficial mayor* of the secretariat of defense at the same time Gutiérrez Barrios was heading the government secretariat. Juárez Carreño is a member of the military power elite.

tory, and PAN leaders more influential, the Technological Institute of Higher Studies (ITESM) in Monterrey will become an increasingly influential source of contact between capitalists and politicians.[64] This linkage has already been demonstrated in the Fox cabinet.[65] Had PRI presidential candidate Luis Donaldo Colosio, a graduate of the ITESM, not been assassinated in 1994, he would have advanced the influence of this institution, having made friendships with the children of many influential capitalist families and PAN leaders.[66]

The only exceptions to this pattern, which occurs among a small group of politicians and military officers, are Mexicans who meet in the selective advanced program at the Colegio de Defensa Nacional (CDN). Top military officers graduate from this program and have come to know mid-level administrators in government agencies. These contacts are too recent to be translated into links across power elites from the political side, but these classmates do establish close personal ties. Civilians who were students in the program remark that these officers continue to maintain contact with them, and officers automatically place a higher level of trust in a civilian graduate of the CDN.[67]

INSTITUTIONAL NETWORKING SOURCES

Institutional positions held by power elites account for more than a third of all networking sources. For military and religious power elites, organizational positions are the crucial settings through which contacts are fostered with the other power elite groups. They have used formal institutional posts to establish three-quarters of their friendships with other elites. (See table 8.) Numerous bishops establish frequent contacts with

64. Many leading capitalists have not only graduated from ITESM, but are very actively involved on the university's boards. Members of the Council of Teaching and Advanced Research and the Governing Board of the ITESM have included Eugenio Garza Laguera, Eugenio Garza Sada, Lorenzo Zambrano, Andrés Garza Sada, Dioniso Garza Medina, Federico Sada González, Alejandro Garza Laguera, Max Michel Suberville, Andrés Marcelo Sada Zambrano, and Alejandro H. Chapa Salazar. Sonia López, "Nueva era para el Tecnológico de Monterrey," *Integratec*, November/December, 1997, 31.

65. Luis Ernesto Derbez, the economic development secretary, was Fox's chief of staff's economic professor at ITESM. See *Mexico Business*, January/February, 2001, 39.

66. Such as Ernesto Ruffo and Carlos Medina Plascencia. See *Proceso*, August 21, 1992, 15.

67. Personal interviews with former graduates.

influential political elites as leaders of the episcopate, which often consults with the secretariat of government, a source of many members of Mexico's political power elite.[68]

The military's contact with politicians, with rare exceptions, has been facilitated almost completely through formal institutional posts.[69] The most significant source of these organizational contact points occur through the presidential staff, a body of the military which is autonomous from the national defense secretariat and reports directly to the president. Nearly three out of ten top officers held a post in this organization. Ten leading officers, all in the power elite sample, have served as the chief, assistant chief, or section head of the presidential staff, including one who was secretary of national defense. Many of these officers, while in those positions, became career mentors to members of their staff. Staff officers provide logistical assistance, security, intelligence, and staffing for the president in his day-to-day functions, which brings them into direct contact not only with the president but cabinet officials as well. Many members of the military power elite have served as personal adjutants to presidents, including a former national defense minister and a naval secretary.[70]

Embassy posts are a second influential source of organizational contact with future political elites, especially for officers serving as military attachés in the United States, France, and the United Kingdom. Most ambassadors assigned to these three countries are political appointees, and many are members of the power elite. Such experiences serve as a personal bridge between young, fast-rising officers and well-established public figures. One out of four officers in the present sample served in the Mexican embassy in Washington, D.C., between 1951 and 1988. Those individuals included three navy secretaries, one air force head, and two national defense secretaries.[71]

68. Adolfo Suárez Rivera, president of the episcopate, and Fernando Gutiérrez Barrios, secretary of government in the initial Salinas cabinet, established such a friendship.

69. A unique exception to this pattern is that of Augusto Gómez Villanueva, who lived at the Heroic Military College in the early 1950s, where he came to know generals Carlos Bermúdez Dávila, Arturo Cardona Marino, and Miguel Godínez Bravo, all members of the military power elite. *Excélsior*, May 23, 1983, 20, and May 22, 1983, 23.

70. For example, General Juan Arévalo Gardoqui and Naval Secretary Ricardo Cházaro.

71. Among those ambassadors whose appointments coincided with those of these military officers are Hugo B. Margáin, 1964–70, 1976–82; Bernardo Sepúlveda Amor, 1982; and Gustavo Petricioli, 1988–92.

In the United States, the most important networking among political, corporate, and cultural figures occurs within organizational bureaucracies or governing boards. Boards in the policy and/or civic sector have served as an influential means of integrating leading members of the corporate and cultural communities. As Thomas Dye concluded, "to the extent that high government officials are interlocked at all, it is with civic and cultural and educational institutions. It is *within* the corporate sector that interlocking is most prevalent. If there is a 'coming together' of corporate, governmental, and military elites as C. Wright Mills contended, it does not appear to be by means of interlocking directorates."[72]

Interlocking directorates, specifically corporate boards of directors, provide virtually no network ties between Mexican corporate elites and other elite groups. Of the hundreds of individuals who appear as members of the boards of Mexico's top companies, only three non-capitalist elites— Enrique Krauze, one of Mexico's most prominent intellectuals who was recently appointed to the Televisa board, and two politicians—are listed for the years 1970–2000. This is surprising given the fact that in other countries, including Spain, many top politicians have been corporate executives.[73]

The other form of organizational contact is that which occurs within governmental organizations. As Harold Salzman and G. William Domhoff point out, "the continuous circulation of corporate officials into and out of government, which has been documented in more general terms in other studies, means that the major corporations constantly are 'interlocked,' through different persons, with the federal government."[74] Non-capitalist power elites do not appear on Mexican corporate boards, but do corporate leaders tend to pursue influential governmental careers? Some Mexican analysts suggested in the early 1970s that an increasing number of prom-

72. Thomas R. Dye, *Who's Running America? The Bush Era*, 5th ed. (Englewood Cliffs: Prentice-Hall, 1990), 186.

73. Salustiano del Campo et al., "The Spanish Political Elite: Permanency and Change," in Moshe M. Czudnowski, ed., *Does Who Governs Matter? Elite Circulation in Contemporary Societies* (DeKalb: Northern Illinois University Press, 1982), 144.

74. Harold Salzman and G. William Domhoff, "The Corporate Community and Government: Do They Interlock?" in G. William Domhoff, *Power Structure Research* (Beverly Hills: Sage, 1980), 251. Peter J. Freitag, in his examination of U.S. cabinets, concluded that 41 percent held management posts before and after their appointment, 22 percent only before, and 13 percent only after. "The Cabinet and Big Business: A Study of Interlocks," *Social Problems*, 23 (December 1975), 148.

inent business leaders from lobbying organizations, as well as capitalists, occupied important positions in the Mexican government.[75] In the 1980s, in a more comprehensive, empirical study, Miguel Centeno discovered that a sizeable number of middle-level Mexican politicians, through career experiences in the private sector, established potential connections to businessmen.[76]

The circulation of lower-level governmental officials in and out of the corporate world, or mid-level corporate management in and out of government, is significant to power elites only if it leads to future ties. The networking potential within the separate organizational worlds of the five power elite groups is limited. Mexico's most influential capitalists and clergy have typically had almost no experience in a career other than their own. As we have seen, clergy use their own institutional positions to come into contact with, and develop friendships among, other power elites, but no member of the inner core of bishops has ever worked in an institution other than the Catholic Church.

The so-called organizational interlock between the corporate and political worlds in the United States is essentially nonexistent for their Mexican counterparts. Only three out of a hundred leading capitalists have held governmental posts, and two of these worked in professional careers before assuming positions as CEOs. Military officers are restricted in their organizational networking ties to career assignments in government, and these assignments always occur while they are on active duty, even if they are granted temporary leaves. Only eleven of the hundred officers in the present sample have held political office, usually at the apex of their careers.

Only two of the power elite groups, intellectuals and politicians, could be said to have had a significant opportunity to establish networking contacts with their peers while working in different organizational settings. One out of ten intellectuals in Mexico have worked in the public sector, in some cases, for many years. Two leading intellectuals, Enrique Krauze, who has directed his own family business and has organized successful publishing ventures, and Gabriel Zaid, who runs a consulting business,

75. Alonso Aguilar Monteverde, "La oligarquía," in Jorge Carrión and Alonso Aguilar Monteverde, eds., *La burguesía, la oligarquía y el estado* (Mexico City: Editorial Nuestro Tiempo, 1972), 193.

76. Miguel Centeno, *Democracy within Reason, Technocratic Revolution in Mexico* (University Park: Penn State University Press, 1994), 130. Centeno combined family, school, and professional experience to reach a figure of 60 percent for his examination of middle-level figures in 1983.

have spent their entire careers split between two worlds, business and culture. Both are unusual because they were educated as industrial engineers.[77]

Politicians, in terms of potential interlocks, boast the most eclectic careers. One out of ten politicians has held management-level positions in the private sector, although none are wealthy capitalists who owned or controlled the largest Mexican firms. Politicians are equally well-represented in the cultural world, where one out of ten directed cultural institutions or publications, putting them into direct contact with Mexico's prominent intellectual figures. One politician, who began his military career in 1943 as a cadet at the Heroico Colegio Militar, resigned as an infantry captain in 1959 to pursue a highly successful career in government internal security.[78]

The most significant finding in this chapter is that Mexican power elites are linked through network ties. The present data suggest a minimum of 500 of these ties, a figure which indicates the significant extent of power elite friendships. In fact, because of the difficulty in identifying these ties empirically in detail, this figure most likely underrepresents the actual number by a large margin. The number of these personal friendships across power elite groups would be expected to be as extensive as those revealed by a single member of the power elite.

These findings, while of major significance, cannot be used to conclude that the broader concept of a power elite, defined as individuals from one policy sector holding top decision-making positions in a second policy arena, exists in Mexico. What they do suggest, however, *is the real possibility of power elites from multiple leadership groups, through extensive friendships, having the potential for exercising policy-making influence*

77. Krauze, the child of Polish Jews, grew up with a father in the printing business. Zaid, the child of a Palestinian immigrant, grew up in Monterrey, where he established friendships with the children of northern capitalist families. Personal interview with Enrique Krauze, Mexico City, May 26, 1982, and Gabriel Zaid, Mexico City, October 6, 1983.

78. Fernando Gutiérrez Barrios was this individual. It is not surprising that his father was in the military, having fought in the 1910 Revolution and retired as a colonel before going into a business. Also, Gutiérrez Barrios, like so many of his influential military peers, served in the Presidential Assault Battalion under the command of the presidential chief of staff in 1948–49. *Mexico Journal*, December 16, 1988, 16, and Roderic Ai Camp, *Mexican Political Biographies, 1935–1993*, 3rd ed. (Austin: University of Texas Press, 1995), 330.

through informal networking ties. It further demonstrates the value of the methodological approach of identifying informal network relationships, which through family and education alone account for nearly two-thirds of all known ties across Mexico's power elite.

Surprisingly, organizational contacts are responsible for only slightly more than a third of important friendships among power elites. The almost exclusive concentration of networking analysis on organizational contacts in other countries thus probably seriously undermeasures the most influential networking sources. The present findings suggest that examining the potential policy influence of elites outside of a policy circle by identifying the holders of significant organizational positions does not provide an accurate reflection of elite interlocks.

A second significant finding is that influential mentors, who often serve as crucial networking links within power elite groups, also provide their disciples with important contacts outside of their own elite circle. These individuals, who number among the most important members of the power elite, pass on these tasks to the next generation of power elites, who learn mentoring and decision-making skills.

The third finding is that the five Mexican power elite groups network with their peer groups in different ways. The structure and preparation of individual power elite circles influence the sources which play the most important role in facilitating influential friendships. Structures which are advantageous to increasing networks within one elite group are often major obstacles to providing linkages across power elites.

As was the case within individual power elite groups, the most structured groups, the military and clergy, make much greater use of organizational linkages. The structural conditions within the Catholic Church and the armed forces in Mexico which encourage educational contacts *within* their two institutions through professional education in military academies and Catholic seminaries, limit educational ties with other elites. Because clergy and the military are rarely related to other elites through their families, the only remaining source which offers them networking possibilities are shared career experiences, which occur in organizational settings.

For the clergy, these are positions in the Catholic hierarchy. As we have seen, serving in the post of bishop facilitates many contacts with national leadership in the political and business worlds. This is particularly the case for bishops who were assigned or elected to administrative positions on the executive committee of the Mexican Council of Bishops. For the military, positions in quasi-military settings, typically on the presidential staff, the national defense staff, and in embassies, bring military personnel into contact with present and future political power elites.

A potential change for both of these groups may be the result of broad political trends sweeping Mexico, particularly the revival of regionalism and the increasing importance of state capitals as the source of future power elites. Influential officers are assigned zone commands throughout Mexico, the most important post involving direct command of troops, and bishops direct dioceses which are in close proximity to every capital. Bishops and generals, therefore, are increasingly coming in contact with future political elites who will move on to the national scene.

A fourth major point about networking ties across power elites is that social class background contributes to the importance of certain types of family linkages. Specifically, kinship becomes an especially influential source of networking between certain power elite groups whose parents are from wealthy backgrounds. Socioeconomic background, therefore, has a significant impact on the importance of one source of networking versus another. Wealth, as a background variable, enhances the influence of "informal" versus more formal channels of networking contacts, increasing the overall ranking of family as a major networking source.

A fifth significant conclusion about power elite networking is that among the many potential non-career social institutions which provide environments favorable to cementing friendships among future leaders, none are as influential as education. Most of the networking linkages initially providing access across power elite groups in Mexico are concentrated in a handful of public or private universities. This finding suggests that educational institutions are fertile grounds for establishing long-term informal networks. These same institutions also have been crucial in the mentor–disciple relationship, since many intellectual and career mentors began their relationships with future Mexican elites as professors.

An exploration of adult residence among Mexican power elites suggests an additional significant finding. Mexico's power elite is concentrated heavily in three urban centers, Mexico City, Guadalajara, and Monterrey. These geographic concentrations facilitate networking through other sources. Only two of the power elite groups, clergy and to a lesser degree the military, can be said to have come from regional backgrounds.

An important finding among political power elites is that a new type of politician at the end of the twentieth century, the hybrid politico, is increasingly characterized by provincial roots and experiences outside the three urban centers. This pattern is likely to increase in importance, as represented by the presidential victory of Vicente Fox, who comes from provincial origins. If large numbers of his collaborators are drawn from regional sources, it may alter somewhat future networking sources.

Part II

HOW POWER ELITES
ARE FORMED

5 Origins of Socialization
Sources among the Power Elite

From 1970 through 2000, Mexico has witnessed exceptional alterations in social, economic, and political attitudes; it has been perhaps the most dynamic period since the revolutionary decades from 1910 through 1929. It is important, therefore, to explain how that shift came about, what it involved, and what socializing sources were most responsible for crafting fresh attitudes among power elite members.

In the previous two chapters, I examined the networking characteristics of Mexican power elites, arguing that mentors play a crucial role in creating and recruiting power elites and in generating networking ties to each other. The way in which power elites establish friendships, and the means through which they potentially influence the allocation of resources and leadership values through networking, is an essential part of their structure and behavior.

Many of the same sources which are essential to networking among power elites are crucial to the development of their attitudes and ideologies. In other words, sources such as family, career, and education also significantly influence the formation of power elite values. Most circumstantial literature suggests that elites, as a consequence of their shared status, view numerous issues in the same light. Most empirical studies, however, conclude that elites are as diverse in their views as is the general population.[1]

This book does not argue that Mexican power elites share similar attitudes within each group or across all groups. It does suggest that leadership

1. For example, Michael Useem, who researched leading American capitalists, concluded that they "were not found to have a political ideology more homogeneous than the remainder of the capitalist class." "The Inner Group of the American Capitalist Class," *Social Problems*, 25 (1978), 237.

is often responsible for significant shifts in public opinion, shifts that have remarkable consequences for redirecting society in many policy areas. For example, G. John Ikenberry and Charles A. Kupchan argue that "case studies confirm that socialization is principally an elite and not a mass phenomenon. For norms to have a consequential effect on state behavior, they must take root within the elite community."[2] This work further argues that mentors and networks contribute significantly to these influential shifts in power elite attitudes.

Strangely, we know little about adult socialization or the sources which contribute most significantly to altering beliefs and opinions of individuals after their childhood and adolescent years. Most students of socialization assume that the greatest changes in values take place during those younger years. We know even less about elite adult socialization.[3]

The most extensive examination of adult behavior over time is Theodore Newcomb's classic two-decade survey, which concluded that attitudes are maintained by creating either environments which block new information, or environments which reinforce a person's original point of view.[4] If an open environment produces fresh sources of information which conflict with an initial interpretation, it could alter an individual's attitudes. If an individual's circle of friends alter their views, they might affect their friend's perceptions.

We know from a small number of previous studies that contextual variables interact with background variables to produce differing socialization patterns in societies. For example, an individual's religious background (or lack of it), hometown, father's occupation (and for younger elites, mother's as well), and type of school all contribute indirectly to developing and reinforcing his or her views.[5]

In addition to such background variables, the events through which a young person or adult passes generate equally important consequences. They might be political (such as a divisive presidential campaign), violent (such as a civil or foreign war), or economic (such as a deep depression).

2. "Socialization and Hegemonic Power," *International Organization*, 44, no. 3 (summer 1990), 314.

3. Jack Dennis, "Major Problems of Political Socialization Research," in Jack Dennis, ed., *Socialization to Politics* (New York: Wiley, 1973), 24.

4. Theodore Newcomb, "Persistence and Regression of Changed Attitudes: Long-Range Studies," in Jack Dennis, ed., *Socialization to Politics* (New York: Wiley, 1973), 422.

5. Allen H. Barton, "Background, Attitudes and Activities of American Elites," in Gwen Moore, ed., *Studies of the Structure of National Elites*, 1 (Greenwich: JAI, 1985), 201.

It has been shown that several types of sources are important in socializing Mexican political elites, and some of these same sources appear to be influential for all power elite members.[6]

It also has been hypothesized recently that major international powers may produce a socializing effect, even indirectly, on other societies and their leaders. Specifically, has the United States "Americanized" other elites?[7] Recent research suggests, using the example of the burgeoning emphasis on economic privatization among dozens of countries, that a common "international policy culture" buttressed its dispersion among policymakers from those societies.[8] The impact of foreign sources of socialization, including education abroad, will be taken up in the following chapters. In the present sample, the testimonies of many members of Mexico's power elite suggest that three main domestic sources appear to be most important in constructing their values and molding their views as influential adults. Those sources are family, career, and education. This chapter will explore the importance of the first two sources, as well as several experiential social processes that have an impact on socialization (e.g., residence and major societal events).

THE FAMILY

Mexican power elites, not surprisingly, have identified family as their most important source of values. Mentors within the family play a significant socializing role, just as they do as recruiters and networkers. Family, generally (but not exclusively) parents, has been identified in nearly every examination of socialization as a crucial source of children's values. Adolescents, despite their natural rebellion against parents and adults, retain many essential values learned within a supportive family environment.

The family socialization process goes well beyond general attitudes about morality, politics, and culture; it includes professional values, too. A strong predisposition toward specific professions exists among children of

6. Roderic Ai Camp, *The Making of a Government: Political Leaders in Modern Mexico* (Tucson: University of Arizona Press, 1984), 1–7.

7. G. John Ikenberry and Charles A. Kupchan, "Socialization and Hegemonic Power," 313.

8. G. John Ikenberry, "The International Spread of Privatization Policies: Inducements, Learning, and 'Policy Bandwagoning,'" in Ezra Suleiman and John Waterbury, eds., *Political Economy of Public Sector: Reform and Privatization* (Boulder: Westview, 1990), 105. Historically, Ikenberry notes that the spread of Keynesian economic policy was fostered by the power and prestige of the United States.

professionals. In the United States, for example, students whose fathers were medical doctors began thinking in terms of a medical career at an early age, and one study found that 50 percent had fathers or other relatives who were physicians. This was also true for lawyers, who are most likely as a group to become politicians.

The military has also long been a family tradition. At West Point, the United States elite army academy, 83 percent of the cadets who had decided on a military career before the age of fifteen had a father who was career military or relatives at West Point. Sons of military fathers alone accounted for 63 percent of the cadets. Over a third of the graduating class in 1965 were children of career officers.[9] Among Mexico's military power elite, one-third were the sons of career military fathers.

In England, among Anglican diocesan bishops, one of the few religious leadership groups to be studied in detail, more than half claimed fathers who were in the clergy, and nearly a third married women whose fathers were clergymen.[10] Politicians, especially those who become "professional" or life-long politicos, are also strongly influenced by family members in the same profession.

Studies from Europe concluded that "psychologically speaking, political involvement is for many men and women a family legacy. Nearly half of the members of the British, German, and Italian parliaments report that some older relative of theirs had been active in politics, half recall that politics was a prime topic of conversation in their childhood, and three quarters say that they became actively interested in politics before the age of twenty-five."[11] Studies of United States politicians discovered that anywhere between 41 and 59 percent of American politicians reported one or more family members as being active in politics.[12]

Mexican power elites, regardless of the group they represent, report a

9. J. P. Lovell, "The Professional Socialization of the West Point Cadet," in Morris Janowitz, ed., *The New Military: Changing Patterns of Organization* (New York: Russell Sage, 1964), 136–37.

10. D. H. J. Morgan, "The Social and Educational Background of Anglican Bishops—Continuities and Changes," *British Journal of Sociology*, 20 (1969), 297.

11. Robert D. Putnam, *The Beliefs of Politicians: Ideology, Conflict, and Democracy in Britain and Italy* (New Haven: Yale University Press, 1973), 76. Kenneth Prewitt, Heinz Eulau, and Betty Zisk found a direct relationship between the age at which an individual entered politics and the importance family played in that individual's career choice. The younger the choice was made, the more overwhelming the role of parents. "Political Socialization and Political Roles," *Public Opinion Quarterly*, 30 (winter 1966–67), 575.

12. Heinz Eulau, "Recollections," in John C. Wahlke et al., eds., *The Legislative System* (New York: Wiley, 1962), 82.

similar level of linkage between their parents' occupations or active interests and their own career choices. In the case of Mexican religious elites, the difference of course is that Catholic bishops are not the products of fathers who were priests. Nevertheless, the incidence of relatives whose careers were associated with the Catholic Church, and more importantly, family religious environment, played significant roles in encouraging Mexicans to become priests, a characteristic present among other Latin American priests.[13]

The principal difference between members of the religious power elite and all other Mexican elites is the frequency with which their mothers influenced their values and career choices.[14] The bishop of Ciudad Juárez for nearly four decades, is typical:

> What influenced me most toward my vocation as a priest principally was my mother, first because she was a very strong, practicing Christian who prayed every day, and generally assisted mass every day, praying in the mass and staying to 5:00 P.M. to give thanks to Jesus Christ during the following mass. . . . Moreover, she professed a great respect for all priests to such a degree that she would never enter her own home before a priest, exclaiming, "I never enter before a priest!" She created a great Christian environment in the home, adorning it with images of the Virgin Mary and other saints, and continually using occasions to illuminate family or social events evangelically. Also, I had a clearer idea of what it was to be a priest because from the age of eight or nine I served as an altar boy in the Chihuahua cathedral. My father, Félix Talamás Sapah, was a good Christian and never failed to attend mass on Sundays or holidays.[15]

Power elites from other categories recall similar familial experiences among both grandparents and parents. Octavio Paz, a member of the in-

---

13. Gustavo Pérez Ramírez and Yván Labelle, *El problema sacerdotal en América Latina* (Madrid: FERES, 1964), 77.

14. This is not to suggest other elites were not equally influenced by their mothers. In fact, Vicente Fox recently revealed that his mother's enthusiasm for politics generally, and his aunt's strong support of the National Action Party, is what led to his partisan interest in PAN. See Antonio Jáquez, "Tensiones, diferencias y recelos entre Fox y el PAN," *Proceso,* July 16, 2000. www.proceso.com.mx.

15. Personal letter from Bishop Manuel Talamás Camandari, October 18, 1996. Talamás's family religious environment obviously was both special and strong. Three of his brothers attended seminary as well, although none became priests. His parents came from a unique religious background, having been born in Bethlehem, Jerusalem (Israel), and having been attended by Franciscan priests. They were married in Saint Catherine the Martyr parish, next to the Christmas Basilica in Bethlehem, arriving in Chihuahua as newlyweds.

tellectual power elite, considered both his grandfather and father to have exerted a significant influence, as mentors, on his ideas. His father introduced him to one of Mexico's most influential figures in the 1920s, an outspoken critic of the regime who later became Paz's mentor and professor in college.[16] His father's friend influenced Paz both because of his intellectual views and because he was an "honest and courageous man."[17] President Miguel Alemán, political mentor to several influential members of the power elite and father of Miguel Alemán Velasco, a leading capitalist in the present sample, considered his own father, a revolutionary general, to have been the most important mentor in influencing his values:

> My father was the person who most influenced my ideas. In my home, as a child, I heard the propaganda of Flores Magón, and others, which circulated in tiny pamphlets or booklets. I think the environment of my home affected me substantially. . . . I was with him a lot during those years of postrevolutionary activity. My mother was a person of great character, and she influenced me in this respect rather than in my intellectual ideas.[18]

Similarly, Miguel Alemán Jr pointed to his father, President Alemán, as having exerted the most influence on his attitudes. Miguel Alemán Jr. wanted to be a politician, like his father:

> I always wanted to be like my father, to be a politician. My father was my most important political mentor. We had a wonderful relationship as friends, not just as father and son. He was very open with me about discussing politics. I think this is why he often took me on trips, to witness political events, and he introduced me to his friends, many of whom were the most influential political figures of that era.[19]

16. Antonio Díaz Soto y Gama founded the National Agrarian Party in the 1920s, was a leading orator of his generation in Congress, and supported an important opposition party as a party official in the 1946 presidential campaign.

17. Personal interview with Octavio Paz, Mexico City, June 29, 1978.

18. Personal interview with President Miguel Alemán, Mexico City, October 27, 1976.

19. Personal interview with Miguel Alemán Jr., Washington, D.C., June 22, 1999. The example of Alemán does not contradict the father-son professional pattern. Miguel Alemán Jr. has had an on-off political career for many years, having served on the National Executive Committee of PRI in 1968, and again in 1992, as senator from his home state, 1991–97, and governor of Veracruz since 1998. He was seriously considered as a PRI presidential candidate in 1999. But Alemán's career in the private sector and as a leading capitalist takes precedence over his political career. His father, who built the fortune inherited by Miguel Alemán Jr., made a life career in politics, after a short period in legal practice, the same profession initially pursued by Miguel Alemán Jr., and used his political connections

Family, as can be seen from the multigenerational examples of Miguel Alemán and his father and son, exerts a very important influence over the socialization of future elites. First, the parent's professional occupation often flavors the child's choice. Second, and solidly linked to the parent's profession, the parent exposes the child to other prominent figures.

The resulting friendships are not only crucial to networking, as we have witnessed previously, but reinforce the impact of the parent's experiences and professional values, providing a deep source of intellectual cross-fertilization and socialization. A leading politician and power elite member who was raised in a low-level bureaucrat's family and who became a close friend of Miguel Alemán Jr. was greatly influenced by his own father, and especially his father's friends:

> My father's generation had a close and important relationship with me—his friends always talked to me. My mother's brother was a judge. Because my father only held a modest position in government, his friends were real friends of the family, not like Miguelito's father, where many friends were seeking favors from his father through Miguelito. On my mother's side, her father was a doctor from Campeche, who practiced medicine into his eighties—he too had a reputation for honesty, and served as a model to me.[20]

This father-child professional linkage can be found most commonly among Mexican capitalists. Eighty percent of the capitalist elite pursued the same profession as their fathers. Another component of familial socialization is the family's social status, which may be linked to a parent's occupation but is not necessarily the product of the parent's profession. Scholars have argued that social backgrounds are insufficient for predicting decision makers' policy positions, yet we know that personal wealth is causally linked to selected attitudes.[21] For example, "net financial worth was a powerful conservative influence, particularly on economic issues," among American elites.[22]

---

to achieve his wealth. The analogy could be stretched to the relationship between President Alemán and his father, who, although he was a revolutionary general, was an important political figure who died in the 1929 rebellion against the government. He wanted his son to have a civilian profession, the profession (law) which produced the postrevolutionary political leadership.

20. Personal interview with Pedro Ojeda Paullada, Mexico City, December 14, 1998.

21. Nelson Polsby, *Community Power and Political Theory* (New Haven: Yale University Press, 1974), 106.

22. Allen H. Barton, "Determinants of Elite Policy Attitudes," in B. A. Rock-

The author of this study went on to say that adult institutional environments often overcome presumed initial differences stemming from class or social origin, but those background variables initially strongly channel people into different elite groups.[23] This pattern in itself is significant because certain class origins dominate elite professions, as in the case of Mexican capitalists. Occupation or profession socializes individual members, and class norms become part of that socialization process.

The socializing influence of elite family backgrounds originates from the fact, about which there is no dispute, that privileged backgrounds occur disproportionately among power elites as compared to the general population.[24] It is also indisputable that families, wealthy and poor alike, transmit general cultural values.[25] Psychologists have determined that even when children are young, wealthy social status exerts "considerable psychological significance."[26]

Observations regarding the specific ways in which wealthy family background affects socialization vary. Some scholars suggest that an elite class background creates an ethos which affects elites' behavior toward each other.[27] Nelson W. Aldrich Jr. suggests that children of "old money" inherit a kind of "spiritual security" as well as social and economic security.[28] Many scholars have asserted that a wealthy family background produces conservative individuals. Such conclusions are often impressionistic, however; the reality of familial socialization is more complex.

One of the few empirical studies of elite socialization indicates that American capitalists, compared to other professions, did not produce more

man and R. H. Linden, eds., *Elite Studies and Comparative Politics* (Pittsburgh: University of Pittsburgh Press, 1984), 213.

23. For example, in D. H. J. Morgan's study of Anglican bishops, not one from 1860 to 1960 was found to have a father who was a manual worker. "The Social and Educational Background of Anglican Bishops," 298.

24. Harold R. Kerbo and L. Richard Della Fave, "The Empirical Side of the Power Elite Debate: An Assessment and Critique of Recent Research," *The Sociological Quarterly*, 20 (winter 1979), 18.

25. Dean Jaros, *Socialization to Politics* (New York: Praeger, 1973), 81.

26. Robert Coles, *Privileged Ones: The Well-Off and the Rich in America* (Boston: Little, Brown, 1977), 418.

27. In an examination of Polish leadership, for example, George J. Szablowski argues that "since Polish political elites originate predominantly from the intelligentsia [true of most political elites worldwide], the ethos of this class prevails in working relations of all political institutions. . . ." "Governing and Competing Elites in Poland," *Governance*, 6, no. 3 (July 1993), 354.

28. *Old Money: The Mythology of America's Upper Class* (New York: Alfred Knopf, 1988), 69.

conservative children who became business leaders.[29] On the other hand, Barton took into account an individual's current institutional affiliation (for example clergy versus politicians), their net worth, and their background, finding that the three variables combined sway elite attitudes significantly.[30] Raymond Aron's classic work on French intellectuals claimed these same variables played a vital role in determining their attitudes.[31] The importance of family wealth is, therefore, that it is often passed on to the next generation, thus determining the power elite member's wealth or socioeconomic circumstance.

Family social status as measured by a father's occupation and / or income also determines the degree of influence socializing sources wield. One of the few studies of socialization among Mexican children found that the father's occupation had a fundamental impact on a child's orientation toward and interest in politics, and that it affected who the child talked to outside the family. As Rafael Segovia expresses it, "teachers lose out in this contest with parents who are professionals."[32] The professional parent, it seems, is more likely to create an environment which influences a child's intellectual values, attitudes, and experiences. The Russian revolution is instructive in this regard: one out of six leaders in Russia attributed their role as revolutionaries to parental attitudes, second only to the impact of books and literature in their personal formation.[33]

I am not suggesting that each member of Mexico's power elite automatically inherits a parent's culture. In fact, testimony from some members of the elite contradicts parental influence. For example, a leading intellectual who grew up in a family dominated by a father who mentored other members of the power elite and who played a crucial role in Mexican

29. Allen H. Barton, "Determinants of Economic Attitudes in the American Business Elite," *American Journal of Sociology,* 91 (1985), 72. Richard Center's classic study of depression generation children cites a survey of public high school students which demonstrated striking differences in attitudes toward collectivism versus individualism based on parents' occupation. "Children of the New Deal: Social Stratification and Adolescent Attitudes," in R. Bendix and S. M. Lipset, eds., *Class, Status and Power* (New York: Free Press, 1953), 361.

30. Allen H. Barton, "Background, Attitudes and Activities of American Elites," 213.

31. Raymond Aron, *The Opium of the Intellectuals* (New York: Doubleday, 1957), 213.

32. Rafael Segovia, *La politizacíon del niño mexicano* (Mexico City: El Colegio de México, 1975), 16.

33. Jerome Davis, "A Study of One Hundred and Sixty-Three Outstanding Communist Leaders," in Glenn Paige, ed., *Political Leadership* (New York: Free Press, 1972), 271.

democratization has suggested that he did not inherit his father's intellectual culture.[34]

But a father like this can offer an extraordinary intellectual milieu. Hugo B. Margáin's father, a prominent physician, provided one of the most remarkable familial surroundings. In fact, one of his father's friends was the brother of Margáin's most influential mentor:[35]

> My grandfather bought a ranch in the nineteenth century which today is where University City sits. We had great intellectual gatherings there. Such men as Nabor Carrillo [leading physicist and rector of UNAM], Carlos Lazo [prominent architect and secretary of public works], Carlos Graf Fernández [notable mathematician and professor], Fernando Benítez [member of the intellectual power elite and political essayist], Carlos Fuentes, and all sorts of scientists and writers came to visit and stay with us. We finally sold this home in 1937. But I grew up in this environment, meeting all of these people. My father was also a professor. My sister married Manuel Sandoval Vallarta [a student of Albert Einstein who taught at MIT]. European intellectuals also gathered at our home on Sundays, and such men as Compton [president of Harvard] and Oppenheimer from the United States.[36]

Elites from working- or even middle-class families would rarely have access to such unique social opportunities, or exposure to numerous personal models and intellectual influences. An elite who follows in the footsteps of prominent parents has not only enjoyed his or her predecessor's fame and influence, but also has been raised in an ambience conducive to the internalization of professional values.[37] These patterns are reinforced, as the examples illustrate, by other immediate family members who may

34. Pilar Jiménez Trejo and Alejandro Toledo, *Creación y poder: Nueve retratos de intelectuales* (Mexico: Contrapuntos, 1994), 169. The intellectual is Federico Reyes Heroles. His father, Jesús Reyes Heroles, was a member of the political power elite and former president of the PRI and secretary of government, who taught at the National University from 1946 to 1963; his former students include President Miguel de la Madrid. Federico's brother, Jesús Jr., served in President Zedillo's cabinet before becoming his ambassador to the United States. His maternal grandfather, General Roque González Garza, was president of the Convention government during the revolution.

35. Margáin's political mentor was Antonio Carrillo Flores, one of the most influential figures of his generation and the brother of Nabor Carrillo Flores, his father's friend.

36. Personal interview with Hugo B. Margáin, Mexico City, March 14, 1977.

37. Alfred B. Clubok, Norman M. Wilensky, and Forrest J. Berghorn, "Family Relationships, Congressional Recruitment, and Political Modernization," *Journal of Politics*, 31 (November 1961), 1036.

Table 12. Occupational Backgrounds among Mexican Power Elites' Relatives

Profession of Immediate Family Members	*Power Elite Group*				
	Intellectuals (%)	*Capitalists (%)*	*Military (%)*	*Clergy (%)*	*Politicians (%)*
Clergy	9	1	0	50	1
Business	18	81	9	7	16
Military	9	1	60	0	10
Government	22	13	13	7	43
Cultural	21	0	0	7	6
None	21	4	18	29	24

NOTE: Based on published sources, correspondence, and interviews. *Cultural* refers broadly to intellectual activities such as education, journalism, arts, etc. (N = 398)

also be active in the same professions. It is not a coincidence that 50 percent of clergy, 81 percent of capitalists, 60 percent of the military officers, and 43 percent of the politicians could claim immediate family members in their same profession (table 12). In other words, such individuals receive the values of their institutional affiliations before they actually set foot within the profession's organizational apparatus, thus extending and linking together family and career socializing influences.

CAREER

The second most influential source of values among Mexican power elites, according to their own published and unpublished testimonies, lies within their career institutions. Career organizations, somewhat like a large, formal family, provide these socializing influences in two ways. First, a career mentor, who may have actually recruited the future elite in the first place and been instrumental in enhancing that individual's networks within and beyond their elite circle, exerts an important influence. This individual transmits the organizational culture, and the skills necessary to succeed within the culture, to his disciple. He also directly influences his disciple's values, but those values are typically tied to broader policy issues which dominate the agenda of a specific power elite circle, whether religious, political, or economic.

The future power elite also learns the organizational culture, skills, and policy preferences indirectly, from a peer environment and from informal institutional rules. In other words, these values and preferences are not necessarily conveyed directly by a mentor, but are observed by an astute participant within the organization.

Extensive research in Europe and the United States has produced evidence to support the importance of organizational influences on individual elite values and attitudes. Most of these studies come from the political world.[38] Nevertheless, it would not be unwarranted to transfer their conclusions to other power elite groups. The general argument that specializing functions in different institutional settings create leaders who respond to the institution's particular interests and to professional responsibilities is convincing.[39]

Professional socialization is so powerful that scholars have discovered organizational differences *within* elite groups. For example, in the United States the economic sector a businessperson represents determines many of his or her attitudes toward public policies.[40] Among French cabinet members, the striking differences in cast of mind can be traced to different career origins—parties, parliament, or the government bureaucracy.[41]

Organizational studies from different professions also suggest that individuals who succeed inside an institutional structure are more likely to have been socialized by their profession's norms. In a recent exploration of military socialization based on a study of cadets at the Royal Canadian Military College, the author concluded that those promoted to higher positions changed their values in a direction congruent with military professionalization. Those changes occurred in a chronological progression based on time spent within the organization. However, the author also concluded that the values and professional orientation the individual brings to an organization are more important than what that individual learns from the socialization process within an institutional atmosphere.[42]

Mature, successful participants within an institution's profession tend

38. A serious, broadly conceived attempt to do this for Mexico is Peter Cleaves, *Professions and the State: The Mexican Case* (Tucson: University of Arizona Press, 1987), especially chapter 5.

39. Allen H. Barton, "Determinants of Elite Policy Attitudes," 230.

40. Allen H. Barton, "Determinants of Economic Attitudes in the American Business Elite," 57.

41. Mattei Dogan, ed., *Pathways to Power: Selection Rules in Pluralist Democracies* (Boulder: Westview, 1988), 36.

42. Serge Guimond, "Encounter and Metamorphosis: The Impact of Military Socialization on Professional Values," *Applied Psychology: An International Review*, 44, no. 3 (1995), 253, 269. Guimond concluded that the organizational socialization process did not have a major impact on the individual's fundamental values or attitudes by the rank of lieutenant or captain.

to support the institution's procedural rules of the game. This is true in politics as well as within the military and clerical bureaucracies.[43] One of the explanations for this type of behavior can be found in reference group theory, which argues that cues picked up from peers determine how individuals view the world and their place in it.[44]

Institutions alter elite values learned in family environments and educational settings. An economist who began his career in the Bank of Mexico after graduating from the National University, eventually reaching the apex of the public financial world as treasury secretary, recalls his initial institutional setting: "I can tell you that the bank changed the views I learned while at the National School of Economics. I came away from the school with a strong ideological orientation. Ideology, of course, is all right, but you have to understand the practical techniques and processes for achieving your goals. This is something the bank taught me which I did not learn in college."[45]

The business world has taught other members of the power elite similar lessons, suggesting the important socializing consequences of professional activities. Vicente Fox, the first presidential candidate to have defeated the PRI and a man whose professional career remained almost exclusively in the private sector until the 1990s, commented on his own socialization:

> At the university, they taught me to reflect and to analyze. But working at Coca-Cola was my second university education. I learned that the heart of a business is out in the field, not in the office. I learned strategy, marketing, financial management, [and] optimization of resources. I learned not to accept anything but winning. I learned an iron discipline for getting results.[46]

An institutional environment not only influences the values and attitudes of those who have sought initially to make an institution their career, but it can prompt a person established in one career to shift laterally to another. The only Mexican in the power elite to have switched from the military to another profession after graduating from the Heroico Colegio Militar recalled going "to the security area [as an employee of the secretary

43. John L. Sullivan et al., "Why Politicians Are More Tolerant: Selective Recruitment and Socialization among Political Elites in Britain, Israel, New Zealand and the United States," *British Journal of Political Science*, 23 (1993), 70.

44. Kenneth Prewitt, Heinz Eulau, and Betty H. Zisk, "Political Socialization and Political Roles," 574.

45. Personal interview with Jesús Silva Herzog, Riverside, California, November 19, 1998.

46. *New York Times*, May 9, 1999, Section 3, 1.

of government in charge of information] as just another military commission. With the passage of time, . . . first I was attracted to, then became passionate about, politics."[47]

RESIDENCE AND MAJOR SOCIAL EVENTS

In addition to the major influences exerted by family, career, and, as we shall see, education on Mexican power elite socialization, there is experience. Experiential socialization processes can be direct or indirect, and unlike the three primary sources of socialization, are not influenced by a mentor. Although they are even more difficult to measure, and even to separate from the three primary forms of power elite socialization, they deserve mention.

The first of these influences is early residence, which commonly reinforces family values. Birthplace and early residence flavor Mexicans' cultural experiences. The effect of this variable was particularly acute when internal transportation was limited, strongly influencing an older generation of Mexican power elites. Distinct local features of economic development and social sophistication affected numerous Mexican leaders' experiences. The childhood residence of the late Heberto Castillo Martínez is an example. He was a power elite from the political opposition who grew up in the Veracruz highlands among Otomi Indians in a culture of extreme poverty and physical violence, where men often traveled armed, including the local priest. This experience exercised a profound impact on his attitudes, and as he suggested, contributed to his posture as a mediator between Congress and the indigenous guerrillas in Chiapas in the 1990s.[48]

Adult residence is equally influential. A comprehensive survey of American elites revealed that a person's views on foreign policy and civil liberties were related to their geographic origin, "the South and Southwest being more hawkish and repressive, the Northeast and Far West being more dovish and libertarian."[49] Comparable survey research on Mexican elites is unavailable, but we know that place of residence is an important variable among ordinary Mexicans in determining differing interpretations about social, economic, and political issues.[50] For example, among

47. Former government secretary Fernando Gutiérrez Barrios. See the *Los Angeles Times*, June 30, 1999, A8.
48. Personal interview with Heberto Castillo Martínez, Mexico City, July 12, 1993.
49. Allen H. Barton, "Determinants of Elite Policy Attitudes," 213.
50. For a detailed analysis, see Peter Ward and Victoria Rodríguez, "Learning

Mexicans in 1998 responding to the question of what democracy means to them, only 13 percent of those living in small villages (fewer than 5,000) compared to three times as many (42 percent) living in cities of 500,000 to 1 million conceptualized democracy as form of government.[51]

We also know from the most comprehensive surveys of Mexican values that regional differences are significant in explaining economic views. For example, in the late 1980s Mexicans residing in the North expressed notable differences of opinion compared to all other Mexicans on the issue of whether or not the government should reduce its participation in the economy. Northern Mexicans strongly favored this concept compared to Mexicans residing in all other geographic locales.[52]

What is important to understand is that geographic residence does affect both elite and mass views. Second, both groups are affected in the same way. The argument can be made that regional elites help to form mass attitudes, and mass attitudes in return reinforce those same values.

The commonality shared by these studies of ordinary Mexicans and elite Americans is that geography contributes to specific values or opinions. In Mexico, one of the few locales where that seems most apparent among elites and ordinary citizens alike is in the North, compared to all other regions. In northern Mexico, the proximity of residents to the United States also affects their attitudes toward many issues, including their northern neighbor.[53] For example, capitalists who reside in Chihuahua, which borders the state of Texas, are influenced by the United States and frequently send their children to elementary school as well as high school or university in El Paso or Austin.[54] Growing up in the North affects attitudes among members of Mexico's power elite as well, including attitudes about where they choose to be educated. Among all Mexican power

Democracy in Mexico: Does Space and Place Matter?" paper presented at Conference on Democracy and Political Learning in Mexico and the United States, University of Texas, Austin, April 4, 2001.

51. See Roderic Ai Camp, "Democracy through Latin American Lenses," CD-ROM, available in my *Citizen Views of Democracy in Latin America* (Pittsburgh: University of Pittsburgh Press, 2001). This is a three-country survey of Chile, Costa Rica, and Mexico sponsored by the Hewlett Foundation in 1998. The survey sample and methodology are described in detail in the data set.

52. See Enrique Alduncin Abitia, *Los valores de los mexicanos: México en tiempos de cambio* (Mexico City: Fomento Cultural Banamex, 1991), 193.

53. Edward J. Williams, "The Resurgent North and Contemporary Mexican Regionalism," *Mexican Studies*, 6, no. 2 (summer 1990), 299–323.

54. Carlos Alba Vega, "Los empresarios y el estado durante el salinismo," *Foro Internacional*, 36 (January/July 1996), 66.

elites, 31 percent were educated both in the United States and Mexico. But among those power elites who were born in the North, nearly two-thirds more received their education in both countries, suggesting the importance which northern power elites place on American education.[55]

The types of Mexican power elites who are most influenced by where they live, according to their own recollections, are the capitalists and the clergy. Capitalists who grew up and resided in Monterrey have noted the cultural stereotype of the city, popular among ordinary Mexicans, representing a distinctive Mexican work ethic, providing a strongly supportive ambience for the entrepreneurial spirit. This spirit yields, according to many capitalist elites, differing attitudes between capitalists and other leadership groups, especially intellectuals and politicians. Specifically, it sets capitalists apart in their support of private sector values. Once younger politicians began to study in the United States, their residential and educational experiences abroad began to reinforce economic attitudes which coincided more closely with those of northern capitalists.

Religious power elites, however, come from many regional origins. What is apparent from their testimonies is that the effect of adult residence, in terms of the specific geographic setting of a diocese, can be dramatic, sharply reversing attitudes developed over long periods by an elite's parents. Samuel Ruiz García, the controversial defender of indigenous rights in Chiapas, fits this pattern of a conservative priest changed by his experiences with indigenous laity. Even bishops who came from wealthy families and who were identified as conservative early in their careers were often changed by their direct observations of and experiences with poverty. For instance, Sergio Méndez Arceo, Mexico's leading progressive bishop in the 1960s and 1970s, was the product of a wealthy family.[56] José Rovalo Azcué is another example. Raised in a middle-class family, he was educated in the 1940s by the Society of the Brothers of Mary in a depressingly poor *barrio* located behind the Basilica of the Virgin of Guadalupe on the outskirts of Mexico City. He believes the residents' social problems "strongly marked me. I consider these years a true gift of God in modeling me as a priest."[57]

55. For power elites, such an emphasis has little to do with the proximity of U.S. universities along the border. Northern power elites who study abroad attend schools similar to those attended by other Mexican elites.

56. Personal interview with Sergio Méndez Arceo, Mexico City, June 21, 1989, and with Samuel Ruiz García, April 30, 1992, Mexico City; Carlos Fazio, *Samuel Ruiz: El caminante* (Mexico City: Espasa, 1994), and *Letras Libres*, January 1999, www.letraslibres.com.

57. Letter to the author from Bishop José Rovalo Azcué, May 13, 1997. Rovalo

In addition to residence, broader societal events also indirectly and directly influence the values and attitudes of prominent figures. As Lewis Edinger noted in his classic study of post-World War II Germans, elite values may be dramatically altered by major social events, and these elite values may turn out to be more important than elites per se.[58]

In the Mexican case, several historic periods were undoubtedly important in forming the values of an entire generation, including future power elites. Again, as in the case of adult residence, these are larger experiential passages for individual elites. They do not involve mentors, but rather indirect and direct personal experience or observation. They also may well reinforce family situations and parental attitudes, especially when the parents are participants or are directly affected by such events.

For older Mexican power elites, the overwhelming political event of their lifetime was the 1910–20 revolution, a complex event including a violent social upheaval. My earlier work on prominent politicians and intellectuals from that era repeatedly demonstrates the revolution's decided impact on their lives and on the lives of ordinary Mexicans. A recent study based on survey research concluded that even stories of the revolution produced a significant impact on the attitudes and behavior of those who listened, even though they personally did not experience the suffering and loss, thus explaining how it is possible for a third generation of Mexicans after the end of the war to still be greatly influenced by their elders' collective memories.[59]

Few members of the 1970–2000 power elite experienced the revolution directly. David Alfaro Siqueiros, last of the great Mexican muralists and a leftist political activist, actually participated in combat from 1914 to 1916 as an officer in the Constitutionalist's forces; he was sent to Paris as an aide to Mexico's military attaché in 1919. Siqueiros later joined the Spanish

---

Azcué resigned his position as bishop of Zacatecas in 1972 to travel and advise young people's organizations throughout Mexico. The archbishop of Mexico recruited Rovalo Azcué back into the church hierarchy as one of his auxiliary bishops in the huge Mexico City diocese.

58. Lewis Edinger made this insightful observation four decades ago, suggesting that "rather than argue in terms of circulation of elite personnel, one might consider the circulation of elite values." "Post-Totalitarian Leadership: Elites in the German Federal Republic," *American Political Science Review,* 54 (March 1960), 81.

59. Linda S. Stevenson and Mitchell A. Seligson, "Fading Memories of the Revolution: Is Stability Eroding in Mexico?" in Roderic Ai Camp, ed., *Polling for Democracy: Public Opinion and Political Liberalization in Mexico* (Wilmington: Scholarly Resources, 1996), 74.

Republican Army in 1937, commanding the 29th division.[60] Another prominent member of the intellectual power elite whose brother fought in the revolution stresses in his memoirs how the violence and personal sacrifice characterizing the revolution markedly distinguished his generation from younger Mexicans.[61] Several of Mexico's top military officers were combat veterans who fought against revolts in the transitional decade of the 1920s, including the intense fighting during the Cristero rebellion, a religiously motivated civil war from 1926 to 1929 in which peasants and their sympathizers opposed a central government they considered to be anti-religious and oppressive. In some regions, priests and nuns were persecuted by civil and military authorities.

The Cristero rebellion plays a special socializing role. Like the revolution, it is beyond the experiences of most power elite members, but a large core group of clergy and a smaller but influential number of military officers have direct recollections of those experiences. Equally important, the events became part of the twentieth-century historical lore of the armed forces and the Catholic hierarchy, a lore yielding opposing perspectives from these two groups. As I have suggested elsewhere: "The Cristero rebellion fostered a unique set of conditions on Mexican Church-state behavior, leaving a significant residue of mutual distrust and resentment on the part of the clergy, secular elites, and the officer corps."[62]

Many members of the religious power elite underwent their vocational preparation in an environment of persecution and repression. Indeed, the interdiocesan seminary in Montezuma, New Mexico was founded in 1937 precisely in response to this adverse climate. One bishop actually smuggled guns to the Cristeros as a teenager. Another archbishop who served three terms as secretary general of the Mexican episcopate grew up in the heart of the Cristero rebellion, and vividly captures these feelings:

> The first recollection I have of my childhood was that of a persecuted Catholic Church. . . . The only thing which influenced me to become a priest, if anything at all, because it wasn't a person or some experience, was the environment of the religious persecution itself. I remember the death of some priests, and the repression of others, and in our home we actually hid persecuted priests who were fleeing from the

---

60. Orlando S. Suárez, *Inventario del muralismo mexicano* (Mexico City: UNAM, 1972), 49 ff. He also studied art in France, Spain, and Italy during those years.

61. Daniel Cosío Villegas, *Memorias* (Mexico City: Joaquín Mortiz, 1976).

62. Roderic Ai Camp, *Crossing Swords: Politics and Religion in Mexico* (New York: Oxford University Press, 1997), 28.

authorities, as well as having secret masses in the house. I think for my generation this was by far the single most important event of our lives.[63]

Secular elites too, who came from western Mexico, remember the deaths of many friends associated with the violence of this period, but they are part of an older generation of elites who preceded those politicians found among the present elite sample.[64]

The older Mexican power elites who were more directly influenced by these two significant historical events, both characterized by intense civil violence, can be distinguished from their younger peers in two significant ways. Among prominent political elites, the revolution reinforced the desire of most public figures after 1929 to seek out peaceful means of governing and to develop pragmatic solutions to social and economic problems through political continuity and stability. Over time, this generation came to place a higher value on stability than it did on political participation, only giving up political space to other parties under intense societal pressure.

The clergy's experience with the Cristero rebellion produced a similar long-term conservative posture among the oldest generation of bishops. Bishops who witnessed these events as children and young adults were extremely hesitant to alter the constitutional pattern of church-state relations proposed by President Carlos Salinas in 1992. They were more willing to maintain the status quo despite the lack of legal recognition and basic rights such as voting, rather than risk threatening the established relationship which had permitted clergy, sometimes in violation of the existing regulations, to regain their influence among the laity.

The other contemporaneous event affecting this older generation, which again touched only a minority of the power elite, was the 1929 world depression. The generation which mentored many of the leading intellectual figures and politicians in the present sample point to the depression as a major socializing experience in their lives. We know that those in the United States who attended college during and immediately after the Great Depression report that they were somewhat more "left" in their student

---

63. Personal interview with Archbishop Manuel Pérez Gil, Tlanepantla Archdiocese, Tlanepantla, México, February 18, 1991.

64. For example, Alfonso Pulido Islas, who was born in 1907 and completed his preparatory education at the University of Guadalajara in the 1920s, recalled that twelve of his companions died as soldiers in the Cristero army. Personal interview, Mexico City, August 12, 1974.

days than any other college-age cohort, earlier or later.[65] A leading figure in the generation of 1929 and mentor to numerous members of the political power elite believed the depression forged a group of leaders who sought "economic development with social justice" and who were "pragmatically oriented to solving the problems of Mexico, rather than being concerned with dogmatic or ideological solutions . . ."[66] This orientation is significant because a large percentage of the current power elite's mentors came from this generation and passed on their views to the younger group.

These important historical events typically provided indirect socializing influences on the power elite, and were followed chronologically by an important event in 1938, President Lázaro Cárdenas's decision to nationalize the foreign-dominated petroleum industry. Half of the members of the power elite were born between 1910 and 1929, and consequently many of them were students at the time of the actual decision. As is well known from socialization studies generally, adolescents and young adults are at their most impressionable stage to receive formative influences.

Unlike the Cristero rebellion, which sharply divided Mexicans, Cárdenas's decision quickly and overwhelmingly united the country, including the Catholic hierarchy, who had little good to say about the president prior to 1938.[67] As Hugo B. Margáin recalled, it produced a strong feeling against North Americans and foreigners generally and consolidated Mexicans "behind Cárdenas 100 percent."[68] One of those Mexicans who was a teenager during the nationalization was President José López Portillo, whose father, an engineer and admirer of Cárdenas, was a member of the presidential commission to examine the petroleum companies immediately prior to 1938.[69] This experience, as the president himself has admitted, affected his own decision to nationalize Mexican banks five decades later.[70]

A much smaller group of power elites from a comparable generation of intellectuals was caught up with the Spanish civil war in Europe. Mexicans

65. Everett C. Ladd and Seymour M. Lipset, *The Divided Academy: Professors and Politics* (New York: W. W. Norton, 1976), 195.

66. Personal interview with Antonio Carrillo Flores, Mexico City, June 26, 1975.

67. For a Mexican historian's view, see Héctor Aguilar Camín and Lorenzo Meyer, both members of the power intellectual elite, *In the Shadow of the Mexican Revolution: Contemporary Mexican History, 1910–1989* (Austin: University of Texas Press, 1993), 153–54.

68. Personal interview with Hugo B. Margáin.

69. *Excélsior*, January 19, 1974, 4–5.

70. Personal interview with José López Portillo, Mexico City, February 19, 1991.

were drawn to the Republican cause in 1937 because a number of prominent Mexicans in the intellectual and business communities were children
of Spanish parents. One or both parents of 3 percent of the current power
elite are Spanish. Three power elite members are known to be children of
Spanish Republicans.[71]

Other Mexicans sympathetic to the Republican cause traveled to Spain
to join the Republican army. Octavio Paz tried to volunteer for the famous
International Brigades in 1937. As he recollected, "instead, they thought
I would be more useful in Mexico to the Republicans by publicizing their
cause. I returned to Mexico and collaborated with *El Popular*."[72] One of
Mexico's leading capitalists traveled to Spain on a fellowship to study at
the Meléndez Pelayo International University in Santander. He joined the
Republicans for seven months in 1936–37, although he did not participate
in the fighting.[73]

The issues represented in the Spanish civil war also made their mark
on a generation of Mexicans because many distinguished Spanish exiles
who were welcomed to Mexico by President Cárdenas mentored a crucial
generation of Mexican intellectuals and politicians from teaching posts at
the National University and the Colegio de México. Many members of the
younger generation have identified them as major intellectual mentors.[74]

The 1940s and 1950s, with the exception of World War II, were rela-

71. These include José Córdoba Montoya, a French national and gray eminence
in the Salinas cabinet whose father was a city official in Almería, Spain; Joaquín
Díez-Canedo, who also fought for the Republicans and whose father was a prominent diplomat and Spanish intellectual; and Ramón Xirau Subias, whose father,
Joaquín, a distinguished philosopher, helped found the Colegio de México and
taught at Oxford while in exile. Jesús Silva Herzog's father helped to found the
Academia Hispano-Americana, a school for the children of Spanish exiles in Mexico. He sent his son there. The entire environment of the school, which brought
together Mexican and Spanish children, flavored his values and attitudes, even as
a young child. Personal interview with Jesús Silva Herzog, November 19, 1998,
Riverside, California.

72. Personal interview with Octavio Paz. Paz believed these experiences marked
his intellectual formation in a unique way and distinguished him from many of
his generational peers.

73. This describes the early experiences of Juan Sánchez Navarro y Peón. *Líderes*, 4 (1993), 74–79.

74. For example, Héctor Fix Zamudio, a leading Mexican jurist and president
of the Inter-American Court of Human Rights, considered Professor Niceto Alcalá-
Zamora y Castillo, son of the first president of the Spanish Republic, a major source
of his ideas; and President Luis Echeverría was one of many Mexicans indebted to
Professor Manuel Pedroso, an influential figure in the 1940s, born in Cuba and
educated at the University of Madrid. Personal letter to the author, July 3, 1997.

tively uneventful in producing a domestic influence having a significant and broad impact on the whole range of Mexican leadership.[75] These decades were characterized by substantial economic growth, often referred to as Mexico's "Economic Miracle," and political stability, where supporters of a single organization, the Institutional Revolutionary Party (PRI), monopolized government at all levels.

It was not until 1968 that an event occurred which had a formative influence on a younger generation of Mexican leaders, an event which unquestionably divided the power elite into two substantially different generations. That event, which initially involved a conflict between student groups in Mexico City, led to government intervention and ultimately to a massive peaceful student demonstration in Tlatelolco Plaza. The students presented a list of demands and wanted to resolve their differences without official interference. President Gustavo Díaz Ordaz, concerned about his government's image as it related to political stability, wanted to control student behavior. Instead of negotiating peacefully with the students, he manipulated the army to violently suppress the demonstrators, killing hundreds, including numerous bystanders.[76]

The Mexican government's failure to respond peacefully to student protests generated serious reverberations in many communities, raising much broader questions about the political and social model. The impact was most decisive on the intellectual elite, but many future Mexican politicians responded similarly with grave doubts.[77] Miguel Centeno, in his examination of mid-level political leadership from that era, wrote:

> The socialization by both the success and failure of the "Miracle"
> and the problems experienced thereafter must have helped shape
> generational attitudes toward the relative roles of public and private
> investment, democracy, and political legitimacy. Even if we cannot
> define exactly what these may be, it is likely that the common
> experiences contributed to a shared perspective that would further

75. For evidence of this see Carlos J. Sierra, *Crónica de una generación* (Mexico City: DDF, 1983), 33–35.

76. Further details of the decision-making process, and the president's purposeful efforts to spark a violent confrontation, have been revealed in new research from national archives. See Sergio Aguayo Quezada's revealing insights in *1968: Los archivos de la violencia* (Mexico City: Grijalbo, 1998).

77. Based on numerous interviews with intellectuals and politicians. For such consequences, see my "Political Modernization in Mexico: Through a Looking Glass," in Jaime Rodríguez, ed., *The Evolution of the Mexican Political System* (Wilmington: Scholarly Resources, 1992), 211–28.

strengthen the social, educational, and professional homogeneity of the elite.[78]

For Mexican intellectuals, the events of 1968 reinforced two continuous threads in Mexican social policy: political liberalization (democracy) and social and economic equality (social justice). Mexico's failure to produce satisfactory results in either camp rapidly pushed intellectuals into a more proactive posture, bringing some political and religious leaders along with them. As a member of the intellectual power elite told an interviewer, "it became an obsessive question for my generation—a traumatic experience—why did this happen—where does this lead us—why did the Revolution lead us to such a socially unequal society?"[79] Analysts of Mexican intellectual life have concluded that after 1968, "perhaps consensus existed on only one point: the political system was broken."[80]

A renewed commitment to political pluralization within the intellectual community, among some members of the political establishment, and among Mexican opposition figures, can be dated from this benchmark event. The student massacre resulted in a serious decline in the legitimacy of the presidency, an increased demand for representation among autonomous interest groups, the growth of political opposition outside the governing elite, and a dramatic increase in inter-elite conflicts over political and economic strategies.

The socializing sources described above have exerted a significant influence on the formation of power elite attitudes. The most influential sources of socialization among Mexican power elites are direct, and administered by mentors, commonly family members and career superiors. While experiential sources of socialization, such as an influential historic event, exerted tremendous influence in the past, most of the prominent Mexicans from 1970 through the end of the century experienced those historical passages indirectly rather than directly.

Familial socializing influences are as important to Mexican power elites

78. Miguel A. Centeno, *Democracy within Reason: Technocratic Revolution in Mexico* (University Park: Penn State University Press, 1994), 110.

79. Héctor Aguilar Camín, quoted in Pilar Jiménez Trejo and Alejandro Toledo, *Creación y poder*, 13.

80. José Antonio Aguilar Rivera, *La sombra de ulises: Ensayos sobre intelectuales mexicanos y norteamericanos* (Mexico City: CIDE, 1998), 86.

as they are to the population generally. One of the most important discoveries of familial influence among power elites is the role which parents have played in determining career choices and reinforcing professional values *before* a prospective power elite begins his adult journey. This is particularly noteworthy among capitalists and military officers. If we conceptualize familial influences as consisting of relatives beyond the immediate nuclear family, it becomes clear that extended kin play equally important roles in the career determinations of top Mexican clergy.

Family mentors, therefore, play all three mentoring roles, as recruiters, networkers, and as socializers. If they are in the same profession as their child, they may directly affect their professional as distinct from their basic moral values and attitudes. Family influences can also be linked to indirect historical experiences; whether a parent or relative was a participant or a victim of those events, the ongoing events were formative in the construction of a family ambience. This type of influence, without question, molded an important generation of clergy.

It is also evident that major social, economic, and political events influence power elite values. As Mexican power elites have revealed in numerous interviews and published testimonies, notable historical experiences contributed to individual and generational views. The three most notable events for all power elite groups are the revolution of 1910–20, the Cristero rebellion of 1926–29, and the violent suppression of student demonstrators in Mexico City in 1968.

As we have seen, the revolution's impact is largely indirect, having formed the most important generation of mentors to Mexico's power elite, rather than the power elite itself. The values handed down by those mentors contributed strongly to the way in which the older generation of power elites responded to political and social change in the 1970s. The student movement of 1968, which many members of the power elite witnessed as students, shifted their emphasis away from the traditional views of the preceding generation, stimulating many of those power elites to explore alternative political solutions to Mexico's economic and social problems, and in some cases, to seek out new parties to achieve their goals.

Family-based socialization is also complemented by another indirect and even more amorphous influence: the local community. Place of residence can reinforce family patterns, which are also affected by peer experiences and attitudes. The role of historic events, since the impact of the latter varies greatly from one locale to the next, also complements other well-established socialization processes.

Until the 1990s, the historic trend in Mexico during the twentieth century was to reduce the importance of regionalism on cultural values and attitudes in favor of an increasingly homogenizing pattern of centralization and urbanization. This pattern was encouraged through state-supported public education, which used nationally approved and distributed textbooks to convey a set of universal values. The geographic origins of Mexican power elites shifted dramatically from the provinces to Mexico City and, to a lesser extent, several other large urban centers.

As political pluralization has seeped into the fabric of the Mexican political model in the 1990s and into the 2000s, dramatically legitimized by Vicente Fox's presidential victory, it is likely to have long-term consequences on cultural and economic centralization. It will strengthen, rather than weaken, local cultural autonomy, and weaken economic centralization from Mexico City. The influence of local and regional roots takes on added importance culturally and politically. This shift is not likely to reverse the definitive geographic centralizing trends occurring in the last half century, but it will reinvigorate the importance of provincial differences among power elites, further accentuating the political pluralism set into motion in the 1990s.

Mentors also have exercised an influential socializing role within power elite institutions, similar to family mentors, functioning as recruiters, networkers, and socializers. This brief analysis of the importance of a power elite's career and profession on the formation of his attitudes confirms the impact of indirect institutional environments in establishing, reinforcing, and generating new professional attitudes that influence elite policy decisions. The importance of a professional organizational milieu will be examined in greater detail in chapter 9, where the policy consequences of interactions between networking and socialization are analyzed. It is evident, however, that organizational and family cultures both determine influential elite Mexican values.

6   Socialization through Education the Mexican Way

Family, career, residence, and major social events all contributed to the socialization of Mexico's power elite. But for many elite members, education has exerted a decisive influence the exact nature of which varies considerably from one group to another. Education can be conceptualized as a shared career experience for clergy and military officers since it occurs primarily within their respective professional or institutional environment, the Catholic Church and the Mexican armed forces.[1]

The socializing role of education on Mexican power elites is enhanced by the fact that many of the mentors identified by the power elite established contact with their future disciples in the classroom. Education provides a significant institutional setting for combining mentoring, networking, and socialization in Mexico. The importance of those activities among power elites reinforced the impact of select educational institutions in comparison to all other sources of influence.

A close examination of the power elite dominating Mexico in the last three decades of the twentieth century suggests the importance of two broad educational sources: Mexican and foreign. This chapter is devoted

---

1. According to Kenneth Prewitt's major work on American local politicians, more than half of those who traced their interest to politics before they became adults mentioned the importance of school experience, and nearly a third mention *only* school influences as important. Since most Mexicans in the political, clergy, and military categories selected their career interests in their teenage years, one would expect education to exert an even greater influence there. *The Recruitment of Political Leaders: A Study of Citizen-Politicians* (Indianapolis: Bobbs-Merrill, 1970), 70.

to an analysis of the role of mentors in national education and education's important influence on power elite values and attitudes.

EDUCATION AND SOCIALIZATION

A survey of the theoretical literature on education and elite socialization reveals several important characteristics. In the first place, educational experiences can moderate the socializing influences attributed to family background and wealth. Barton discovered in his elite studies that while wealthy families had the resources to send their children to elite Ivy League universities and small liberal arts colleges, attendance at these institutions produced a more liberal product, counteracting the conservative influence of family wealth.[2]

University education generally exerts a liberalizing influence on students regardless of discipline.[3] Plenty of evidence exists to suggest that students of private or Catholic parochial schools and products of public schools in Latin America have different political ideologies. This is the case among the Argentine intelligentsia, for example.[4] Second, young adults are highly vulnerable to shifts in attitudes, which stabilize as they age.[5] Third, of the many variables Barton analyzed in his examination of American elites, one of the three most influential was attendance at elite schools and colleges.[6]

2. Allen H. Barton, "Determinants of Elite Policy Attitudes," in B. A. Rockman and R. H. Linden, eds., *Elite Studies and Comparative Politics* (Pittsburgh: University of Pittsburgh Press, 1984), 201.

3. Reo M. Christenson and Patrick J. Capretta, "The Impact of College on Political Attitudes: A Research Note," *Social Science Quarterly,* 49 (1968), 320; and W. Paul Vogt, *Tolerance and Education: Learning to Live with Diversity and Differences* (Beverly Hills: Sage, 1997).

4. See Juan Marsal and Margery Arent, "Right-Wing Intelligentsia in Argentina: An Analysis of Its Ideology and Political Activity," *Social Research,* 37 (autumn 1970), 473, where they conclude that parochial schools produced 62 percent of rightist intelligentsia compared to secular schools graduating 85 percent of the non-rightist. Of course, the preselection variables of family background and wealth would have played a role in who attended these schools. Data from this period are relevant because most of the figures in our study attended schools and colleges in the 1950s, 1960s, and 1970s.

5. Duane F. Alwin and Jon A. Krosnick, "Aging, Cohorts, and the Stability of Sociopolitical Orientations over the Life Span," *American Journal of Sociology,* 97 (1991), 189.

6. Allen H. Barton, "Determinants of Economic Attitudes in the American Business Elite," *American Journal of Sociology,* 91 (1985), 70.

The educational discipline a Latin American student takes, or the school the student attends, also exerts an ideological influence, "precisely because [schools] provide a social and physical environment within which students with similar backgrounds and interests group together."[7] This is true among Guatemalan political elites, for example.[8] In other words, family socialization and intellectual interests can be reinforced by student peers and faculty. Even the prestige ranking of a graduate's professional school exercises a powerful influence on the student's subsequent career.[9]

As will become evident in this analysis, teachers have played an extraordinary role as mentors and recruiters in Mexican life; they are in the enviable position of exerting a major influence on the values and attitudes of their disciples, elite and non-elite. Students of American politics have found many politicians who "maintained life-long contact with the teacher first responsible for their political introduction."[10] There is no reason to expect that other professions would behave differently. The degree to which education plays a measurable role in the formation and networking of influential power elites is determined largely by a leader's level of education. Put simply, the greater the level of contact between any individual and an institution, the greater its potential impact on that person. The educational setting takes on added importance among the Mexican power elite because, in the broadest terms, it is the most universally shared experience.

The leaders of virtually any society are better educated than the average citizen.[11] What is striking about Third World countries is that elites often

7. Arthur Liebman, Kenneth Walker, and Myron Glazer, *Latin American University Students: A Six Nation Study* (Cambridge: Harvard University Press, 1972), 125.

8. Joel Verner, "The Guatemalan National Congress: An Elite Analysis," in Weston H. Agor, ed., *Latin American Legislatures: Their Role and Influence* (New York: Praeger, 1971), 318–20.

9. John P. Heinz and Edward O. Laumann, *Chicago Lawyers: The Social Structure of the Bar* (New York: Russell Sage, 1982).

10. Kenneth Prewitt, Heinz Eulau, and Betty H. Zisk, "Political Socialization and Political Roles," *Public Opinion Quarterly*, 30, no. 4 (winter 1966–67), 574.

11. In fact, these differences are sometimes more pronounced in post-industrial than in developing societies. For example, Mattei Dogan notes that only 1 percent of the French population between eighteen and twenty-five take college courses, yet 85 percent of its cabinet ministers were college graduates, suggesting that "a fraction of 1 percent of the population furnished 85 percent of the ministers." "Career Pathways to the Cabinet in France, 1879–1986," in Mattei Dogan, ed., *Pathways to Power: Selecting Rulers in Pluralist Democracies* (Boulder: Westview, 1988), 43.

achieve very high levels of advanced education, obtaining academic credentials that exceed those of comparable groups in postindustrial societies.[12]

Mexican power elites are no exception to the general Third World pattern. For example, 86 percent obtained a college degree in a society were fewer than 10 percent of all citizens boast such a credential. (See table 13.) More remarkable is the fact that among prominent Mexicans in the last three decades, more than a third obtained graduate degrees (22 percent M.A.'s and 15 percent Ph.D.'s). These figures are comparable to those for United States elites.[13]

The most highly educated group among these Mexicans are Catholic clergy, 44 percent of whom obtained Ph.D.'s (typically in theology), followed by intellectuals, nearly a third of whom obtained doctorates. More than half in each of these two groups obtained graduate degrees. It is not surprising that Mexicans whose tasks are more intellectually oriented, whether religious or secular, place a greater value on higher levels of formal education. Influential capitalists were the least educated formally among elite Mexicans; they tend to place a higher emphasis on practical experience in a firm than on technical or theoretical education.[14] Fewer than one out of seven captains of industry obtained graduate educations.[15]

The level of educational achievement suggests several important patterns among older power elites. Contrary to the general educational trends

12. This pattern is especially strong in India. For example, among prominent public figures in Indian cabinets prior to 1980, some two-thirds or more possessed a postgraduate degree. Richard Sisson, "Pathways to India's National Governing Elite," in Mattei Dogan, ed., *Pathways to Power*, 185.

13. Thomas R. Dye found that 31 percent held advanced academic or professional degrees. *Who's Running America? The Bush Era*, 5th ed. (Englewood Cliffs: Prentice-Hall, 1990), 193.

14. Interestingly, businessmen coming up through the managerial ranks in Mexico, in contrast to capitalists, are extremely well educated. According to a study of 100 director generals from the top 500 firms completed by Mexico's leading business magazine, *Expansión*, 61 percent had bachelor's degrees, 32 percent had master's degrees, and 4 percent held doctorates. *Expansión*, June 8, 1988, 48–49.

15. Among chief executive officers in the United States in the late 1970s, from a comparable group of firms, 14 percent had received only a high school diploma or less education. The author notes that an explosion in postgraduate training occurred among U.S. executives after 1950. Forty percent had M.A.'s or Ph.D.'s at the time of this study. See Charles G. Burck, "A Group Profile of the Fortune 500 Chief Executives," *Fortune*, May 1976, 175. In Hungary, higher education continues to be as important for success in the private sector as it was earlier in public-sector careers. See Rudolf Andorlka, "Selected Papers from the Tenth World Congress of Sociology," *Social Indicators Research*, 14 (April 1984), 368.

Table 13. Level of Education Achieved among Mexican Power Elites

Education Level Completed	Power Elite Group				
	Politician (%)	*Intellectual* (%)	*Capitalist* (%)	*Military* (%)	*Clergy* (%)
Secondary	12	28	23	6	0
University	46	19	60	60	42
Graduate	24	19	15	31	14
Doctorate	18	34	2	3	44

NOTE: $N = 398$.

among all elites, intellectuals and capitalists opened their ranks to non-college graduates. (Almost all of the Mexican intellectuals without university degrees are in the plastic arts, requiring physical, aesthetic, and visual skills.) The fact that a fourth of their members succeeded without a college degree suggests several significant characteristics. First, they are the only two power elites where a substantial percentage of their members could reach their professional apex without formal credentials. Second, the lack of emphasis on formal credentials, specifically higher education, is a product, in part, of the lack of formal structures. In other words, neither capitalists nor intellectuals rise up the elite ladder through well-developed institutional settings comparable to those found in political, military, and clerical bureaucracies. Instead, their success depends almost exclusively on their skills and other resources. Third, both capitalists and intellectuals share greater opportunities to be self-made, without using formal, institutional channels. As the plastic arts professions become more structured, for example, they too will require the universal credential of a college degree.

The other surprising figure in the data is that a fifth of politicians obtained doctorates. As I shall discuss in the next chapters, power elite mentors who valued increased technical skills and expanded theoretical alternatives encouraged their disciples to obtain graduate training, typically abroad. This training became increasingly necessary as complex economic decisions dominated the Mexican political agenda in the 1970s, 1980s, and 1990s.

Not only is the level important for determining education's potential influence as a source of socialization and networking, but power elite choices of where to study can also affect both patterns. In Mexico, there are substantial differences in the curricular content and ideological setting of private and public universities, and even *within* specific institutions, regardless of funding sources.

THE ROLE OF PUBLIC EDUCATION

In Mexico, the decisive educational influence in the formation of the power elite lies with the differences between public and private or parochial institutions. Background data for the present study indicate that two public institutions have educated the largest and most diverse group of Mexican power elites, the National Preparatory School and the National University.

As I have argued elsewhere, the National Preparatory School (ENP) for many years performed a role similar to that of leading public schools in England. It provided a common experience and meeting place for future Mexican leaders—particularly intellectuals and politicians, and to a lesser extent capitalists from the Federal District and the state of México. Because influential professors typically were successful national politicians or intellectuals, as well as notable mentors to the power elite, the National Preparatory School became a breeding ground for their disciples.

As was the case for English public schools or the Turkish Mulkiye, public service and active participation became a norm passed on by generations of teaching mentors.[16] A companion of President Luis Echeverría at the National Preparatory School pointed out that the school greatly influenced the future president's initial formation, and it was here "where his vocation toward public service was first accentuated."[17] In addition to its networking function, the "long-standing ties of friendship and trust increase the ability of an elite to cooperate effectively."[18] Unlike elite British public schools, however, the National Preparatory School never drew

16. Joseph S. Szyliowicz found the same pattern in Turkey's Mulkiye, where "students were effectively socialized into an acceptance of the values, attitudes, and patterns of behavior that were necessary for success within the administration." See his "Elite Recruitment in Turkey: The Role of the Mulkiye," *World Politics*, 23 (April 1971), 389–90.

17. Letter to the author from Mario Colín Sánchez, May 3, 1974. Its influence was also confirmed by former president José López Portillo, a boyhood companion of Luis Echeverría who also attended the National Preparatory School. Personal interview with the author, Mexico City, February 19, 1991.

18. Robert D. Putnam, *The Comparative Study of Political Elites* (Englewood Cliffs: Prentice-Hall, 1976), 96. The best description of the socializing role of British public schools can be found in Rupert Wilkinson, *Gentlemanly Power: British Leadership and the Public School Tradition: A Comparative Study of the Making of Rulers* (New York: Oxford University Press, 1964), and Byron G. Massialas, ed., *Political Youth, Traditional Schools* (Englewood Cliffs: Prentice-Hall, 1972).

its students from wealthy families, indeed, most students came from middle and lower middle class backgrounds.

One of the special attributes of the National Preparatory School and the National University is that both their academic environments were infused with political debate.[19] Many former graduates recall the importance of the environment outside the classroom and its impact on the formation of their attitudes and interests. The excesses engendered by this politicized atmosphere (strikes, missed classes, ideological biases, etc.) eventually led to the migration of a younger generation of power elites to private schools.

One member of the intellectual power elite attributes many influences to his pre-university years in Mexico City public schools. He argues that his teachers at these schools, not the university, were the most important influences on his personal values and intellectual ideas, and that the "flavor of the public school curriculum was crucial" in his formation.[20] He bemoans the fact that unlike his generation, most of whom also attended public schools, the majority of younger Mexican intellectuals have attended private institutions.[21]

It is impossible to specify the important social, economic, and political values that were taught at the National Preparatory School in the years during which members of the power elite attended, but in the 1940s and 1950s, when the largest percentage of the power elite took classes, many students were exposed to three broad themes: a brand of nationalism that placed the United States in a negative light; an anti-clericalism that questioned the motives of the Catholic Church; and an anti-capitalism that directed suspicion toward the private sector.[22] These views, remembered by former students, also appear in public school textbooks provided by the Mexican government that were used universally in elementary schools.[23]

---

19. Rafael Segovia, *La politizacíon del niño mexicano* (Mexico City: El Colegio de México, 1975), 12, 79.

20. So do other power elites, but not necessarily those who attended public schools in the capital. Jorge Carpizo, who graduated from a distinguished provincial school in his home state, the Instituto Campeche, attributes the social and liberal thoughts which form the roots of his present ideas to the experience. *Líderes*, 2, 1991, 42.

21. Personal interview with Carlos Monsiváis, Claremont, California, November 18, 1998.

22. Personal interview with Jesús Silva Herzog, Riverside, California, November 18, 1998. He attended the ENP from 1951 to 1953.

23. See, for example, the work of Mary Kay Vaughan, "Ideological Change in Mexican Educational Policy, Programs, and Texts, 1920–1940," in Roderic Ai

Only six undergraduate schools can be said to have had the potential to exercise a pronounced influence on Mexican power elites, since all other universities, domestic and foreign, graduated fewer than 1 percent of these individuals. Those institutions are the National University, the Higher War College, the Heroic Naval College, the Gregorian University in Rome, the Monterrey Institute of Technology and Higher Studies, and the Montezuma Seminary in New Mexico.[24] These six institutions have provided the undergraduate education of 77 percent of influential Mexicans in the last thirty years.

The most influential of these undergraduate institutions, as suggested above, is the National University (UNAM). It has educated three out ten individuals in the power elite, and it is the only undergraduate institution in Mexico to have educated a significant percentage of power elites in three of the five groups: politicians, intellectuals, and capitalists. A similar pattern is found in Japan, where the concentration of elites in a single institution is the highest among all industrialized countries. As a leading Japanese specialist suggests:

> The most important Japanese elites, in all sectors of the society, are very likely to have attended Todai [University of Tokyo], or at least one of the few other top universities, and because age ranking requires that they move into elite positions at about the same age, *most Japanese elites at one point in time were university classmates who knew each other,* lived together around campus, got drunk together, and created bonds which normally last a lifetime. The evidence for this is overwhelming.[25]

The intellectual influences associated with the National Preparatory School are also present in the National University. One of the differences in the two experiences is that until the early 1950s all ENP students attended classes in the same physical location, which meant that young people with many distinct interests were brought together. At the National University, students pursued separate professional programs. The majority of future power elites who attended the National University were concentrated in several faculties, namely law, economics, and philosophy and

Camp, Charles A. Hale, and Josefina Vázquez, eds., *Los intelectuales y el poder* (Los Angeles: UCLA Latin American Center, 1992), 507–26.

24. There are two naval academies in Mexico, one in Veracruz, Veracruz, and the other in Mazatlán, Sinaloa. The majority of top-ranking naval officers in this study have attended the academy in Veracruz.

25. Harold R. Kerbo and John A. McKinstry, *Who Rules Japan? The Inner Circle of Economic and Political Power* (Westport: Praeger, 1995), 140.

letters. Until the 1960s, there was considerable cross-fertilization among disciplines—especially among students who were interested in university politics.

The most important professional program at UNAM—in terms of socializing influence and consequent impact on shifts in intellectual ideas and public policy—is unquestionably the school of economics. The National School of Economics, initially created within the law school in the 1930s to meet the country's need for trained economists, dominated Mexican educational production of economists for many decades. By the 1950s, the program increasingly emphasized Marxist economics:

> Even in the early 1950s, economics students at the UNAM were required to take three full years of Marxist economic theory, with limited to no exposure to neo-classical . . . thought. In 1976 the students take an even longer seven-semester sequence, prudently re-titled "political economy," which centers around labor value theory, dialectical and historical materialism, the theory of surplus value, imperialism, and the economics of socialism. . . . The quantitative area remains light.[26]

The Marxist emphasis at this school drove away many students to other colleges beginning in the 1960s, enhancing a trend favoring private university training, especially in economics. Sophisticated students understood the differences between the National University schools and other, highly reputed, private institutions. One important figure in the democratic non-governmental organization movement in the 1990s who graduated from both the National Schools of Law and Economics in 1955 and 1956, respectively, actually chose to attend those schools even though he believed he could obtain a stronger professional education from the Free Law School, a prestigious private alternative in the Federal District. He believed UNAM was "a good preparation for understanding the whole country because it was a reflection or mirror of the entire country."[27]

The son of a scion of the capitalist class, a graduate of Jesuit schools and the Monterrey Technological Institute of Higher Studies (ITESM) preparatory school who became president of Nestlé of Mexico and a member of the capitalist elite Mexican Council of Businessmen, also chose to obtain his economics degree from UNAM in the mid-1960s despite its extreme

26. Richard A. LaBarge and T. Noel Osborne, "The Status of Professional Economics Programs in Mexican Universities," *Inter-American Economic Affairs*, 31 (summer 1977), 9.

27. Letter to the author from Julio Faesler, July 2, 1975.

Marxist orientation. Unlike the NGO leader, he did so because he wanted to be exposed to macroeconomics, an emphasis not then offered at ITESM.[28] He is an exceptional case in the capitalist class, but his experiences illustrate the clear differences between the Mexican public and private university experiences.

Mexican power elites receive their educational influences in two ways, which are analogous to the ways they are influenced within professional organizations. First, these elites have noted the impact of general socializing intellectual influences characterizing the setting of the larger institution and its specific schools. Second, they are socialized by intellectual mentors.

Each power elite group, depending on the dominant institutions in its educational background, collectively identifies certain individual mentors who stand out because of their impact on multiple generations of influential Mexicans. These *magnet mentors* provide linkages across generations via networking to cement personal relationships and socialize various personalities intellectually.

In the world of public universities, Mario de la Cueva is a classic example of the magnet mentor. As a member of the political power elite fondly recalls, de la Cueva's influence was decisive on his own personal formation, and his impression of de la Cueva's classes was "one of enormous and profound beauty."[29] The following members of Mexico's power elite are disciples of Mario de la Cueva; also listed, when available, are the classes these men attended:

Jesús Reyes Heroles	Theory of the State
Rubén Bonifaz Nuño	
José Campillo Sáinz	Labor Law
Héctor Fix Zamudio	Theory of the State
Carlos Fuentes	Constitutional Law and *Medio Siglo*[30]
Miguel de la Madrid	Constitutional Law

28. Personal interview with Carlos Eduardo Represas de Almeida, Mexico City, March 3, 1986.

29. This recollection was expressed by Jorge Carpizo. See *Líderes Mexicanos*, 2 (1992), 42. Carpizo's laudatory view is confirmed by many other distinguished Mexicans interviewed by the author. For the extent of his influence, see his disciples' recollections in *Testimonios sobre Mario de la Cueva* (Mexico City: Porrúa, 1982).

30. Salvador Elizondo, Carlos Monsiváis, and Eduardo García Maynez were also active collaborators of *Medio Siglo*, a publication de la Cueva personally promoted.

Sergio García Ramírez   Constitutional Law and *Medio Siglo*
Jorge Carpizo MacGregor   Theory of the State
Porfirio Muñoz Ledo

Other prominent mentors also taught at the National University, many of whom became or formerly were power elites.[31]

THE ROLE OF PRIVATE EDUCATION

Among secular, non-military power elites, private educational experiences have expanded rapidly in Mexico, shifting from secondary and preparatory school to the university level. To some of the prominent graduates from public institutions, this trend marks a significant and detrimental change in Mexican life. To others, it has introduced positive changes. This shift in educational location is crucial for understanding the ideological shift among many Mexican power elites in the 1980s.

31. They included Jesús Reyes Heroles, professor of general theory of the state; Manuel Pedroso, a Cuban-born Spanish exile who mentored President José López Portillo, President Luis Echeverría (thesis director), and Reyes Heroles, among others, in his general theory of the state class; Ramón Beteta, a political economy professor who influenced the economic ideas of Hugo B. Margáin's generation; Antonio Carrillo Flores, in his philosophy of law and administrative law classes; Jesús Silva Herzog, the father of the treasury secretary, who taught an influential course on Mexican economic history and founded the National School of Economics; and Manuel Gómez Morín, who taught public law, mentioned by capitalists and politicians alike. According to many of his students, Beteta also introduced them to North American economics literature. He received his undergraduate economics training, then unavailable in Mexico, at the University of Texas, Austin. Carrillo Flores was one of those Mexicans who crossed many elite circles because his father was a leading Mexican musician, and his brother was one of Mexico's foremost mathematicians and rector of the National University. He served in numerous cabinets and was one of the most influential political power elites of his generation. Silva Herzog was viewed by his biographer as providing "a large part of the spirit of the National School of Economics . . ." Fedro Guillén, *Jesús Silva Herzog* (Mexico City: Empresas Editoriales, 1969), 67. Members of the intellectual power elite also viewed him as a patron to many cultural leaders through his decades-long editorship of *Cuadernos Americanos*, a major multidisciplinary journal. Personal interview with Jaime García Térres, Mexico City, August 9, 1978. Manuel Gómez Morín was one of the most important figures in Mexico in the 1920s and 1930s, and co-founder of the National Action Party in 1939. His students also included two of the other influential mentors, Ramón Beteta and Mario de la Cueva. For a discussion of his intellectual influence on students, and his own intellectual mentors, see *Testimonio en la muerte de Manuel Gómez Morín* (Mexico City: Editorial Jus, 1973). For an understanding of his crucial contributions to Mexico, see Enrique Krauze's classic *Caudillos culturales en la revolución mexicana* (Mexico City: Siglo XXI, 1976).

If Mexico could be described as having a select private preparatory school for influential members of the power elite, that school would be the Centro Universitario de México (CUM), which from the 1910s to 1973 produced at least twenty-one leading figures. CUM is a parochial school administered by the Brothers of Mary order. It has made room for students from the lower middle and working classes through scholarships, including such notable politicians as Porfirio Muñoz Ledo and Mario Moya Palencia.

The most important private universities in the educational backgrounds of Mexico's power elite are the ITESM, commonly known as Monterrey Tech; the Autonomous Technological Institute of Mexico (ITAM); the Ibero-American University, a Jesuit institution; and the Colegio de México, a publicly funded institution which operates like a private university. With the exception of the ITESM, all are located in the capital.

The social composition of students at private universities in Mexico is quite different from that found in public institutions. The majority of students come from upper-class backgrounds, and these schools provide very few scholarships to talented students whose socioeconomic level does not permit them to attend. Class background alone does not account for differences in attitudes between private and public institutions in Mexico or elsewhere; the curriculum and general environments also produce students with differing perspectives.[32]

In 1943, the Monterrey business community decided to create the Monterrey Technological Institute of Higher Studies.[33] In only eight years time it became the first Mexican university accredited by the Southern Association of Colleges and Schools (a U.S. institution). It has been described as a staunch supporter of laissez-faire economics, and has even been called the MIT of Mexico.[34] Leading Monterrey capitalists are represented on the board of this institution and all other private universities in Nuevo León.[35]

32. Allen H. Barton, "Determinants of Economic Attitudes in the American Business Elite," 74.

33. For background on the founding, see Daniel C. Levy, who remarks that "political and social conservatism figured in its founding, but economics was the foremost determinant." *Higher Education and the State in Latin America: Private Challenges to Public Dominance* (Chicago: University of Chicago Press, 1986), 121; and Charles N. Myers, *Education and National Development in Mexico* (Princeton: Princeton University Press, 1965), 105.

34. Richard A. Labarge and T. Noel Osborne, "The Status of Professional Economics Programs in Mexican Universities," 13.

35. Francisco Ortiz Pinchetti, "El Grupo Monterrey crea sus propias fábricas de hombres," *Proceso*, June 23, 1980, 12. The first board of trustees at ITESM is suggestive of capitalists' influence, and included: Eugenio Garza Sada (president), Bernardo Elosúa, Jesús J. Llaguno Jr., Andrés Garza Sada, Ricardo Quirós, and

The VISA holding group was especially powerful in the university's governance. According to Daniel Levy, the rector, who was handpicked by local business leaders, exercised a major role in setting general academic policy.[36] Graduates, including members of the capitalist power elite, believe their student days formed them as adults and provided many life-long friendships.[37] ITESM has graduated seventeen members of the power elite, most of whom are leading capitalists.[38] Four members of the political power elite also attended this school, two of them important figures in the National Action Party. Only one leading intellectual, Gabriel Zaid, has attended this institution.

ITAM, which might be considered a counterpart institution in Mexico City, was founded in 1946 by a group of capitalists and academics, including several power elite members. One of the founders defined the institution's mission: "We are preparing young people who in thirty to forty years can begin the transformation of a statist country to a liberal capitalist country."[39] It is often referred to as Mexico's University of Chicago because of the presence of Milton Friedman's disciples on campus.[40]

ITAM's curriculum is comparable to that of a U.S. liberal arts college; all students, including economics majors, are required to choose from a distributive selection of electives.[41] The university's devotion to high-quality applied economics attracts children of prominent political families, some of whom have gone on to achieve national prominence themselves.[42]

Roberto Guajardo Suárez. Eugenio Garza Sada is one of the influential capitalists included in this study, and three other board members are related to other influential capitalists included in this sample. Eugenio's son, Eugenio Garza Laguera, took business administration classes from ITESM, and all four of his children graduated from this institution. *Integratec,* September/October 1993, 16.

36. Daniel C. Levy, *Higher Education and the State in Latin America,* 133.

37. Sonia López, "Semblanza de Lorenzo H. Zambrano," *Integratec,* September/October 1994, 26.

38. Prominent capitalists from Monterrey who attended ITESM are following a pattern established by members of the "Monterrey Group," the city's original industrial families. According to one scholar, one-third of the old family members working at this group's companies graduated from either ITESM or MIT in the United States. George R. Andrews, "Toward a Reevaluation of the Latin American Family Firm: The Industry Executives of Monterrey," *Inter-American Economic Affairs,* 30 (winter 1976), 37.

39. The power elite members were Raúl Bailleres and Aníbal de Iturbide. *Expansión,* April 13, 1994, 38.

40. *Proceso,* May 17, 1982, 24–26.

41. Richard A. Labarge and T. Noel Osborne, "The Status of Professional Economics Programs in Mexican Universities," 11.

42. Daniel C. Levy, *Higher Education and the State in Latin America,* 162.

The economics program, however, did not achieve a national reputation until the mid 1960s.

The economics curriculum itself was patterned after North American college programs. As Sarah Babb points out, "the evidence suggests that the source of this Americanization was not the businessmen who financed the ITAM and sat on its board, but rather the Mexican central bank. The Banco de México constituted a professional 'sub-constituency' within the Mexican state that provided the ITAM with resources by supplying its professors and hiring its graduates. It was principally through the Banco de México that new foreign models were transmitted to the ITAM in the 1960s and 1970s."[43]

Many students and professors from ITAM, as its founders predicted, achieved success in the public financial and banking sector. ITAM has graduated two treasury secretaries—Gustavo Petricioli Iturbide, 1986–88, and Pedro Aspe Armella, 1988–94, architect of economic neoliberalism in Mexico—as well as the influential head of the Bank of Mexico (Mexico's Federal Reserve), Miguel Mancera. Pedro Aspe, who chaired ITAM's economics program from 1978 to 1982 after receiving his Ph.D. from MIT, reformed the curriculum, moving it away from its extreme emphasis on microeconomics and quantitative theory and adding requirements in economic history and income distribution.[44] He can be viewed as a magnet mentor to the youngest generation of technocratic power elites, who guided Mexico's economic fortunes during the Salinas administration.

Mancera is to the ITAM economics program what de la Cueva was to generations of UNAM law students. He attended the university only five years after it was founded, from 1951 to 1956, probably because one of the key co-founders, a former treasury secretary and head of the Bank of Mexico, was a close friend of Mancera's father, who served as assistant secretary of the treasury from 1948 to 1958.[45] Furthermore, during Mancera's first year as an undergraduate, the university was led by Antonio Carrillo Flores, who served as treasury secretary (and was Mancera's father's boss) for six years in the 1950s.

Mancera taught international trade at his alma mater from 1958 to

43. Sarah Babb, *Managing Mexico: From Nationalism to Neoliberalism* (Princeton: Princeton University Press, 2002).

44. Stephanie R. Golob, "Making Possible What Is Necessary: Pedro Aspe, the Salinas Team, and the Next Mexican Miracle," paper presented at the Latin American Studies Association meeting, Atlanta, March 1994, 14.

45. The friend was Luis Montes de Oca, treasury secretary from 1927 to 1932 and director of the Bank of Mexico from 1935 to 1940.

1964. He first worked as a government economist in the Committee of Public Investment of the Secretariat of the Presidency under the direction of President Salinas's father, himself a mentor to an important generation of older economists. Mancera eventually gathered a group of influential Mexicans under his own wing, mentoring such disciples as Guillermo Ortiz Martínez, treasury secretary and his replacement in the Bank of Mexico, and President Ernesto Zedillo.

The Ibero-American University was established in 1943. In part, it was created in response to the politicized environment at UNAM.[46] Given its Jesuit administration, the presence of Catholic curricular influences, especially the Christian Democratic ideology which began sweeping Latin America in the post–World War II era, is not surprising. Ibero attracted an influential group of Catholic philosophers as well as an important generation of politicians from the National Action Party who held to similar Catholic ideological tenets.

Those prominent figures included the son of PAN's first presidential candidate, who left the Jesuit seminary to pursue an interest in politics after having studied under a distinguished Jesuit historian. He eventually followed in his father's footsteps as the party's presidential contender. Another figure was the PAN presidential candidate in 1994, who had taught at Ibero since 1964. Both men did their secondary and preparatory studies at the Jesuit Institute of Sciences in Guadalajara, and both were linked to Manuel Gómez Morín, a magnet mentor to dozens of prominent Mexicans and the leading PAN figure of his generation.[47]

The Colegio de México, originally a unique public-private hybrid in Mexico,[48] was organized in 1940 as a civil association with the participation of the government, the Bank of Mexico, the Fondo de Cultura Económica (government publishing house), and the Casa de España (cultural institute).[49] In the eyes of some observers and its founders, the institution is

---

46. Daniel C. Levy, *Higher Education and the State in Latin America*, 121.

47. *El Financierio* (international edition), October 18, 1993, 20, and *Líderes*, 6 (1994), 65–71. The two leading Panistas are Efraín González Morfín, who ran for president in the 1976 presidential race, and Diego Fernández de Cevallos, who opposed Zedillo in the 1994 election. Fernández de Cevallos participated as a teenager in González Morfín's father's presidential campaign in 1952.

48. Daniel Levy describes other institutions which have since followed this pattern, including other regional "colegios," in his *Building the Third Sector: Latin America's Research Centers and Non-Profit Development* (Pittsburgh: University of Pittsburgh Press, 1996).

49. El Colegio de México, *El Colegio de México* (Mexico City: El Colegio de México, 1976), 5.

oriented toward the use of ideologically neutral historical methodologies, and it therefore does not attract students who desire a broad social experience typical of public institutions. The Colegio, while critical of the state, expresses itself more objectively and with a less radical tone than the National University.[50] In an interview, one of its prominent intellectual graduates in the power elite, a co-founder of the magazine *Nexos*, described the intellectual ambience from 1969 to 1975 as open and supportive of research on little-known topics.[51]

Daniel Cosío Villegas, one of its most influential founders and a member of the cultural power elite, viewed the Colegio's mission as having three main components: to prepare intellectual leaders, to train university professors, and to stimulate and carry out research. His biographer concludes that Cosío Villegas never made clear how the Colegio would actually accomplish this mission, but he wanted to produce individuals with independent views, original ideas, and critical thoughts.[52] Enrique Krauze, his disciple and managing director of *Vuelta* for many years, vividly describes the Colegio's contribution:

> El Colegio opened intellectual territories in the academic field by creating a new kind of social researcher unknown, until then, in our country: the professional intellectual. Since then, El Colegio de México has had a fundamental influence on our cultural scene: one of moderation, of avoidance of ideological nonsense (one of our main sicknesses), of scholarly outlook, method, theories and styles. In short: a new intellectual *ethos*.[53]

The degree to which the Colegio has achieved these aims can be measured in several ways. First, three past presidents of the Colegio are members of the intellectual power elite.[54] All seven graduates in the present sample are prominent intellectuals, and although the Colegio is the small-

50. Personal interview with Arturo Warman, Mexico City, August 10, 1978.
51. Héctor Aguilar Camín, quoted in Pilar Jiménez Trejo and Alejandro Toledo, *Creación y poder*, 13.
52. Enrique Krauze, *Daniel Cosío Villegas: Una biografía intelectual* (Mexico City: Joaquín Mortiz, 1980), 101, 214.
53. Enrique Krauze, "The Intellectual as Cultural Entrepreneur: The Case of Daniel Cosío Villegas," paper presented at the International Symposium on Intellectuals as Agents of Change in Mexico and Latin America, Central College, Pella, Iowa, October 19, 1980, 5. Of course, this does not suggest that the Colegio's intellectual product reflects these qualities, nor that it is inherently stronger. The same pattern of clientelism and infighting is present at the Colegio as in other institutions.
54. They are Daniel Cosío Villegas, Silvio Zavala, Víctor Urquidi.

est of the universities elites frequented, at least eighteen individuals in the power elite have taught there, half of whom were intellectuals. Second, the Colegio uses full-time faculty almost exclusively; its student-to-faculty ratio is only 2–1. Virtually every student receives sufficient funds to support full-time study, and at the height of its influence among the present power elite during the mid-1970s, only 250 students were enrolled, 50 of them undergraduates.[55]

SOCIALIZATION IN MILITARY SCHOOLS

The public and private educational settings produce two broad sets of power elites in Mexico, but there are further educational divisions among prominent Mexican leaders, which have their origins in professional schools. Two kinds of professional schools are responsible for educating a large portion (more than a third) of Mexico's leaders: military academies and religious seminaries.

Military academies differ significantly from all other elite educational institutions because of their emphasis on discipline, loyalty, and acceptance of authority. Officers who attend these schools are totally immersed in their institutional values twenty-four hours a day, since they reside on campus, and movement on and off campus is controlled. Another important difference is that military academies worldwide deindividualize students through intense indoctrination programs and remold them within their institutional framework.[56]

None of the Mexican universities discussed above provide any on-campus housing, and thus the on-campus residence at military academies is all the more striking. Finally, as one military scholar notes, since World War II, the average Latin American military professional spends more of his or her career attending professional schools than any world counterpart.[57]

It is important to pay increased attention to military leadership because in the last decade the size of the armed forces increased 35 percent. This expansion has dramatically affected the size of the officer corps. In 1988,

55. El Colegio de México, *El Colegio de México*, 14.
56. T. M. McCloy and W. H. Clover, "Value Formation at the Air Force Academy," in C. C. Moskos and F. R. Woods, eds., *The Military: More Than Just a Job?* (Washington, D.C.: Pergamon, 1988), 135.
57. Russell Ramsey, "Forty Years of Human Rights Training," *Journal of Low Intensity Conflict and Law Enforcement*, 4, no. 2 (autumn 1995), 254.

approximately 925 individuals graduated from all military schools combined; by 1997, that figure had grown to 7,981 graduates.[58]

The military ethos fascinates scholars not just in Mexico but worldwide, and consequently a fairly generous literature exists on it and the socialization process it engenders. Analysts have summarized the fundamental values of the military subculture as including acceptance of all-pervasive hierarchy and deference patterns; extreme emphasis on dress, bearing, and grooming; specialized vocabulary; focus on honor, integrity, and professional responsibility; stress on brotherhood; special reverence for history and traditions; and nationalism.[59]

As they do in the secular educational venue, young people who choose military careers affect the socialization process by self-selection before they darken the doors of any military academy. High school seniors in the United States "who expect to serve in the military are more promilitary than those who do not, and those who anticipate military careers are the most pro-military."[60] Second, officer cadets who are children of fathers and mothers in the military, and who have thus been previously exposed to the military, are more likely to share the military ethos.[61]

Evidence about the military socialization process is somewhat contradictory. Studies universally point to a general conservatism and intolerance among military officers compared to their civilian counterparts, but on many influential policy issues, military officers do not differ significantly from civilians.[62] For example, one study found that the so-called military

58. Presidencia de México, *Sexto informe de gobierno, September 1, 2000* (Mexico City: Presidencia, 2000), 5. As of August 2000, the armed forces totaled 238,985, of which 183,296, or 77 percent, were army personnel. In 1996–97, 725 regular cadets and 107 other students were enrolled in the Heroic Military College, 143 officers in the three-year Higher War College curriculum, and 26 high-ranking officers from all services, including several civilians, in the National Defense College. A dramatic increase occurred from 1995 to 1996, when the total number of graduates of all service training programs went from 1,659 to 5,300.

59. Gary L. Wamsley, "Contrasting Institutions of Air Force Socialization: Happenstance or Bellwether?" *American Journal of Sociology*, 78 (1972), 401.

60. J. G. Backman, L. Sigelman, and G. Diamond, "Self-Selection, Socialization and Distinctive Military Values: Attitudes of High School Seniors," *Armed Forces and Society*, 13 (1987), 182.

61. Serge Guimond, "Encounter and Metamorphosis: The Impact of Military Socialization on Professional Values," *Applied Psychology: An International Review*, 44, no. 3 (1995), 270.

62. Ted Goertzel and Acco Hengst, "The Military Socialization of University Students," *Social Problems*, 19 (1971), 262; R. Priest, T. Fullerton, and C. Bridges also found that cadets were less committed to the outside world and more strongly

mind was not substantially different from the mind-set of leading businessmen.[63] However, some connection does exist between authoritarian personalities and acceptance of military ideology.[64] The traits of the military subculture are straightforward, rather than intellectually complex, and are characterized by "overt, patterned ways of behaving, feeling and reacting," as distinct from views on any specific social issue.[65] A study of West Point cadets, who provide a disproportionate share of army leadership, also suggests that their attitudes are not overly homogeneous.[66]

Perhaps because of the historical circumstances peculiar to Mexico's heritage, Mexican military academies accentuate some of the socializing influences found in military culture in other countries, particularly discipline and social control. Two historical phenomena, the 1910 Revolution and Mexico's animosity against the United States—which invaded Mexico both in the nineteenth and twentieth centuries, seizing more than half of its national territory—have been formative. In general, though, the military academies produce attitudes similar to those found in other military subcultures.

It is noteworthy that the level of discipline and subordination to authority inculcated among cadets who successfully complete training at its Higher War College, which graduates most army officers reaching general rank, is extreme.[67] The academies are more successful at achieving these

---

committed to a closed form of nationalism. They too found dramatic increases in conservatism over the four years cadets attended West Point. "Personality and Value Changes in West Point Cadets," *Armed Forces and Society*, 8 (1982), 637, 640–41.

63. Bruce M. Russett, "Political Perspectives of U.S. Military and Business Elites," *Armed Forces and Society*, 1 (fall 1974), 97.

64. Elizabeth G. French and Raymond R. Ernest, "The Relationship between Authoritarianism and Acceptance of Military Ideology," *Journal of Personality*, 24 (December 1955), 190.

65. Gary L. Wamsley, "Contrasting Institutions of Air Force Socialization," 401. For example, Ted Goertzel and Acco Hengst found that ROTC cadets scored higher on measures of personality authoritarianism, misanthropy, and punitiveness, which would be anticipated on the basis of studies of the correlates of militarism. "The Military Socialization of University Students," 260.

66. J. P. Lovell, "The Professional Socialization of the West Point Cadet," in Morris Janowitz, ed., *The New Military: Changing Patterns of Organization* (New York: Russell Sage, 1964), 146.

67. See my "The Educating and Training of the Mexican Officer Corps," in Elliott V. Converse, ed., *Forging the Sword: Selecting, Educating, and Training Cadets and Junior Officers in the Modern World*, vol. 5, Military History Symposium Series of the United States Air Force Academy (Chicago: Imprint Publications, 1998), 336–46.

levels because discipline, not technical knowledge, is at the forefront of their mission.[68] Furthermore, as is true in the smaller academies in the United States, small class size facilitates different and more effective methods of social control.[69]

The Heroico Colegio Militar (HCM), the army's entry-level institution for officer cadets, has graduated more members of Mexico's power elite than any other institution, with the exception of the National University. It also has graduated the second largest percentage of any individual elite group. Sixty-eight percent of the 100 leading officers count the HCM as their alma mater, compared to the 73 percent of Mexican politicians who graduated from UNAM. It has produced every defense secretary since 1970. The present facility, built at the end of Luis Echeverría's administration, is a three-story building which houses fifty-four small classrooms, each of which can seat thirty-five students. The simply furnished classrooms have green blackboards and plain wooden desks.[70]

Within the military, the traditional occupational specialties of infantry, cavalry, and artillery have produced most defense secretaries, who have in turn favored other high-ranking officers from those specialties. But among the post-1940s graduates, a distinctive shift in professional backgrounds has occurred. Among those officers who are members of the power elite, slightly over half specialized in administration, not the combat arms occupations. Their recent influence is symbolized by the fact that the secretary of defense from 1994 to 2000 was the first "admin" officer to reach this post.

The HCM captures the largest number of future officers because it serves as the entry-level funnel among military educational institutions for army and air force officer aspirants; but the most influential socializing experiences take place at the Escuela Superior de Guerra (ESG) and the

68. William S. Ackroyd, "Descendants of the Revolution: Civil-Military Relations in Mexico," unpublished Ph.D. dissertation, University of Arizona, 1988, 110.

69. Sanford M. Dornbusch, "The Military Academy as an Assimilating Institution," *Social Forces*, 33 (May 1955), 316.

70. The secretariat of national defense itself describes the products of this school with its own rhetoric as joining a peaceful army which serves institutions, converting a citizen to a soldier who serves national development and draws his ideals from the Mexican Revolution. *La evolución de la educación militar en México* (Mexico City: Secretaria de Defensa Nacional, 1977). For a description, see Vicente Leñero, "Estrenando Colegio Militar," *Talacha periodística* (Mexico City: Editorial Diana, 1983), 190. For a reevaluation of Lovell's findings, see Volker C. Franke, "Warriors for Peace: The Next Generation of U.S. Military Leaders," *Armed Forces and Society*, 24, no. 1 (fall 1997), 33–57.

two equivalent naval academies. The ESG's primary mission is to weed out officers who are unwilling to submit to abusive treatment at the hands of their instructors, to sacrifice for the benefit of the group, or to subordinate themselves, for whatever reason, to higher authority.[71]

The ESG can closely control the environment in part because an individual class never exceeds fifty individuals. The fifty-eighth class, which graduated in 1990, consisted of thirty-seven Mexican officers, two from the navy and two from the air force, and six foreign guest officers, including one from the United States.[72] The second year of the three-year program consists of a course load of twenty-three subjects that range from tactics at the division level to sociology and statistics. It is the rough equivalent of a U.S. Army basic or advanced course in all combined arms with several semesters of a university administration education thrown in. A recent guest officer described the ESG's purpose:

> to develop in the graduate a capacity to perform a limitless amount of work, albeit inefficiently done and many times senseless in nature, blind obedience to authority and unquestioned loyalty to the institution. I must add that an unstated goal is for the ESG student to pay his "dues" which leads to the enjoyment of a lifelong career as a special class of officer who will receive faster promotion and a lot more pay. This represents an oligarchy over the Mexican army and exercises almost complete power over all those who are not graduates regardless of rank.
>
> Students are forced to memorize incredible quantities of text to negotiate the over 120 exams the student takes during the academic year. The students know they cannot do this, which leads to a cheating culture. The testing process becomes a vicious circle with the instructor's job to make the tests impossible and the student's job to find any and all means to pass the test. This led one instructor to acknowledge that the job of the student is to cheat and the instructor's is to discover the cheating.[73]

71. The ESG remains a man's domain. Women took the higher arms course at the ESG in the 1980s at the rank of lieutenant colonel. Allegedly one was allowed to start the staff and command course (DEM), but didn't have the physical ability and washed out. All of these goals, which were repeatedly described by guest officers in the 1980s and 1990s, are contained in their official reports as viewed by the author, and cited in great detail by Michael Dziedzic, in "Mexico's Converging Challenges: Problems, Prospects, and Implications," unpublished paper, U.S. Air Force Academy, Colorado Springs, Colorado, 1989, 28–34.

72. *Revista de Ejército y Fuerza Aérea,* August 1990, 68–69.

73. Letter from Major Michael Knutson to the author, February 23, 1999.

The failure rate at the ESG during the three-year course is 60 percent.

Higher war colleges attract attention from civil-military theorists because of the perceived tendency in the region to produce officers with social and political interests who become involved politically. The classic, much studied case of this was the 1964 military coup d'etat in Brazil.[74] Some Mexicans have intimated that the armed forces in their own country are following a similar path, and that the ESG will play a crucial role in producing politicized officers.[75] For a variety of reasons, this has never been an issue in Mexico, distinguishing it from other Latin American countries, including Peru and Brazil.

The curriculum at the ESG includes subject matter which unquestionably could influence officer values. Those officers who will be achieving top command positions in the 2000s have read confidential texts on internal security issues which include significant political interpretations. Their course materials identify and discuss a Mexican oligarchy, they explore deficiencies in public administration, including electoral fraud, and they consider cultural and economic imperialism as well as Catholicism and socialism, suggesting that all are potentially destabilizing influences in Mexican society.[76]

After the 1986 economic crisis, the program administrators changed their recruiting requirements. The typical class in the 1980s consisted of eight majors, twenty-five first captains, and twelve second captains. The post-1987 classes increasingly admitted first lieutenants and junior captains, on the premise that their younger age would make them more susceptible to ESG influence. The perceived sympathy of many officers for Cuauhtémoc Cárdenas in the 1988 presidential race only increased the ESG's emphasis on younger officers. An American army officer in the 1989–91 class noted that fellow officers were openly expressing the belief that they could do a better job than their civilian counterparts in managing the country's political affairs. When members of the second-year program

74. Christopher Brogran, "Military Higher Education and the Emergence of 'New Professionalism': Some Consequences for Civil-Military Relations in Latin America," *Army Quarterly and Defense Journal*, no. 112 (January 1982), 25.

75. Raimundo Riva Palacio, a Mexican military analyst, claimed that the army has been expressing an attitude of superiority toward civilian politicians and that they have 3,000 officers who can do a better job than civilian cabinet secretaries. Personal interview, Mexico City, February 13, 1991.

76. Escuela Superior de Guerra, *Compendio de seguridad interior. Libro primero: El estado mexicano y los factores desestabilizadores* (Mexico: Escuela Superior de Guerra, 1985), 84–95.

were asked to rank their institutional loyalties, they ranked the army above country.[77]

Despite earlier efforts to keep politicizing influences from creeping into the Escuela Superior de Guerra classrooms, this has become an ingrained pattern which is condoned by many in administrative posts. A guest officer in 1997–98 reports: "We had respected instructors stating in front of class that officers should vote for PAN. Some of my peers told me that PRI had their chance for the last fifty years and now it was time for someone new. Some of the more radical officers said a revolution was necessary. I must say there was not widespread support for Cárdenas."[78]

The ESG expanded the breadth of views to which the students were exposed by replicating a mainstay of the curriculum of the prestigious Colegio de Defensa Nacional, the guest speaker program. "This really took off last year [1998] at ESG. . . . There are rumors that the director was replaced because he brought in too many National Action Party speakers. Vicente Fox was scheduled to deliver a presentation and was canceled one day prior to the presentation."[79]

As the analysis of the mentoring process among Mexico's elite suggested, education provides a source of many future military mentors, career officers who themselves offer the vast majority of instruction in the armed forces. The military produces magnet mentors similar to those found in civilian institutions, but given the institutional secrecy surrounding the armed forces they are more difficult to identify.

The most notable magnet mentor, who is also a member of the military power elite and who taught many peers from this group, is the late General Antonio Ramírez Barrera. General Ramírez Barrera received a eulogy and a detailed obituary in the official armed forces magazine unlike any other officer during the last three decades. The authors of that tribute indicated that "the Colegio Militar and the Escuela Superior de Guerra had the good fortune of being nurtured with his teachings and guidance as a mentor of the highest professional quality and moral integrity."[80] The article goes on to discuss his impact on numerous generations of officers. General Ramírez Barrera was a two-time zone commander, a military attaché to France and Brazil, and served in Congress after retiring, where he chaired the national

77. Letter to the author from Major Richard James Kilroy Jr.
78. Letter to the author from Michael Knutson.
79. Ibid.
80. *Revista de Ejército y Fuerza Aérea*, October 1994, 68.

defense committee. Twenty-nine of his fifty-one years of active duty were spent in military higher education as a student, professor, and administrator:[81]

1970–72	Director General of Military Education
1961–66	Director of the Escuela Superior de Guerra (ESG)
1961–65	Professor of Engineering, Escuela Superior de Guerra
1960–61	Counter-Insurgency Course, Ft. Gulick, Panama Canal
1949–53	Director of the Police Academy of the Federal District
1946–53	Instructor in Strategy, Escuela Superior de Guerra
1943–44	Staff and Command Course, Ft. Leavenworth, Kansas
1939–42	Higher Arms and Staff and Command Course, ESG
1938–39	Instructor, Heroico Colegio Militar (HCM)
1936	Instructor, HCM
1931–34	Cadet, HCM, graduated as Second Lieutenant Infantry

The educational training of leading officers in the armed forces, unlike that of any other power elite group in Mexico, continues well into their professional careers, when they are middle-aged and poised to achieve the highest ranks in their respective services. Most of the officers who experience late career training have reached the rank of colonel or general and are in their forties. This middle-aged educational experience epitomizes mature, adult socialization.

According to a former director of the Colegio de Defensa Nacional (CDN), the secretary of national defense from 1976 to 1982 perceived the armed forces education to be seriously deficient:

> He realized that most of his general officers didn't really understand various aspects of Mexico, including social, political, and economic conditions, especially in broad terms. He thought it was impossible for men of this rank and responsibility to carry out their functions effectively without such general knowledge. So it was his desire to help modernize the military by introducing this type of preparation. In the old days, before the establishment of the CDN, a well-designed

---

81. Biographical details, in addition to his obituary, are taken from *Revista de Ejército y Fuerza Aérea*, July 1961, 30; September 1961, 43; November 1968, 54; November 1972, 39, 49; August 1975, 118; *Directorio del poder ejecutivo federal, 1971* (Mexico City: Secretaria de la Presidencia, 1971); and *Directorio del poder ejecutivo, 1965* (Mexico City, 1965).

program to increase strategic and general education beyond the higher war college level had never existed.[82]

The Colegio de Defensa Nacional initiated its first class in 1981. One of the hallmarks of this elite program, which grants an M.A. degree in national security, is its small size. The ninth generation (1989–90), for example, consisted of ten generals, fourteen colonels, one navy captain, one rear admiral, and two civilians.[83] The overall class size remains small. Every member of that generation's lower ranking participants since has reached general or admiral rank. Within the present sample of power elites, the number of graduates is small because most officers reached positions of influence prior to the program's existence. Six of the officers in the sample are graduates, five of them from the first class (1981–82), and one of those became head of the air force.

The unique feature of this professional program is that it includes civilian students, carefully selected from mid-career in government agencies, usually those agencies represented in the national security cabinet along with national defense and the navy.[84] The civilian presence has been expanded, reaching six students in the 1998–99 class. The commandant of the Colegio de Defensa Nacional has suggested that they will increase those numbers further.[85] The final feature is that many of the college's professors are civilians, but because they do not lecture throughout the course, they are usually unable to develop close personal ties to the students.

A recent graduate from the Colegio de Defensa Nacional describes the calibre of the program as equivalent to that found at the Colegio de México or the ITAM. Its curricular sources are very diverse, including military and political bibliographic materials from the United States and Mexico. The first half of the course exposes students to broad social, economic, and political issues. Most of the lecturers on these topics are civilians. Students are addressed by prominent Mexicans from all walks of life, as well as by some foreign experts. The entire cabinet spoke individually to this class, and for the most part, they did not delegate that responsibility to an as-

---

82. Personal interview with General Gerardo de la Vega, Colegio de Defensa Nacional, Mexico City, August 19, 1990. De la Vega was appointed secretary of national defense by President Fox in December 2000.

83. *Revista de Ejército y Fuerza Aérea*, August 1990, 58.

84. These would include the attorney general, government, and foreign relations.

85. Personal interview with General Rafael Paz del Campo, a graduate of the 1985–86 generation, Mexico City, December 12, 1998.

sistant. Most of the prominent foreign military attachés also lecture to the students.

The methodology of the course, devoted to completing a group project on a significant national security issue, is conceptualized differently from a civilian approach. The military typically formulates ideas following a continuum beginning with military policy, then broad strategy, then tactics; whereas a typical civilian approach reverses the order to strategy, then policy, followed by tactics. Students also have noted differences between the military and civilian terminology, differences which they believe create serious obstacles to clear communication between these groups.[86]

SOCIALIZATION OF CATHOLIC CLERGY

It is much easier to capture the general flavor of the curriculum and environment for the secular elite groups than for the religious elites, whose educational experiences at the national level are more diverse and therefore make generalizing more difficult. From the 1930s through the early 1960s, about half of the bishops attended the diocesan seminaries in Puebla, Morelia, Guadalajara, and Mexico City. Many of these bishops, as suggested in the previous chapter, lived through formative historical events while enrolled in seminaries, adverse experiences that flavored their attitudes and values more strongly than anything conveyed in the classroom.

I have described the prevailing ambience of these seminaries elsewhere, but a short summary of characteristics is worth repeating here:

1.   In the 1930s and 1940s, most seminaries which reopened after the persecution fostered during the Cristero rebellion tried to close off student minds to outside social and political news.

2.   In the late 1960s and early 1970s, large numbers of students were washed out of seminary programs for showing an excessive zeal favoring a social ministry and service to the poor.

3.   Mexican seminaries, similar to secular college environments, witnessed widespread diversity in seminarians' changing attitudes toward institutional authority.

86. Personal interview, September 15, 1998. The source gave the example of the military students repeatedly confusing the term *social mobility* with *social migration*. In policy terms, the culture of the military prefers that they be given a well-defined mission or task. Mexican civilian policymakers prefer to sketch only the broadest outlines of their responsibilities. Such differences may lead to serious misunderstandings.

4. The crucial difference from one seminary to another focused on the basic definition of a priest's pastoral role.

5. Seminaries with greater financial resources and the ability to provide a stronger theological preparation were favored in sending their students abroad for advanced training.[87]

The clergy has produced its own magnet mentors in Catholic seminaries. The most notable Mexican seminary in the educational backgrounds of the bishops in the power elite is the Palafoxian Seminary in Puebla. For many years, a major figure at the seminary was Octaviano Márquez y Toriz, who from 1928 until 1951 served consecutively as a professor, spiritual director, and rector of the seminary.[88] He mentored numerous prominent bishops when they were students and, in many cases, after they became priests in his diocese—including the bishop of Atlacomulco, who served as his secretary; the bishop of Tlaxcala, who replaced his mentor as spiritual director of the seminary; the archbishop of Durango, who also became spiritual director of the seminary; the archbishop of Puebla, who served in many posts in the seminary; the cardinal archbishop of Mexico, who studied under Márquez y Toriz in the 1930s and replaced him as archbishop; and the archbishop of Yucatán, who returned from Europe in 1940 to study at the Palafoxian seminary.

The national educational experiences of leading civilians, military officers, and clergy suggest several shared general patterns. The most important finding is that, according to the recollections of Mexican power elites, preparatory and especially university education played a significant role in the formation of their values, whether they attended public, private professional, or nonprofessional schools.

A more detailed analysis of these socializing experiences clarifies mentors' fundamental role in the socializing process. Most power elites were aided by individual mentors at certain points in their careers. A select group of individuals within each of the policy circles are known to have mentored multiple figures within the power elite. Given the fact that I have tried to identify the inner core within Mexico's power elites, and that their numbers are quite small, the impact of these magnet mentors, as I

87. Roderic Ai Camp, *Crossing Swords: Politics and Religion in Mexico* (New York: Oxford University Press, 1997), 162–64.

88. Luis Nava Rodríguez, *Octaviano Márquez y Toriz* (Mexico City: Editorial Jus, 1978).

have labeled them, is rather extraordinary. If a single bishop, for example, mentored five out of fifty leading clergy, that person directly influenced one out ten prominent clerics. The same can be said for the other magnet mentors described above.

This analysis definitely demonstrates that magnet mentors have used their educational responsibilities as teachers and administrators to identify and promote talented students. Not only have they taken disciples under their wings as intellectual mentors, but in many cases they have combined their socializing functions generally with socializing functions relevant to career success. In short, they have taught disciples the informal rules of those professions in addition to influencing their broader political or economic views.

Detailed examination of these magnet mentors makes it clear that they have combined all three mentoring functions—socialization, networking, and recruitment. Indeed, it is difficult to separate these mentoring tasks, as they are often complementary.

As I suggested earlier in this work, mentors are themselves important figures among the present or past power elite. What is also apparent from this analysis is that many magnet mentors were disciples of an older generation of magnet mentors. Mentors within the Mexican power elite are an ingrown and a self-perpetuating phenomenon.

The structure of social development, the investment of public resources, and the role of the state have all contributed to the peculiar structure of higher education in Mexico, a pattern found in every other country in Latin America and most of the Third World. The most relevant structural condition in education, reinforcing the mentoring task and undoubtedly enhancing magnet mentors' roles, was the lack of full-time teachers at public preparatory schools and universities. This deficiency led to many top professionals teaching part time, but for long durations. It also led to legitimizing teaching as a normal task of a successful professional career. Within more structured professions, such as the armed forces or the clergy, full-time teaching or administration became essential to career success.

One of the educational differences across power elite groups is the breadth of their exposure to prevailing social, economic, and political ideologies. A tension appears to exist between a focus on the more "professional" or "technical" aspects of one's preparation versus an exposure to broader intellectual issues which provide the larger setting for a particular professional preparation.

Some institutional settings view outside influences as threats to the purity of their professional or intellectual message. Viewed in that light, power elite intellectuals received the broadest, most eclectic education in major social and political issues, followed by politicians, while the military and clergy were exposed to the narrowest range of nonprofessional influences. Capitalists, who typically majored in engineering programs in private universities, tend to fall somewhere in between.

It should be noted, however, that by virtue of their spiritual teachings, a focus lacking among all other leadership groups, the clergy are provided with a strong underpinning potentially favorable to political change and social justice. This moral underpinning came to play a role when the progressive currents of Vatican II reached the curriculum of Mexican and foreign seminaries. Despite the fact that Mexican clergy were only moderately influenced by those views, their presence flavored the spiritual and theological content experienced among a younger generation of priests.[89] There is no question that active clerical support for Mexican democratic participation and electoral competition in the mid-1980s was grounded on those currents seeping into the Catholic educational system in the 1960s and 1970s.

Another pattern which emerges from power elites' educational experiences in Mexico is that a deep concern for social change, expressed in many ways—including declining loyalty to existing institutions, professional or national; an emphasis on economic and social inequalities; and a desire for increasing pluralism in Mexican society—began to influence future power elite groups other than the clergy in the 1960s. The intellectual and political class, who were automatically drawn to the political debates of their generation, often beginning during their preparatory or college student days, were most exposed to these issues, and were often mentored by older professors with similar concerns.

The military, despite the existence of influential magnet mentors, might be viewed as being the least influenced in their political and social views by educational socializing experiences. A younger generation of officers slowly altered its own professional culture after witnessing society's reaction to the military's role in the 1968 student massacre. The topic of the massacre was taboo in the classroom, but its unpleasant consequences, discussed privately, molded a generation of officers who desired an armed forces with a better grasp of the societal setting. Those desires were reflected indirectly in the social and political content of new military text-

89. I am not suggesting that all members, and all groups, were equally affected by this issue, but rather that, for a large number among those elites expressing such concerns, education provided an influential source.

books available in the 1980s. New civilian instructors in the National Defense College could not serve as mentors to leading officers, but they did discuss this and other controversial political and social issues in the classroom, exposing future decision makers to views their civilian counterparts were considering.

Mexican power elites use education to identify, reinforce, and remold values which form the basis of an elite subculture. Some subcultures, because they directly control their own educational institutions, are most easily described for military and clerical elites. But magnet mentors, regardless of educational environment, as former or present power elites, are significant contributors inside the organizational structures of their own professions, reinforcing and adding to "institutional cultures," and thereby altering long-term institutional and cultural values.

7 Globalizing Mexico's Power Elite
The Role of Education Abroad

In Mexico and in Third World countries generally, education abroad has contributed significantly to the credentials and experiences of top leaders from many sectors of society. Mentors, both within the family and in higher education, contributed strongly to these socializing influences. The implications of those foreign influences have been taken up in classic fictional accounts, especially in African writings (or writings set in Africa), as indigenous intellectuals explore the impact of the postcolonial "been to."[1] They have also been emphasized in the scholarly literature, which suggests that Latin American and other "elite groups are more oriented economically and culturally, towards North American and Europe than to their own countries."[2]

Study abroad was an international phenomenon throughout the entire twentieth century, as well as earlier, but it became noticeable in terms of numbers in the early 1960s. Both Europe and the United States have attracted foreign students for decades, but the United States has dominated the list of host countries in recent decades.[3] In 1962, the United States

1. For examples see Chinua Achebe, *Things Fall Apart* (New York: Anchor, 1994), and V. S. Naipaul, *A Bend in the River* (New York: Vintage, 1989). In his novel *Guerrillas* (New York: Vintage, 1990), 237, set in a different geographic context, Naipaul offers an insightful comment on the psychological explanation for foreign education: "We're a dependent people, Peter. We need other people's approval. And when people come to us with reputations made abroad we tend to look up to them. It's something you yourself have been complaining about."

2. Vicky Randall and Robin Theobald, *Political Change and Underdevelopment: A Critical Introduction to Third World Politics*, 2d ed. (Durham: Duke University Press, 1998), 15.

3. For example, one of the oldest figures in the intellectual elite, Daniel Cosío Villegas, studied at Cornell University, Harvard University, and the London School

attracted the most foreign students of any country, nearly 65,000; in 1990 it remained the top host country, enrolling 408,000 students in colleges and universities. The two dominant trends in global study abroad patterns during these years were an increasing flow of students from "peripheral" to industrialized nations, and an increasing percentage of international students choosing the United States.[4]

Mexico has not been immune to these universal trends. Mexicans in the power elite have been heavily exposed to the socializing influences of international education. Of the individuals whose preparatory and higher educational experiences are known, over half studied abroad at some point in their life. (See table 14.) Not surprisingly, only a minuscule number of power elites have studied exclusively abroad (both preparatory and college education), so Mexican institutions remain at the forefront of their educational socialization.

The fact that more than half of Mexico's leadership received part of their education abroad is nevertheless a remarkable statistic. It establishes beyond a doubt that the majority of Mexican leaders are potentially exposed to the classroom and cultural influences which accompany foreign study. What is particularly extraordinary is that more than one out of three Mexican elites studied in the United States. European countries, primarily France and England, have contributed to the education of one out of five power elites. Only seven individuals have studied in Latin America, one of those exclusively.

The data also suggest important differences among power elites' level of international exposure and where it occurs. The leadership group with the most international education are Catholic bishops, eight out of ten of whom attended school abroad. Unlike the majority of Mexican leaders from the other four groups, most clergy studied in Europe. By contrast, fewer than half of all politicians studied abroad, and only a fifth did so in Europe. Europe also exerted a greater impact on the study abroad experiences of Mexican intellectuals, distinguishing intellectuals from three of the other groups. Military officers and capitalists remain essentially un-

---

of Economics in the 1920s. He recalls being influenced by the Webb brothers and by Harold Laski. Other Fabians in England also influenced him and he studied from 1926 to 1928 under a Fabian who was very popular during this time. The U.S. and the impact of economic geography on economic policy also had some effect on his attitudes. Letter to the author, May 14, 1974.

4. Mary E. McMahon, "Higher Education in a World Market: An Historical Look at the Global Context of International Study," *Higher Education*, 24 (1992), 466.

Table 14. Power Elite Education Abroad

	Country Where Power Elite Studied			
Power Elite Group	Mexico Only (%)	United States (%)	Europe (%)	Latin America (%)
Politician	53	29	15	3
Intellectual	49	32	17	2
Capitalist	40	50	8	2
Military	45	53	0	2
Clergy	21	7	72	0

NOTE: A small number of elites, 5 percent, studied in both the United States and Europe. For purposes of the table, and the growing influence of the United States on Mexican elite education, I am including that figure as part of the United States column. (N = 398)

touched by European educational experiences. The only individuals in the entire sample of power elites to have received all of their higher education in the United States were four capitalists, suggesting the group's strong orientation toward North American professional values. Military officers were the most likely to have studied in the United States, something one out of two officers experienced, but *exclusively at military institutions*.

Why do foreign students in general and Mexican students in particular seek education abroad? Why have such students increased their focus on the United States? Students typically have studied abroad for two reasons: the unavailability of comparable programs in their country of origin and the quality of programs available in their own country.[5] For example, in Mexico, many of the students who came to study graduate-level economics in the United States did so because such doctoral programs were unavailable until the mid-1970s at UNAM and the National Polytechnical Institute.

5. Pedro Ojeda Paullada, who graduated with an important generation of lawyers in the 1950s, explains why most Mexicans in that era who became politicians did not study abroad: "As is my own case, most of us did not study abroad after completing law school. . . . But really, we completed law school at about the same time López Mateos was campaigning for the presidency. Most of us joined the campaign, and we participated in the formulation of his campaign platform in 1957. This really was an important political event for us—we were formed through this direct political experience. [Mario] Moya Palencia was involved in this too. My M.A. and Ph.D. are in campaign politics, which took us to all parts of the republic before producing the final document. Also remember that we did not have a graduate program in law until 1951. It did not have much prestige yet." Personal interview, Mexico City, December 14, 1998.

Another reason which applies in the Mexican case is that the government itself made a policy decision to increase advanced technical education in all areas, providing scholarships first through the Bank of Mexico, as early as the 1950s, and then, beginning in the 1970s, through the National Council of Science and Technology (Conacyt), which began funding hundreds of students during Luis Echeverría's administration (1970–76).[6]

As one beneficiary of this program pointed out, Conacyt grants "allowed thousands of Mexican students to study abroad, and many of these foreign-educated Mexicans would eventually constitute the new cadres of the Mexican ruling elite, displacing traditional politicians from Echeverría's era. . . . These academic institutions nurtured the neo-liberal ideas that would transform Mexico's history."[7] But other observers believe that President Echeverría had an ulterior motive for the fellowship program: to remove a radicalized generation of students from the country.[8] The irony is that the program produced a technocratic elite who introduced economic policies completely contrary to the president's own philosophy.

The origins of a formalized foreign study program, and the crucial role of the Bank of Mexico, date back to the early 1940s. Nelson Rockefeller proposed a scholarship program through the Institute of Inter-American Affairs. Rockefeller was a friend of the director of the Bank of Mexico, an important entity in the development of Mexican economics.[9] The primary adviser to the program was another key official of the bank who for many years directed the industrial planning department.[10]

These initial scholarships were designed to support Mexicans in obtaining practical knowledge in a business setting. What is essential to under-

6. By 1997, Conacyt was funding over 18,000 students, a fifth of whom were studying abroad. This proportion of students studying abroad was consistent from 1985 through 1997. *México social, 1996–1998* (Mexico City: Banamex, 1998), 334. Daniel Levy argues that Mexico, like Argentina, stayed clear of direct fellowship assistance from the Agency for International Development, Ford, and the Inter-American Development Bank in the 1960s. Personal communication to the author, June 1, 2000.

7. Sergio Aguayo, *Myths and [Mis]Perceptions: Changing U.S. Elite Visions of Mexico* (La Jolla: Center for U.S.-Mexican Studies, University of California, San Diego, 1998), 171.

8. Miguel A. Centeno, *Democracy within Reason: Technocratic Revolution in Mexico* (University Park: Penn State University Press, 1994), 152.

9. The initial selection committee was made up of Eduardo Villaseñor, director of the Bank of Mexico; Carlos Martínez Ulloa, head of the Federal Electric Commission; an American, the president of American Smelting, who presided over the group; and Víctor Urquidi, who functioned as executive secretary.

10. That individual was Gonzalo Robles.

stand is that well-placed Mexican mentors used their influence to encourage students to study abroad, as well as to obtain government fellowships for their protégés.[11]

When World War II ended, the international scholarship program was not renewed. Shortly thereafter, Daniel Cosío Villegas, who had studied at Cornell, Harvard, the University of Wisconsin, and the London School of Economics, and who had co-founded the economics program at the National School of Law with his close friend and patron Eduardo Villaseñor, joined the bank's subdirector general, Rodrigo Gómez, in proposing that the Bank of Mexico sponsor its own program. According to Víctor Urquidi, who managed the program, they suggested sending several economists abroad.[12]

After its initial success, Gonzalo Robles suggested expanding the program across various specialties; he drew up a list of fields in Mexican engineering and the sciences lacking technical expertise. Urquidi implemented the expanded program, bypassing all other federal agencies and dealing directly with universities in the United States and elsewhere. The bank converted his personal efforts into a permanent fellowship program.[13]

In the 1960s and 1970s, the bank continued to select students for fellowships who were recommended by sponsors. If students were accepted by the university the bank had chosen, they were sent there; if rejected, they were sent to another institution. At the beginning, Harvard and Yale were the primary destinations among economists. No one was "sent to get

11. One of the participants in this program was Jorge Díaz Serrano, a member of the power elite who studied internal combustion engines from 1943 to 1945 and became director of Petróleos Mexicanos, the state-owned oil industry, in 1976.

12. One of the first three individuals sent on the new program was Jorge Espinosa de los Reyes, ambassador to the United States in the 1980s, who worked with Urquidi in the bank's economic studies department. Also in the early days of the program, Urquidi sent Héctor Hernández Cervantes to study at the University of Melbourne in 1949. Hernández Cervantes, a member of the power elite, became secretary of commerce in 1982. Urquidi could also be viewed as a magnet mentor, both as a professor, a key figure in the bank's technical departments, and as a director of the Economic Commission for Latin America in Mexico. Urquidi graduated from the London School of Economics at age twenty-one, had lived abroad as the child of a diplomat, and was a member of the Club of Rome. He was one of the most influential economists of his generation, having edited *El Trimestre Económico* for nearly twenty years. He directed the Colegio de México during the years it achieved educational prominence, from 1966 to 1985. His networking ties reach broadly across intellectual and political boundaries, as well as among influential international elites.

13. Personal interview between Theodore Mesmer and Irwin Baskind, and Víctor Urquidi, Mexico City, September 17, 1997.

a Ph.D. . . . A better use of resources was to send an additional person instead. Many obtained their M.A. degrees and did the course work to qualify for the Ph.D., but the Ph.D. was not included in the scholarship."[14]

The most influential figure in the decision of a Mexican power elite to study abroad is his or her mentor, who is largely responsible for career success and graduate training. As suggested previously, mentors convinced their disciples to choose such an educational path, and they made it feasible, through government-supported funding, to explore those opportunities.

The educational levels of past and present power elite members are quite high, and it is clear that well-educated mentors pass on their preferences for higher education to their younger disciples. Fewer than one out of ten of their disciples stopped their education at a pre-college level. Among the disciples of non-elite mentors, who did not boast their higher levels of education, four times that number did not pursue advanced education, an extraordinary difference.

Mentors who were power elites not only shared a preference for higher levels of education, including graduate studies, but also for studies abroad. Among power elite mentors, only a minority were educated exclusively in Mexico. Nearly two-thirds studied either in Europe or in the United States, and of those, two-thirds received part of their education in the United States.

The shift from Europe to the United States among the present power elite in the 1960s and 1970s was anticipated by an earlier generation of power elite mentors, whose increasing educational experiences abroad, especially in the United States, were complemented by foreign training in non-educational internships or professional assignments.

Half of power elite mentors born prior to 1945 studied or trained in the United States; nearly two-thirds of those born after 1945 had direct experience with Mexico's northern neighbor. The disciples of these mentors were the most likely to have obtained graduate education in the United States. One out of four disciples of younger mentors obtained graduate degrees from U.S. universities, compared to only one out of eight disciples of older mentors.[15]

14. According to Ernesto Fernández Hurtado, who for many years assisted Rodrigo Gómez before taking over the helm of the bank. Personal interview between Theodore Mesmer and Irwin Baskind, and Ernesto Fernández Hurtado, Mexico City, September 17, 1997.

15. The influence of elite mentors on the foreign graduate education of their disciples is well illustrated by the last two presidents. President Zedillo is the disciple of Leopoldo Solís, an economist who attended Yale University. Zedillo also

In general, foreign students choose to attend schools in specific countries for many reasons. Those reasons include the political setting within their country of origin, the commercial relations between the potential host country and their country of origin, the level of immigration from their culture to a host country, and the similarity in higher education content and structure between the countries.[16] For example, a member of the intellectual power elite and one of the first three students at the Colegio de México to be sent abroad frankly admits: "You might say I went to study the enemy with my misconceptions about the United States and academia in the U.S. I realized that things were not that simple. My focus as a student abroad was on U.S. foreign policy. I was influenced by the New Left as well as by the conservative response. Essentially, I was interested in U.S. thinking about Mexico."[17]

The geographical proximity of two countries, especially when one is a Third World country and the other a highly developed postindustrial society, decidedly affects educational choices. Even geographic proximity within Mexico influences power elites' choice to study abroad. Among all power elites, slightly more than one out of three studied in the United States, but among power elites who came from the North, those states that

---

attended Yale and graduated in economics. Carlos Salinas was the disciple of Miguel de la Madrid, his predecessor as president, who graduated from Harvard with an M.A. in public administration. Salinas also obtained an M.A. from Harvard in public administration, but continued on for another M.A. and a Ph.D. in political economy. Even if one thinks of Salinas being more influenced by an elite parent, it is not accidental that his father, an influential political figure in his own right, obtained an M.A. in economics from Harvard University, and mentored an important generation of economists in politics. See Roderic Ai Camp, "The Middle-Level Technocrat in Mexico," *Journal of Developing Areas*, 6 (July 1972), 571–82. The older Salinas believed, early on, that understanding the United States was critical, and in 1964 took his two sons on an extensive trip, introducing them to politicians, using his contacts as the former commerce secretary. *Proceso*, November 21, 1999, www.proceso.com.mx.

16. W. K. Cummings and W. C. So, "The Preference of Asian Overseas Students for the United States: An Examination of the Context," *Higher Education*, 14 (1985), 405.

17. Personal interview with Sergio Aguayo, Chicago, September 25, 1998. The other two Mexican students were Roberta Lajous Vargas, who studied at Stanford and became later secretary of international relations of the National Executive Committee of PRI, and Adolfo Aguilar Zinser, another member of the intellectual power elite, an independent congressman in the 1990s and adviser to President Fox, who attended Harvard and was a fellow at the Kennedy School of Government's Mason Program.

border the United States, more than half attended school across the border.[18]

Two factors play a role in the North's disproportionate representation: geographic proximity, including cultural influences attributed to the United States, and the absence of a distinguished regional public university during most of those years.

Mexico conforms with global educational patterns, both in the increasing percentage of elites who study abroad and in their choice of the United States as the site for those studies. Almost half of power elite Mexicans born *prior* to 1945 studied exclusively in Mexico. But among Mexicans born *after* 1945, 72 percent ventured beyond their country's borders for educational training. (See table 15.)

The United States has been a magnet for foreign students, particularly at the graduate level, because of its international prestige in technical fields and empirical social sciences. As an expert on international education explains, "graduate training at a U.S. university has been considered the pinnacle of successful mobility through education and has been correspondingly rewarded in the trainee's home country. Graduates of U.S. universities and professional schools now occupy key positions near the top of the social hierarchy and, what is at least as important, tend to play a critical role in determining who the next generation of U.S.-trained elites is going to be."[19]

Mexicans shifted from a European to a United States-based educational experience in the 1970s. The generational pattern can be viewed through the data presented in table 15. If we look at power elite birth dates, we discover that 1945 serves as a benchmark year in determining where a future Mexican elite studies abroad. Among the pre-1945 generations, a third studied in the United States. Half of younger, post–World War II elites studied in the United States.[20]

18. The North includes six states: Baja California, Chihuahua, Coahuila, Nuevo León, Tamaulipas, and Sonora.

19. Hans N. Weiler, "The Political Dilemmas of Foreign Study," in Elinor G. Barber et al., eds., *Bridges to Knowledge: Foreign Students in Comparative Perspective* (Chicago: University of Chicago Press, 1984), 191.

20. Among mid-level leaders, graduate study abroad shifted dramatically in the 1970s and 1980s. For example, according to data from the Mexican executive branch, among those officials who obtained Ph.D.'s, the figures were as follows: in 1972, 58 percent from Mexico and 13 percent from the U.S.; in 1980, 48 percent from Mexico and 21 percent from the U.S.; in 1984, 31 percent from Mexico and 35 percent from the U.S.; in 1989, 29 percent from Mexico and 48 percent from

Table 15. Generational Patterns in Power Elite Study Abroad

| | Country Where Power Elite Studied | | | |
Date of Birth	Mexico Only (%)	United States (%)	Europe (%)	Latin America (%)
Born after 1945	28	50	20	2
Born before 1945	47	35	16	2

NOTE: A small number of elites, 5 percent, studied in both the United States and Europe. For purposes of the table, and the growing influence of the United States on Mexican elite education, I am including that figure as part of the United States column. (N = 398)

The explanation for this shift in educational experiences from England and France to the United States can be seen in the rationale given by students who pursued economics, the single most important academic discipline represented in this geographic shift.[21] A former treasury secretary and a forerunner of elite emphasis on United States preparation in economics explains why:

> They [United States universities] were considered to be more modern—
> the English universities not only taught a more traditional economics,
> but their system of independent studies resulted in some students
> just having a good time, not learning substantive information. So it
> wasn't really an ideological rationale behind the shift, but a focus
> on practical training. Also, there existed a much closer tie between the
> ministries and U.S. universities.[22]

Students who opted for studies in France and England in the 1960s and 1970s were interested in the intellectual currents in London and Paris compared to those on university campuses in the United States.[23] Jorge

---

the U.S. See Alfonso Galindo, "Education of Mexican Government Officials," *Statistical Abstract of Latin America*, 30 (Los Angeles: UCLA, 1993), 569. Among high-level corporate officials, 52 percent had studied abroad, primarily in the U.S. See *Expansión*, June 8, 1988, 48–49.

21. However, among ordinary Mexican and Latin American students, the most important United States contribution in shifting disciplinary trends occurred in the sciences. Daniel C. Levy, unpublished data (2000).

22. Personal interview with Jesús Silva Herzog, Riverside, California, November 19, 1998.

23. One reader correctly suggests that European universities were at a comparative disadvantage in attracting Mexican students because of a lack of university scholarship funds; however, almost all of the power elites in this sample who studied abroad did so on Mexican government fellowships.

Castañeda, for example, who already had studied at Princeton for four years, became bored and decided to live in Paris from 1973 to 1978, where he obtained a Ph.D. in economic history. He describes those years as formative, and the intellectual currents in France as affecting him profoundly. Among the ideas that strongly impacted power elite linkages and countered the existing pattern in Mexico was the argument that intellectuals should distance themselves from the state. He cites a group of Mexican exiles from the 1968 student movement, and his friendships with such prominent international figures as Carlos Fuentes and Regis Debray, as particularly influential.[24]

In the present context, the central issue of foreign education is the level of influence it exerts on the formation of a student's values and attitudes, in addition to whatever technical expertise the student learns in the classroom. These formative experiences occur inside and outside the classroom and they may be linked to a multitude of socializing agents, including peer influence, reading materials, time spent in the host country, level of contact with fellow students and professors, and the host country's social and political environment.[25]

24. José Antonio Aguilar Rivera, *La sombra de ulises: Ensayos sobre intelectuales mexicanos y norteamericanos* (Mexico City: CIDE, 1998), 145, and Pilar Jiménez Trejo and Alejandro Toledo, *Creación y poder: Nueve retratos de intelectuales* (Mexico City: Contrapuntos, 1994), 191–95. The way educational background and the larger social setting might affect a student's ideological beliefs and career choices is aptly illustrated in the experiences of Ricardo A. Pascoe, a leading member of the PRD: "I completed secondary and preparatory school in an English boarding school, Darlington Hall. I attended NYU, and then I did an M.A. in FLASCO in Chile from 1971 to 1973 [during the Allende years and the coup d'etat] in sociology. I worked on a Ph.D. at the London School of Economics. When I was in Chile I became politically active, joining a political party. I had to seek refuge in the Mexican embassy, and was taken out in a special plane sent by president Echeverría. I returned to Mexico in 1973, and was taken under the wing of my parents' friend Professor Rodolfo Stavenhagen [member of the power elite]. I had thought about being a diplomat like my parents, or a philosophy professor. . . . I taught at Autonomous Metropolitan University of Mexico (UAM) in Xochimilco, where I became head of the sociology department. Union activity at the university was intense during this period. I joined the PRT, having become enthralled with Trotsky's values. My colleagues elected me secretary general of the UAM union. At that point, I had to decide between an academic or union/political career. I resigned from the department and ran for the union leadership, which to my great surprise I won." Personal interview, Mexico City, May 5, 1992.

25. For example, the more time Chinese students spend reading the *New York Times*, the more likely they were to be critical of official Chinese ideology. See Xinshu Zhao and Yu Xie, "Western Influence on (People's Republic of China) Chinese Students in the United States," *Comparative Education Review* 36, no. 4 (1992), 524.

Considering that the United States and Third World countries have expended billions of dollars on study abroad programs, it is shocking that so little is actually known about their impact.[26] Analysts of foreign student experiences have made several findings via selective case studies; some of these are worth considering. First, study abroad confers a certain level of social status to the individual student. As one scholar suggests, it makes those students "part of a very distinct and remarkably persistent upper class in their own countries and will thus help exacerbate the already intractable problem of social equality in those countries."[27]

Second, a foreign student's attitudes toward the host country, including the United States, are largely determined by his or her reactions to experiences in the host country.[28] Third, the longer a student remains in the United States, the less favorable the attitude expressed.[29] Fourth, the younger the student, the more susceptible he or she is to United States influence, a finding supported in the general socialization literature.[30]

Fifth, although a causal, empirical relationship has not been proven, "foreign study does seem to be associated with a greater degree of political openness."[31] Sixth, some authors view the host country's recruitment of foreign elites as part of its effort to create "a subtle system of political control, domination, and dependence."[32] Seventh, the desire among many Mexicans to obtain graduate education in the United States was so strong that it contributed significantly to effecting a changing pattern in domestic education from public to private universities.[33]

26. For example, in the case of military training programs in the United States, which for Latin American officers have provoked controversy for decades, Miles Wolpin calls for detailed analysis of training, prior socialization, and personnel relationships to test the hypotheses of external socialization by the West and its effects on officer corps role playing. See his "External Political Socialization as a Source of Conservative Military Behavior in the Third World," in K. Fidel, ed., *Militarism in Developing Countries* (New Brunswick: Transaction, 1975), 275.

27. Hans N. Weiler, "The Political Dilemmas of Foreign Study," 191–92.

28. Deborah Kay Sell, "Research on Attitude Change in U.S. Students Who Participate in Foreign Study Experiences," *International Journal of Intercultural Relations*, 7 (1983), 142.

29. Xinshu Zhao and Yu Xie, "Western Influence on (People's Republic of China) Chinese Students in the United States," 511.

30. Ibid., 520.

31. Gerald W. Fry, "The Economic and Political Impact of Study Abroad," *Comparative Education Review*, 28, no. 2 (1984), 216.

32. Ibid., 209.

33. I am indebted to Jesús Silva Herzog for identifying this influence. He argued that "it was UNAM graduates who first came to the U.S. But as UNAM became increasingly politicized and marxist, economics students looked elsewhere

Foreign elites often receive significant socializing influences abroad from non-school experiences. Many elites have resided in the United States and Europe as fellowship recipients from foundations or have interned in public and private institutions as part of their career training.[34] A small number have worked and traveled extensively in the United States, and have attributed considerable influence to those experiences.[35] Mexican work and residential experiences between the two countries have been part of the cultural scene for more than a century.[36]

Personal testimonies make it clear that a significant portion of Mexican power elites have resided in the United States. More than one out of three have spent time in the United States in a professional capacity. The power elite group which has spent the most time professionally in the United States is the officer corps, half of whom have had hands-on practical experience at American bases. (See table 16.) They are the only Mexican leadership group which has received direct training in United States government agencies. This specialized experience in the defense department is all the more significant given the fact that two-thirds of the Mexican power elite claim no internship or job training experiences in the United States.

The second noteworthy pattern is that Mexican clergy experienced no residential opportunities in any type of United States institution, religious, private, or public. This is consistent with their foreign educational experience and sets them apart from all other Mexican power elites.

Third, although analysts would point to the dramatic shift in Mexico's macroeconomic policies from a traditional pro-state, deficit-spending strat-

---

for an education, particularly at ITESM and ITAM . . . The UNAM students made this switch because they were being rejected at U.S. graduate schools, not because of ideology, *but because they lacked the technical preparation for those programs abroad.*" [emphasis mine] Personal interview, November 19, 1998.

34. For example, in my study of elite Mexican intellectuals in this century, fully two-thirds had resided abroad. *Intellectuals and the State in Twentieth Century Mexico* (Austin: University of Texas Press, 1984).

35. Claudio X. González, a member of the capitalist power elite, was strongly influenced by his automobile travels with his father in New Mexico, Texas, and Arizona. *Líderes*, 2 (1992), 74.

36. Alfonso Pulido Islas, former dean of the National School of Economics, noted that many Mexicans migrated to the United States during the revolution, returning to Mexico in the 1920s. According to Pulido Islas, "Some of the ideas and things they brought back with them had a direct impact on Mexican culture." Personal interview, Mexico City, August 12, 1974. This is confirmed in Manuel Gamio's classic study, *Mexican Immigration to the United States: A Study of Human Migration and Adjustment* (Chicago: University of Chicago, 1930).

Table 16. Power Elite Experiences Abroad:
Fellowships, Internships, and Work

Power Elite Group	Type of Experience Abroad			
	Fellowship (%)	Intern/Work, Private (%)	Intern/Work, Public (%)	None
Politician	26	2	0	72
Intellectual	44	2	0	54
Capitalist	35	2	0	63
Military	1	0	52	47
Clergy	2	0	0	98

NOTE: N = 398.

egy in the 1970s to a neoliberal, strongly pro-capitalist approach in the 1980s, this shift cannot be attributed to any direct experiences of Mexicans, including government officials and capitalists, who worked in the American private sector. Surprisingly, only five individuals were known to have received direct hands-on training in the world's most powerful capitalist economy (table 16).

Finally, the most typical reason for Mexican power elites to spend time in the United States (other than those who were enrolled in school) was that they obtained foundation or academic fellowships in their fields. Not surprisingly, intellectuals were the most likely to have spent time in the United States, the case for two-fifths of cultural leaders. However, a third of capitalists and a fourth of politicians also resided in the United States under similar programs.

The late Octavio Paz is a notable example. He was awarded a prestigious Guggenheim fellowship in 1944; for the next several years, he lived first in the United States, then in France, and then in Japan. According to his biographer, during this period his ideas changed significantly and his poetry shows many foreign influences.[37]

It is relevant to note here that a power elite's socioeconomic background also has a bearing on the likelihood of acquiring such an experience. Mexican power elites from blue-collar families resided in the United States less often than their peers from middle- and upper-class family backgrounds. For example, although a fourth of all politicians interned or worked in the United States, only 10 percent of those from working-class families did so.

37. Octavio Paz, *De una palabra a otra* (Mansfield: Latitudes, 1992), p. 27.

No capitalists from blue-collar backgrounds worked outside Mexico. Mexican military officers from modest backgrounds did have opportunities for hands-on-experiences in the United States, but they participated in fully subsidized government programs, which were common in their profession.

It is apparent that educational experiences abroad potentially influence the attitudes of Mexico's power elite, regardless of whether they occur in a regular university setting or in a controlled professional environment. Initially, most influential Mexicans who studied abroad sought out institutions in Europe, which for cultural reasons maintained strong ties to Mexico. European educational experiences among elites remained typical for most of the twentieth century, but declined dramatically in the 1960s and 1970s.

Influential power elite mentors began placing a greater emphasis on more specialized academic training, some of which could not be found in Mexico. This changing emphasis occurred across all power elite categories, especially among politicians, career officers, higher clergy, and intellectuals. Their mentors, often members of the previous or present power elite, were themselves a select group, having attended school abroad in far greater numbers than their peers, thus setting the stage for mentors to encourage their disciples to replicate the same pattern of educational preparation.

As power elite circles began placing an increasing emphasis on foreign academic credentials, younger power elites began choosing universities in the United States. This dramatic change did not occur until mentors within the power elite decided to emphasize postgraduate education. Key figures within the Mexican bureaucracy, some of them magnet mentors, advocated government support for advanced studies and were instrumental in choosing the recipients of this support. Without government-subsidized fellowships, it is unlikely that so many Mexicans would have been able to share in these educational experiences, and to have done so as early as mid-way through the last century.

Many future politicians and intellectuals benefited from these scholarship programs. Similarly, leadership within the Catholic hierarchy and the Mexican armed forces began placing greater emphasis on advanced education, sending their most talented recruits to Rome and the United States for advanced education after their initial schooling in Mexican seminaries and military academies.

Governmental institutions undoubtedly exercised a significant influence on power elite educational patterns abroad, but many of the individuals responsible for these programs were personally responsible for mentoring the next generation of leaders. It is indisputable that these mentors' personal qualities included a strong appreciation for high levels of formal education and for the skills and intellectual diversity made available through graduate study abroad. They instilled similar values in their disciples, many of whom became part of the next generation of power elites and power elite mentors.

The importance of higher education as a power elite credential increased the likelihood that greater numbers of Mexican power elites would obtain graduate training. Among power elites who obtained graduate degrees, nearly three-quarters studied outside of Mexico, mostly in the United States and Europe. Of those power elites who obtained postgraduate training, nearly all clergy, four-fifths of capitalists and military officers, seven out of ten politicians, and three-fifths of intellectuals did so abroad.

Ultimately, the question raised by these experiences abroad is whether they affected the attitudes of Mexico's power elites, and if so, whether they contributed to the economic and political transformation in Mexican elite ideology during the 1980s and 1990s. The following chapter explores the socializing consequences of foreign education on Mexican leadership.

8 Socializing Mexico's Power Elite
Educational Experiences Abroad

A fundamental ideological shift occurred among Mexico's power elite from 1970 to 2000: the transformation of the development model from a protected economy, a centralized political system dominated by the executive branch, and a one-party monopoly of political power, to an outward-looking model of economic growth, a decentralized political system, and power-sharing on the state level and in the national legislative branch.

These changes can be attributed to the failures of long-standing political and economic strategies which characterized the Mexican scene from the 1930s through the 1980s. They can also be attributed to fundamental changes in power elite attitudes, the seeds of which can be found in the 1970s and earlier.

Power elites' early recognition of these economic and political failings can be traced, in part, to intellectual influences from educational settings, including foreign educational experiences. The ideological impact of those foreign socializing influences can be seen in two issues that were important in the 1980s and 1990s: economic globalization and political liberalization.

There were two distinct segments of the power elite who led the way in changing Mexico's developmental path in these two directions. In the case of political liberalization, top clergy and intellectuals were most influential. So too were opposition politicians, but they formed only a small proportion of the political power elite. The officer corps, privately, became increasingly receptive to electoral democracy and competitive parties, but it never provided proactive leadership to promote such a change. The proactive elite in support of economic globalization came from the political class, complemented by some influential capitalists. Many leading clergy and intellectuals, on the other hand, were opposed to NAFTA and to neoliberal economic strategies.

One of the interesting questions raised by these socializing experiences is why did specific elites favor one change, but not the other? The answer lies, in part, with the fact that the type of education elites received abroad differed substantially, either in format or disciplinary focus. Most intellectuals and clergy who studied abroad were educated in the humanities and the social sciences. Philosophy, history, sociology, and political science are disciplines which raise fundamental issues about social equality and political pluralism. It is not surprising, therefore, that influential members from these two groups became early advocates of political liberalization.

The second reason for intellectuals and clergy taking on the authoritarian state and the one-party system is that they are the most autonomous of the five elite groups. The clergy's relationship to the Mexican government is built on historical antagonism, and on an abuse of human rights. The constitutional restrictions on the Catholic Church, which remained in effect until 1992, assigned it second-class status, including not granting priests and nuns a legal right to vote. In short, they were treated in much the same way in which the state and the dominant party treated the secular political opposition in Mexico.

A structural change also occurred in the intellectual community in that increasingly younger influential intellectuals began extricating themselves from economic dependence on the state, and thus were no longer, as was the case of their older peers, directly employed by the state. Many remained financially independent, or at least were full-time university employees of publicly funded institutions. This innovative structural change allowed many prominent intellectual figures to loudly voice their criticisms of an authoritarian state.[1]

Most members of the Mexican power elite, with the exception of opposition party figures, differed sharply from their clerical and intellectual colleagues in that the education they sought was focused almost exclusively on economics, a discipline taught in the United States at the graduate level, which did not require prerequisites in American politics. Therefore, while they received constant exposure to intellectual currents criticizing Mexico's economic model, their direct experience with formal socializing influences favorable to political liberalization was exceptional.

Power elite socialization at foreign universities occurred, as I suggested in the previous chapter, typically at the postgraduate level. Consequently, these students were enrolled in specialized academic or professional pro-

1. Including Jorge Castañeda, Enrique Krauze, Gabriel Zaid, Luis Rubio, Carlos Monsiváis, and Federico Reyes Heroles, all members of the intellectual power elite.

grams. This level of academic experience abroad contributed theoretical intellectual influences and professional institutional values.

This chapter focuses on the foreign educational experiences of elite clergy, politicians, and military officers. It explores the experiences of future bishops who played a critical supporting role in persuading ordinary Mexicans to demand fair elections and political accountability. Their views are epitomized by a group of northern bishops in 1986, which became known as the Chihuahua tendency.[2] This chapter focuses heavily on politicians because of their concentrated experience in elite Ivy League schools, and because this group initiated the most dramatic change in the Mexican model, the 1990s shift toward a global economic strategy. Finally, this chapter explores the officer corps, who, more than any other elite group, studied in the United States, yet little is known about these experiences on their political values and their changing ideologies. Moreover, the Mexican military has been a passive but critical actor in the political liberalization process. It was crucial in certifying the electoral victories of both Carlos Salinas in 1988 and Ernesto Zedillo in 1994, respectively, making possible the fundamental economic changes introduced by Salinas and continued by his successor.

Without the military's support, Salinas would have had great difficulty taking office after the highly disputed election. Indeed, it is apparent that Salinas used the military, with its acquiescence, to strongly enhance his presidential image, giving him the political strength to implement his economic strategy.[3] In 1994, the military made it clear to the public that it would recognize the victory of any of the three leading candidates for the presidency as long as they won the electorate's support in a clean election. Their support of Zedillo indirectly made possible the 1996 electoral reforms, which in turn laid the groundwork for the competitive 2000 presidential race and the decisive victory of Vicente Fox.

The role of foreign education in the economic and political transformation of Latin America in the 1980s and 1990s is treated as a given, with only scattered evidence of how it occurred and what was involved.[4] Elsewhere in the region, experts have described a growing pattern of students studying abroad, of returning to their home country to take charge of

2. Cindy Anders, "No Power, No Glory," *Proceso*, June 15, 1989, 19.
3. Roderic Ai Camp, *Generals in the Palacio: The Military in Modern Mexico* (New York: Oxford University Press, 1992), 33–34.
4. The best studies of this phenomenon are of Chile, but Chile shares few similarities with the Mexican experience.

influential institutions, and of introducing their foreign alma maters' orientation into the domestic intellectual debate. Some academics view it as a not-so-subtle form of United States domination.[5]

The literature on American elite socialization, specifically on the influence of elite Ivy League colleges and universities, concludes that college quality is significantly related to American leaders' responses to economic, social, and political policy preferences.[6] There is no reason to expect a different impact on Mexicans. Four U.S. universities have exerted a strong influence on the Mexican power elite, educating thirty of its members: Harvard, MIT, Stanford, and Yale.

Historically, Harvard is the most important U.S. university in the education of Mexican power elites. Harvard acquired this special importance among Mexicans for several reasons. First, it has graduated two generations of Mexican leaders and proved to be an equally important source of influence among power elite mentors. Second, as suggested earlier, it is the only U.S. university to have educated two presidents: Miguel de la Madrid and Carlos Salinas de Gortari, adding to its already existing mystique among future Mexican leaders. Third, of the four institutions mentioned, it is the only one that has attracted prominent figures from political, capitalist, and intellectual circles, providing linkages among all three groups. Fourth, its proximity to the Massachusetts Institute of Technology, attended by other influential Mexicans, has resulted in a cross-fertilization and concentration of Mexican students unmatched elsewhere in the United States.

One of the most influential programs attracting prominent Mexicans to Harvard is the Center for International Affairs. Humberto Hernández Haddad, the first Mexican fellow to be invited to the Center, captures the ambience at Harvard during the 1970s, revealing why Harvard had the potential to exert considerable influence on the intellectual formation of future Mexican power elites:

> My goal to study international economics and Latin America was complemented with Raymond Vernon's lectures and his tutorial supervision of my readings. His classic book *The Dilemma of Mexico's Development* (1963) was revisited and discussed in detail with him

5. E. F. Fuenzalida, "The Contribution of Higher Education to a New International Order," in B. Sanyal, ed., *Higher Education and the New International Order* (Paris: UNESCO, 1982), cites the example of Chile, 139.

6. Allen H. Barton, "Determinants of Elite Policy Attitudes," in B. A. Rockman and R. H. Linden, eds., *Elite Studies and Comparative Politics* (Pittsburgh: University of Pittsburgh Press, 1984), 200.

many times. An influential notion of modern economics for me was to study macroeconomics under the guidance of Lawrence Lindsey, today governor of the Federal Reserve in Washington, D.C.

Vernon replaced Samuel P. Huntington as director of the CFIA at Harvard, at that time the top expert on transnationals and the leading voice anticipating what we now call "globalization." Vernon's book *Sovereignty at Bay: Multinational Spread of United States Enterprises* was everywhere. Having everyday access to the most prestigious members of the American intellectual establishment was extraordinary.

One of the privileges of being a fellow at the Center was the endless array of invitations to meet with Faculty members. I was provided an I.D. with access to the Faculty Club where you could spend marvelous hours listening to the most prestigious members of the Harvard faculty. Small dinners with John K. Galbraith were quarterly events.

The masters of Kirkland House, Evon Vogt and his wife Helen, invited me to be a regular member of their Faculty Room, with weekly meetings on Wednesdays for supper. The Vogts started the Harvard-Chiapas project in San Cristóbal de las Casas in the 1960s.[7]

Mexican students who went to Harvard, regardless of disciplinary interest, usually ended up in history courses taught by John Womack Jr., who established his reputation in Mexico as author of the best-selling classic, *Zapata* (1969). President Carlos Salinas became his most prominent student. Hernández Haddad also took Womack's seminar, the Mexican Revolution, 1910–1940, with seven other students.[8] He describes Womack as using economic history as an apt means for understanding Mexico's past. Another student, Mexico's treasury secretary from 1988 to 1994, recalls this course as a revelation: history presented the "greatest obstacle to equitably-distributed economic development."[9]

Encouraged by Womack and Jorge Domínguez, who taught Latin American politics, many Mexicans enrolled in joint seminars with MIT, which also brought them in contact with Wayne Cornelius, another Mexican

7. Letter from Humberto Hernández Haddad, who at thirty-one became a senator from his home state, January 27, 1997.

8. But not all Mexican students at Harvard, or at the other Ivy League institutions, identified with specific instructors. Some, like Carlos Monsiváis, who spent only a year at Harvard in the mid-1960s, notes the importance of books rather than individual professors. Personal interview with Carlos Monsiváis, Claremont, California, November 18, 1998.

9. Stephanie R. Golob, "Making Possible What Is Necessary: Pedro Aspe, the Salinas Team, and the Next Mexican Miracle," paper presented at the Latin American Studies Association meeting, Atlanta, March 1994, 4.

specialist who taught there. Joseph Nye also offered a joint seminar on political development which focused on "the reasons for political backwardness in different regions of the world."[10]

MIT, a stone's throw down the Charles River from Harvard, served as a home to future leading capitalists, most of whom graduated from the engineering program. The former president of Grupo Cydsa, long-time member of the Mexican Council of Businessmen and descendant of one of the two leading Monterrey families, enrolled in MIT in 1947 after having completed five years of boarding school in the United States. He considered the entire student environment, including attending classes and studying, as a formative experience in his life, particularly in developing a strong sense of responsibility.[11]

All of the MIT graduates in the present sample are leading capitalists, with one exception—Pedro Aspe Armella, architect of President Salinas's neoliberal economic strategy, who received a Ph.D. in economics in 1978 and taught macroeconomics during his last year in residence. There is no question that Aspe put into practice, both as chair of the economics program at ITAM and as treasury secretary, concepts and strategies he learned at MIT. Equally important, he developed a close friendship with Salinas when the president was studying at Harvard.

In the 1970s, MIT's economics department was known for its focus on public policy and for its belief in the benefits of market liberalization tempered by attention to market failures and consideration of limited government intervention to restore equilibrium. This approach "appealed to Aspe who, while doubting the economic wisdom of the statist Mexican development model of the 1970s, was also skeptical about solutions that rejected state intervention under any circumstances."[12]

What did Aspe learn at MIT? According to professor R. S. Eckkaus, one of his instructors, "all graduate students in the Ph.D. program were required to pass examinations in microeconomics and macroeconomics that covered topics included in a set of courses lasting through an academic year. In addition, there were requirements in econometrics and economic

10. Letter to the author from Humberto Hernández Haddad.
11. That was Andrés Marcelo Sada Zambrano. Eugenio Garza Sada, the first of the capitalist power elite to graduate from MIT in the 1910s, used his background there to found and design the Monterrey Technological Institute of Higher Studies in 1943. See *Líderes*, 6, 1994, 123.
12. Stephanie R. Golob, "Making Possible What Is Necessary" (1994), 4.

history. The objective of the Ph.D. program was to train students to understand and use the most advanced concepts and tools in economics."[13]

Aspe developed several close relationships with his professors at MIT, including Rudiger Dornbusch and Franco Modigliani. Modigliani describes in detail how he came to know Aspe and his influence on Aspe's ideas:

> I came to know him well, by serving as a second reader on his doctoral dissertation, which dealt with "Essays on the International Transmission Mechanism: The Mexican Case," and was completed in May of 1978. The thesis adviser was Professor Rudi Dornbusch, and he suggested my name to Pedro Aspe. As a result of that initial connection, we established very friendly relations, which were cultivated by visits to Mexico, before and after he was Minister of Finance, and which was reinforced by the fact that he had a very charming Italian mother.
>
> While working on his thesis, Pedro became aware of the work I was doing on the design of mortgages suitable for a highly inflationary environment. He eventually used my ideas to design a mortgage instrument for Mexico, but in the process, made one very ingenious and significant modification which substantially increased the practical usefulness of the instrument. Basically, he replaced my indexation, based on the cost of living, with an indexation based on the minimum wage. This version of the "inflation-proof mortgage" has been adopted, or considered by several other South American countries. In addition, he used my mortgage idea in setting up a program by which, after the first Mexican crisis, the government took over the foreign liabilities of firms in return for a claim on firms which was gradually amortized, much like a mortgage debt.
>
> I also vaguely recall that, at some point, Rudi and I had some talks with him about a plan under which foreign creditors would agree to reinvest the return from their investment in Mexico.[14]

Professor Dornbusch, Aspe's primary mentor at MIT, had a more profound impact, shaping him as an economist, policymaker, teacher, and international actor. Dornbusch wrote extensively on ways to tackle structural imbalances in Latin America's closed economies as well as on methods to address specific problems such as hyperinflation and external debt, two difficulties which plagued Mexico throughout the 1980s.[15] According to

13. Letter to the author from R. S. Eckkaus, January 29, 1997.
14. Letter to the author from Franco Modigliani, MIT, January 22, 1997.
15. Stephanie R. Golob, "Making Possible What Is Necessary: Pedro Aspe, the Salinas Team, and the Next Mexican 'Miracle,' " in Jorge I. Domínguez, ed., *Tech-*

Golob, Dornbusch turned Aspe into a "cosmopolitan nationalist" and suggested appropriate macroeconomic policies to set economies like Mexico on a viable path toward development.[16]

The Harvard–MIT linkage frequently led to contact with another Ivy League university, Yale. Humberto Hernández Haddad recalls that Jack Womack invited him to attend a weekend seminar at Yale in New Haven, Connecticut, where he introduced him to future president Ernesto Zedillo and to the future commerce and treasury secretary in the Salinas and Zedillo administrations; both were Yale doctoral students in economics. The seminar centered on public economic policies, specifically currency stabilization.[17]

Yale, like MIT, played a very special role as a critical training ground of future power elites in control of Mexican economic policy in the 1980s and 1990s. Yale used its International and Foreign Economic Administration to draw prominent Mexican economists into its intellectual sphere beginning in 1953.[18] Only six power elites graduated from Yale, the smallest number among the four Ivy League schools, but five of those individuals led the three institutions most responsible for formulating Mexican macroeconomic policy and shifting it to an orthodox neoliberal strategy.[19]

American institutions like Yale developed important ties to agencies in Mexico. An analyst of fellowship programs supporting foreign students in the United States argues that foundation staffs specifically send candidates to universities, research centers, and planning offices considered to be of strategic importance. For example, Zedillo, who studied on Conacyt fellowships through the presidency, completed his Ph.D. through assistance from the Ford Foundation.[20]

---

nopols: *Freeing Politics and Markets in Latin America in the 1990s* (University Park: Penn State University Press, 1997), 111.

16. Stephanie R. Golob, "Making Possible What is Necessary" (1994), 11.

17. The other future elite was Jaime Serra Puche. Letter to the author, January 27, 1997.

18. Graduados de Yale, "Yale donde vive usted: Una perspectiva de los enlances entre Yale y México," unpublished paper, Mexico City, April 1976, 2.

19. Those graduates were Miguel Mancera Aguayo, head of the Bank of Mexico, 1982–97; Jesús Silva Herzog, treasury secretary, 1982–86; Gustavo Petricioli, treasury secretary, 1986–88; Ernesto Zedillo, budgeting and programming secretary, 1988–92; and Jaime Serra Puche, secretary of commerce and industrial development, 1988–94. The most important mentor to these and other economic technocrats was Leopoldo Solís, an influential Bank of Mexico official and chair of the advisory economic council to the president, who graduated from Yale in 1959.

20. As did Guillermo Ortiz. Personal interview between Ted Mesmer and Irwin Baldwin with Leopoldo Solís, Mexico City, September 24, 1997.

Typically, Latin American students who are selected for doctoral study have already received a master's degree from an elite university like Harvard or Stanford.[21] But Mexican students emanating from the public sector have traveled abroad courtesy of government fellowships, funded for many years by the Bank of Mexico. Yale established itself as a significant source for educating Mexican economists because the Bank of Mexico created a special relationship with a leading Yale economist of that time, Professor Robert Triffin.[22]

Yale spawned a critical generation of economists, and those graduates, including members of the power elite, trace their intellectual influences directly to their Yale experience. Jaime Serra Puche, for example, believes his classes affected his views on developing an economic policy for Mexico which would help achieve stability, growth, and social justice.[23] Again, former students point to the totality of their experiences, not just to the effect of an individual professor:

> It wasn't a single teacher or book, but collectively the whole set of experiences. *Yale had the strongest impact on me professionally of any experience.* [emphasis mine] I essentially came back to Mexico as a changed person. I came back understanding much broader economic issues, such as trade flows. I overlapped with Mancera my second year— his first. He was very conservative and I was very liberal, and we used to argue constantly in class. But as a result of our year together, the differences between us narrowed considerably.[24]

The only impact shared by Mexican power elites from military and non-military backgrounds who study in the United States is their exposure to a different methodological approach which is typical of American graduate and higher education. Prominent figures identified it at Yale, at Johns Hopkins, and at Harvard. One member of the political elite provides a frank, personally revealing description of the devastating impact this "American approach" wields on foreign students:

> Yale was a terrible shock for me. All my life I was a top student, always in the top five of my class in every level. But I was in for a terrible shock at Yale. When I began doing the readings in my classes,

21. Robert F. Arnove, "Foundations and the Transfer of Knowledge," in *Philanthropy and Cultural Imperialism: The Foundations at Home and Abroad* (Boston: G. K. Hall, 1980), 315.

22. Personal interview with Jesús Silva Herzog, Riverside, California, November 19, 1998.

23. *Líderes,* 4 (1993), 99.

24. Personal interview with Jesús Silva Herzog.

I read the way I had done in Mexico, looking for the ideological content in the analysis rather than the substantive aspects in the essays.[emphasis mine] I was in Bella Belassa's class on trade and immigration, and he provided us with an introductory econ 101. After we took the first test, he announced the top five students, and I puffed myself up expecting to hear my name. I wasn't in that first group. Then he announced the next five highest scores, so I thought, well, at least I'm in that group—no I wasn't. Well, I returned home that night and told my wife we should go back to Mexico, I had failed at Yale. I slept on it, and decided the next morning to start fresh.[25]

Jesús Silva Herzog's willingness to share such an intimate experience points to the tremendous differences in educational and analytical practices between Mexico and the United States. Beyond the difficulties any student initially would face coming from a background similar to Silva Herzog's is a more fundamental consequence: exposing future Mexican elites to analytical arguments and discussions based on differing technical as well as ideologically motivated policy views.

The only group of Latin American students who studied abroad and who have received serious attention from scholars are technocrats, politician-administrators who began to take over leadership from their domestically educated peers.[26] But technocrats in Chile and Brazil, for example, became identified with characteristics which are not necessarily shared by Mexicans because Mexico cast its own imprint on its technocrats.[27] The técnicos, as a group, are worth exploring because they perhaps more than any other power elite group in Mexico influenced the major trends in public policy, trends which confronted and reformed the country's economic and political structures.[28]

In assessing the impact of socialization patterns and the influence of

---

25. Personal interview with Jesús Silva Herzog.

26. The two best works on this are Miguel A. Centeno and Patricio Silva, eds., *The Politics of Expertise in Latin America* (New York: St. Martin's, 1997), and Jorge I. Domínguez, ed., *Technopols: Free Politics and Markets in Latin America in the 1990s* (University Park: Penn State University Press, 1997).

27. The best case study of Chile is Juan Gabriel Valdés, *Pinochet's Economists: The Chicago School in Chile* (Cambridge: Cambridge University Press, 1995). For a fascinating comparison between Brazil and Mexico, see Ben Ross Schneider, "The Material Bases of Technocracy: Investor Confidence and Neoliberalism in Latin America," in Miguel A. Centeno and Patricio Silva, eds., *The Politics of Expertise in Latin America* (New York: St. Martin's, 1997), 77–96.

28. See my "Technocracy a la Mexicana: Antecedent to Democracy," in Miguel Centeno and Patricio Silva, eds., *The Politics of Expertise in Latin America* (New York: St. Martin's, 1997), 186–213.

foreign education, it is important to recognize that a precursor to the técnicos of the 1980s and 1990s was already in place in Mexico twenty years
earlier. Raymond Vernon, the Harvard professor who mentored some of
the very same figures in the new group, was one of the few to recognize
their emergence in Mexico. He accurately described them in the 1960s as
having "a common ideology which, harnessed to the government apparatus, constitutes a strong force in shaping the behavior of the public sector
in Mexico. . . . Accordingly, the strength of the technicians lies not so much
in their powers to shape policy directly as in their capacity to choose the
technical alternatives which are presented to their political masters."[29]

Vernon recognized that these earlier técnicos viewed public investment
decisions as emanating from "reason and study." He suggests that they
thought of themselves as economic technicians, as distinct from politicos,
and although in the 1960s a anti-state faction did not exist, the técnicos
who favored a mixed economy were divided into two groups: those connected with the Bank of Mexico, who believed fiscal and monetary restraint
were crucial to growth, and those connected to spending and investing
agencies, who viewed them as handicaps to growth.[30]

Where did these government technocrats come from? Vernon notes that
generally they were drawn from schools of economics. "Though many of
the *técnicos* are quick to agree that Mexico's schools of economics are far
from providing an ideal training ground for market analysis, locational
studies, and capital budgeting at the level of the individual firm, they tend
to see themselves as well ahead of the private decision-maker in their
training and preparation for activities involving industrial investment and
management."[31]

This view is supported by the fact that the private sector opposed a
major policy decision to link Mexico in a regional market, the Latin American Free Trade Agreement (LAFTA), some twenty-five years before the
North American Free Trade Agreement (NAFTA) took effect in 1994, suggesting early on technocrats' tentative orientations toward regional economic arrangements. The critical actors in that decision were early technocrats, many with ties to the Bank of Mexico, and many of whom
mentored the influential group of technocrats within the power elite.[32] A

29. Raymond Vernon, *The Dilemma of Mexico's Development: The Roles of
the Private and Public Sectors* (Cambridge: Harvard University Press, 1965), 137,
147.
    30. Ibid., 137.
    31. Ibid, 147.
    32. Roderic Ai Camp, "The Role of the Técnico in Decision-Making: A Com-

crucial figure in these deliberations was Rodrigo Gómez, a magnet mentor responsible for the foreign education of numerous leading public figures.

These early economists, interestingly, were mentored by none other than Raúl Salinas Lozano, President Carlos Salinas's father, who studied at Harvard on a government fellowship in 1946, graduating with an M.A. in economics. Salinas senior held a number of influential mid-level posts in the treasury secretariat, was an alternate governor of the International Monetary Fund from 1956 to 1958, and joined the cabinet as secretary of industry and commerce in 1958. He used his six-year tenure to promote the careers of many economists whose upward mobility in government initially concentrated in the commerce rather than the treasury secretariat.[33]

As this technocratic group began to rise up the bureaucratic and political ladder, they developed a number of shared characteristics. In the first place, in recognition of the fact that the National School of Economics was not providing them with the technical training they required, they began to study abroad. A few politicians with economic interests continued to choose Cambridge University or the London School of Economics, but most instead enrolled in M.A. and Ph.D. programs in the United States.

A broad analysis of foreign student applications to Ph.D. programs in economics demonstrates that only 5 percent applied to schools in the United Kingdom, Canada, and nineteen other countries. The rest applied to the United States.[34] Why did these future economists choose the United States? Latin American students claim that they were interested in improving the quality of research, increasing public policy rationality, implementing market-oriented reforms, and creating international networks.[35]

Scholars who have studied this phenomenon among Latin American students have delved deeper into their reasons for choosing the United States. First, the economics profession adopted English as a lingua franca.

---

parative Study of Mexico and the United States," unpublished Ph.D. dissertation, University of Arizona, 1970. For a published analysis of how they influenced the policy process in that era, see my *The Role of Economists in Policy-Making: A Comparative Study of Mexico and the United States* (Tucson: University of Arizona Press, 1977).

33. Roderic Ai Camp, "The National School of Economics and Public Life in Mexico," *Latin American Research Review,* 10 (fall 1975), 137–51.

34. Nahid Aslanbeigui and Verónica Montecinos, "Foreign Students in U.S. Doctoral Programs," *Journal of Economic Perspectives,* 12, no. 3 (summer 1998), 175.

35. Ibid., 176.

Economic knowledge became a form of political power.[36] Most of the theoretical writings in vogue originated in the United States, giving American graduate programs an edge. As the number of economists in government bureaucracies expanded, their sheer density transformed the culture of political elites: "Their language is increasingly common and those who are not professionally trained in it either acquire it on the job or come to feel themselves outsiders."[37]

The language of economics, according to Mexican power elites, has extended well beyond government culture. As a prominent economist suggests, the "other change in the last ten to fifteen years is the importance of economics in everyday discussions. When you used to socialize at a party, no one ever would talk about balance of payments problems—but in recent years, everyone began to discuss these sorts of serious economic issues. What happened is that the politicians who didn't have technical training began to abandon ship when similar discussions took place in the public sector."[38]

A second reason for the attractiveness of U.S. graduate programs in economics was the increasingly abstract nature of American economics education, a quality which validated the claim that economics as a discipline is not an ethnocentric product of Anglo-American traditions, but rather is transferable to distant cultural and institutional milieus.[39] These economists "often see themselves in the service of 'rationality' or 'efficiency' rather than in the service of the goals of their superiors, and at the same time they may even take pride in the claim that they do not serve group interests."[40]

Technocrats elsewhere in the region, defining themselves in similar terms, viewed this approach as guaranteeing that the government would pursue a rational economic model. Their commitment to this scientific and technical approach, as was the case in Chile, led them to believe firmly that their decisions were not inspired by political and ideological postulates.[41]

36. Ibid., 176.
37. John Markoff and Verónica Montecinos, "The Ubiquitous Rise of Economists," *Journal of Public Policy*, 13, no. 1 (1993), 47.
38. Personal interview with Jesús Silva Herzog.
39. Nahid Aslanbeigui and Verónica Montecinos, "Foreign Students in U.S. Doctoral Programs," 176.
40. John Markoff and Verónica Montecinos, "The Ubiquitous Rise of Economists," 51.
41. Patricio Silva, "Technocrats and Politics in Chile: From the Chicago Boys

Mexican technocrats' views reflected an acceptance of the inevitability of global capitalism and its rules. As economists they identified with an international profession based in the U.S., with tools and concepts that were believed to be universally—and locally—applicable.[42] As one source described it, "Economics today is a profoundly transnational profession socialized in a body of thought, that to a considerable degree is skeptical of the claims of culture and history, and that has re-embraced the sacralization of the unimpeded market and the unchallenged integration of the national into the global economy."[43]

The concept of a rational approach is inextricably linked to the methodology of economics learned in United States graduate programs, solutions based on trial and error and economic models, similar to what Pedro Aspe's professor described as part of his learning process at Yale. In his examination of the rising generation of government technocrats, Miguel Centeno captures the critical importance of methodology as ideology:

> The new elite defended orthodox economic policies, not as a direct
> articulation of class interests, but because these programs appeared as
> the only rational option. The definition of that rationale was partly
> determined by social position and exposure to an economic ideology in
> the United States . . . what the elite shares is an epistemological
> rather than economic ideology, an agreement about the source and
> nature of policy knowledge, not its actual content. *How* the *tecnócratas*
> thought was more decisive than *what* they thought. The elite shares
> a cognitive framework, a unique way of analyzing social problems,
> formulating solutions, and implementing policy that limits the potential
> for public participation and that inherently denies the inevitability of
> conflicting social interests. This attitude, more than any specific
> commitment to markets or free trade, determined the fate of Mexican
> democracy in the 1990s.[44]

The pattern Centeno describes can be found elsewhere in the Third World, outside the region. The expectation among Korean students who study abroad, even in Japan, is that they will play an important role in contrib-

---

to the CIEPLAN Monks," *Journal of Latin American Studies*, 23, no. 2 (1991), 393.

42. Letter to the author from Stephanie Golob, Harvard University, Cambridge, Massachusetts, May 13, 1997.

43. Verónica Montesinos and John Markoff, "From the Power of Economic Ideas to the Power of Economists," in Miguel A. Centeno, ed., *The Other Mirror: Essays on Latin America* (Princeton: Princeton University Press, 2000), 48.

44. Miguel A. Centeno, *Democracy within Reason*, 191, 212.

uting to rational approaches and democratization in modernizing their country.[45]

The claim of the universality of industrialized economic models, especially those developed in the United States, has produced the most severe criticism of technocrats in their home environment, both from academics and the popular media. *Excélsior* reported that the Party of the Democratic Revolution addressed them as "inexpert youth from Harvard . . . without any economic social sensitivity."[46] The criticism is aptly expressed by a Latin American economist who argues that

> we have continued to be prisoners of this "alienation," copying
> painfully and without critical adaptations whatever emanates from
> Harvard, Cambridge, and other prestigious universities. . . . the majority
> of young economists who go to industrialized countries for training
> return to their home environment with theoretical schemes that are to
> a greater or lesser extent divorced from objective reality and from
> the economic problems of their own countries, and often with research
> methodologies that have no possibility of being usefully applied.[47]

At least initially, the Bank of Mexico, an institution critical to encouraging and financing students to study abroad, tried to counter the impact of foreign study. The director of the Bank of Mexico understood the dangers of untested theoretical intellectual transfers. Silva Herzog, the first of the influential Mexican economists to travel to Yale, offers a remarkable revelation about Rodrigo Gómez, director general during the eighteen formative years (1952–70) when the shift toward economics training abroad took hold. His long tenure established a reputation for Gómez similar to that of Alan Greenspan as chair the United States Federal Reserve.[48] Gómez "understood that when you come back with a graduate degree, you think

45. Kyu Hwan Lee, "Study Abroad: From Korea to Japan—A Discussion from a Perspective of Modernization," *Education and Society,* 13, no. 1 (1995), 33.

46. *Excélsior,* July 19 1997, A1.

47. Aníbal Pinto and Osvaldo Sunkel, "Latin American Economists in the United States," *Economic Development and Cultural Change,* 15, no. 1 (October 1966), 80, 83.

48. Former president Miguel de la Madrid said the following about Gómez: "Yes, a real 'sabio.' Very straightforward and very firm in his ideas, but also with a great political ability to maintain a very good relationship with the Ministry of Finance, at that time, with Mr. Ortiz Mena and with the presidents. Mr. Rodrigo Gómez had been one of the main architects of the economic policy in Mexico for very long periods. He exercised a positive influence in framing and executing economic policy in Mexico, going further than his character as chairman of the Bank of Mexico. He was a very influential man at that time." Interview with Theodore C. Mesmer and Irwin Baskind, Mexico City, September 13, 1997.

you know everything. He would assign all of those students to a desk, with no responsibility, known inside the bank as being in the 'freezer.' I personally remained in the freezer for five months after returning from Yale. After my generation, and Rodrigo Gómez retired, no one imposed the 'freezing' experience. These newer graduates went directly into high positions."[49]

The third reason for the attractiveness of economics programs in the United States is that U.S.-trained economists who have returned home have played an important networking and communication role in facilitating the recruitment and admission of foreign students to American universities, typically to their own alma maters. My discussion of mentors, and the influence of Ivy League schools, confirms the importance of these personal networking ties in Mexico. Stephanie Golob's examination of the Mexican case, focused on economists tied to Pedro Aspe, concluded that "participation in academic life at Harvard, MIT, Stanford, Yale and the University of Chicago connected them in an international community of scholars and practitioners, interlocutors in future negotiations."[50]

The final reason why American economics programs became so alluring is that a worldwide trend existed to pattern economics programs after the U.S. model. Students, therefore, studied and taught in American graduate programs in order to replicate their structure and curriculum at home.[51] The demand for foreign-trained professors in academia contributed to a more general process of internationalizing Mexican economics.[52] The fact

49. Personal interview with Jesús Silva Herzog. Mancera, Petricioli, and Silva Herzog all were bank scholarship holders under Gomez's tenure.

50. Stephanie Golob, "Making Possible What Is Necessary" (1997), 103.

51. The most notable example is Herminio Blanco Mendoza, who began a full-time career as a professor at the University of Texas, Austin, from 1980 to 1985, before resigning to become an adviser to President Miguel de la Madrid. Another treasury secretary, David Ibarra, who Golob considered to have been a key player in promoting this new generation of technocrats as treasury secretary, directed the graduate program in economics at UNAM and taught numerous courses in the 1950s and 1960s. Jaime Serra Puche, who taught for a year at Stanford, was a full-time researcher and professor at the Colegio de México's economics program for seven years. Both he and Zedillo served on the editorial board of *El Trimestre Económico*, one of the country's leading economic journals.

52. Sarah Babb, "Neoliberalism and the Rise of the New Money Doctors: The Globalization of Economic Expertise in Mexico," paper presented at the Latin American Studies Association meeting, Chicago, September 24–26, 1998, 4, 26. The other key player in the changes at ITAM was Francisco Gil Díaz, a student of Mancera's, a graduate of the Ph.D. program at Chicago, and Aspe's professor, who directed ITAM's economics program from 1973–78. As Babb suggests, he and Petricioli both helped ITAM students study abroad and found them jobs in the bank

that many leading figures among Mexican economist-technocrats were academics is not accidental. Ernesto Zedillo and Pedro Aspe both pursued academic careers before crossing the bridge into public life. Zedillo and especially Aspe published serious economic essays in the academic community, and Aspe contributed directly to refurbishing the economics program at ITAM. Gustavo Petricioli, who began teaching at ITAM while working as an economist at the Bank of Mexico in 1959, presided over his alma mater, becoming more Americanized, rigorous, and mathematical, and recruited more bank officials and economists who studied abroad as faculty.

Table 17 sheds light on why this small group of eleven Mexicans, alone among the power elite, could exert so much influence over public policy. Collectively, they dominated the four essential economic policy-making agencies in Mexico during the 1980s and 1990s. They have continued their impact into the twenty-first century through Fox's cabinet appointments in treasury and economic development.[53] All but one studied at Harvard, MIT, Yale, Chicago, or Stanford.[54]

Ideologically, the Mexican técnicos who gradually seized control of economic policy fostered a number of significant visions on Mexican society. It is erroneous to suggest that their beliefs in empirical methodologies and technical solutions made them value-neutral. They actively used their economic knowledge to foster a macroeconomic strategy which included considerable ideological components and was linked directly to Mexico's political development.

As is so often the case, the trend toward foreign education coincided

---

or the treasury department. Gil Díaz became assistant director of the bank and assistant secretary of the treasury before taking over as CEO of a Mexican company in 1997. President Fox appointed him treasury secretary in 2000.

53. In addition to Gil Díaz, Fox appointed Luis Ernesto Derbez, an Iowa State University Ph.D. in econometrics, who was a visiting professor at Johns Hopkins from 1983 to 1997 and an economist at the World Bank, as secretary of economic development.

54. The University of Chicago played a major role in the technocrat's influence elsewhere in the region, particularly in the case of Chile. The University of Chicago established a study abroad program as early as the 1950s to bring Chilean students to their economics department, comparable to Yale's link with Mexico. As I implied earlier, unlike the Mexican case, Chile's was the result of a concerted effort on the part of the U.S. government, the economics department of the University of Chicago, and the Catholic University of Chile. See Eduardo Silva, *State and Capital in Chile: Business Elites, Technocrats, and Market Economies* (Boulder: Westview, 1996), 98; and Juan Gabriel Valdés, *Pinochet's Economists: The Chicago School in Chile,* 81–108.

Table 17. Foreign Education of Technocrats in Mexico's Power Elite

Agency years of service		University	Degree
Treasury			
1977–82	David Ibarra	Stanford	Economics
1982–86	Jesús Silva Herzog	Yale	Economics
1986–88	Gustavo Petricioli	Yale	Economics
1988–94	Pedro Aspe Armella	MIT	Economics
1994	Jaime Serra Puche	Yale	Economics
1994–98	Guillermo Ortiz Martínez	Stanford	Economics
Programming and Budget			
1979–81	Miguel de la Madrid	Harvard	Public Admin.
1982–87	Carlos Salinas de Gortari	Harvard	Political Econ.
1987–88	Pedro Aspe Armella	MIT	Economics
1988–92	Ernesto Zedillo	Yale	Economics
Commerce and Industrial Development			
1988–94	Jaime Serra Puche	Yale	Economics
1994–00	Herminio Blanco Mendoza	Chicago	Economics
Bank of Mexico			
1982–97	Miguel Mancera	Yale	Economics
1997–00	Guillermo Ortiz Martínez	Stanford	Economics

with dramatic events in Mexico beginning in the mid-1970s, when a succession of presidents, Luis Echeverría (1970–76), José López Portillo (1976–82), and Miguel de la Madrid (1982–88), began encountering serious economic problems.[55] The structural weaknesses in the Mexican economy reached their apex at the end of López Portillo's administration, leaving the country with its largest debt load in generations, with a private sector alienated by an ill-conceived nationalization of Mexico's domestic banks in 1982, and a situation producing hyperinflation under his

55. Mexican economists within the government were already critical of traditional import substitution policies as early as the 1960s. According to Leopoldo Solís, a magnet mentor who molded the most influential group of students around Salinas and Zedillo, economic analysis in the public sector was "led and influenced by people who have gone to do graduate work abroad. Then the fact of price stabilization and equalization theory, something you have to learn in graduate school, is not too difficult to apply to a country's condition." Interview with Theodore C. Mesmer and Irwin Baskind, Mexico City, September 24, 1997.

successor, Miguel de la Madrid. The U.S.-trained economists, particularly in the Bank of Mexico, recognized these problems earlier, but they did not have the president's ear in the 1970s, or control of the treasury secretariat.[56]

The economic crisis facing Mexico in the 1980s was severe, and it confronted the graduates of foreign economic programs head on. This context is significant because scholars have suggested that new policy ideas spread most rapidly following a crisis, when old ideas are discredited.[57] The desperate economic circumstances in which Mexico found itself provided plenty of fuel to support the growing criticism of deficit spending and pro-state strategies pursued by previous government economists. It challenged these new foreign-educated economists collectively to rebuild the Mexican economy.[58]

To prevent outright government bankruptcy, President de la Madrid negotiated an agreement with the International Monetary Fund, a decision that introduced another structural variable supporting the rise of Mexican technocrats.[59] This external actor, requiring Mexico to make specific economic policy decisions, replicated the economic theories offered at the leading American programs attended by Mexican students.[60]

A critical perspective in the técnicos' approach was that the Mexican state, traditionally the major player in the country's economic development, was part of the problem, not the solution. Under de la Madrid's predecessors, the state had acquired literally hundreds of businesses, which, by the time it nationalized the banking industry, put it in control

56. Ironically, these changes were accompanied by a belief that through domestic education, Mexico would attain "a professional society." In fact, the sluggish rates of real upward social mobility, reflected in declining opportunities for college graduates, yielded unexpected change and new political alignments. They helped shape Mexican political culture for years to come. See David Lorey, "The Rise of the Professions and the Dream of a 'Professional Society' in Twentieth-Century Mexico," in Kevin Middlebrook, ed., *Dilemmas of Change in Mexican Politics* (La Jolla: Center for U.S.-Mexican Studies, University of California, San Diego, 2002).

57. G. John Ikenberry, "The International Spread of Privatization Policies: Inducements, Learning, and 'Policy Bandwagoning,'" in Ezra Suleiman and John Waterbury, eds., *Political Economy of Public Sector Reform and Privatization* (Boulder: Westview, 1990), 107.

58. Stephanie Golob, "Making Possible What Is Necessary" (1994), 5.

59. Lourdes Melgar, "The Monterrey Industrial Elite: Ideological Contradictions, Political Alliances and Economic Practices," paper presented at the Latin American Studies Association meeting, Los Angeles, 1992, 17.

60. Sarah Babb also believes that pressures from the World Bank contributed to the increasing influence of economists in Mexico. "Neo-liberalism and the Rise of the New Money Doctors," 48–49.

of more than three-quarters of the economy.[61] The technocrats believed it essential to reverse this statist trend and to reestablish the trust of the private sector, which had been severely damaged in 1982.[62] According to his chief of economic advisers, de la Madrid's own experience at Harvard, and the fact that he spoke English, "changed his whole outlook on life."[63] Contrary to what many observers argued, Mexico's technocrats never believed in a weak state; rather, they hoped to make it a leaner, meaner version of liberalized, state-led development, with the private sector as a helpful partner.[64]

Another fundamental component of their philosophy was a belief that Mexico should play a larger role in the world economy, and that it could no longer remain isolated from changing global patterns through high tariffs and protected, inefficient industries. They also recognized the need to compete vigorously for international capital after repeated debt crises, and to eliminate their preponderant dependence on oil exports. Some authors have given this vision the label of "cosmopolitan nationalism," attributing it specifically to their education abroad.[65] Others have viewed it as a form of denationalization, resting on a belief that social problems are transnational in character.[66]

The técnicos found natural allies in the Monterrey capitalist elites. It

61. Interestingly, the two economists who convinced the president to nationalize the bank relied on a long technical article by two neo-Keynesian economists from Cambridge University to support their interpretations, and one of them, Carlos Tello, a member of the power elite, studied economics under Joan Robinson at Cambridge in 1961–63. The other economist, Andrés de Oteyza, also a member of the power elite, also studied at King's College, but in 1966–68, where he completed a master's in economics. Sylvia Maxfield comments on their role in her *Governing Capital: International Finance and Mexican Politics* (Ithaca: Cornell University Press, 1990), 129, 143–44.

62. Roderic Ai Camp, *Entrepreneurs and the State in Twentieth Century Mexico* (New York: Oxford University Press, 1989), 133.

63. Personal interview between Theodore Mesmer and Irwin Baskind, and Leopoldo Solís.

64. Stephanie Golob, "Making Possible What Is Necessary" (1994), 8.

65. As Jorge I. Domínguez suggests in his intellectual characterization of the technocratic politicians, none "fell into the trap of believing 'my' country is so different that the international norms of technical analysis should not apply, or that 'no foreigner can teach me about my homeland.' All were concerned with universal questions; all addressed their work as professionals whose standards and tools were worldwide and universalistic." *Technopols*, 16.

66. John Markoff and Verónica Montecinos, "The Ubiquitous Rise of Economists," 45.

should be remembered that these elites also increasingly obtained degrees abroad, many in business administration programs. These younger members of capitalist families began taking over their fathers' firms. They shared "common ground with the new generation in their ideas about sovereignty, nationalism and the United States as well. Though very traditional, family-oriented and religious (Catholic), the major business families in Monterrey long sent their children to the United States to study, and saw no contradiction in a sense of openness to the markets and products—educational and otherwise—of the United States, and their sense of national identity or national pride."[67]

The técnicos' belief in their methodological correctness led them to adapt an equal assuredness in manner about the macroeconomic strategies these "theories" convinced them to pursue. They quickly developed, throughout the region, a reputation for arrogance, a belief that any criticism of their strategies was due to the critic's ignorance or promotion of self-serving political interests.[68] Mexicans who were part of this technocratic transition admit that the change in policy direction was accomplished in a "brusque manner, and without the proper groundwork."[69]

Perhaps the most complex ideological preference which emerged amidst the técnicos in Mexico revolved around the relationship between macroeconomic neoliberalism and political liberty. It became readily apparent that Mexican technocratic leadership led by President Salinas made a conscious decision that their orthodox economic strategies were a precondition for democracy.[70] Some of these political technocrats, including Salinas himself, offered few signs that they were committed to a functioning democracy in the immediate future. In fact, it has been convincingly argued by Pamela Starr that economic reform was expected to create growth and

---

67. Stephanie Golob, "Crossing the Line: Sovereignty, Integration, and the Free Trade Decisions of Mexico and Canada," unpublished Ph.D. dissertation, Harvard University, 1997, 40.

68. Patricio Silva, "Technocrats and Politics in Chile," 394.

69. Interview with Jesús Silva Herzog. Some scholars were unsurprised by this quality since they view Mexico as reflecting a general Latin-Iberic ethos founded on a value system and political culture dedicated to hierarchy, order, and absolutes, values which the técnicos did not discard. Howard J. Wiarda has presented this thesis most convincingly. "The Latin Americanization of the United States," *New Scholar*, 7, no. 1 (fall 1980), 65.

70. The Chilean technocrats believed it was a precondition for the very existence of genuine political liberty. See Patricio Silva, "Technocrats and Politics in Chile," 396.

attenuate the public's desire for democratic change. In short, most technocrats never intended to implement political liberalism, only to use their new-found economic strategies to entrench themselves in power.[71]

It is apparent that many of the Mexican economists who graduated from U.S. universities during this era and returned home did not openly express praise for the democratization process.[72] It is also the case that initially many Mexican capitalists, who identified with the economic policies advocated by the political-technocrats in the late 1980s, failed to reached a consensus on using the political arena to achieve their economic agenda, and to encourage a plural, democratic system.[73]

Other prominent Mexicans who were educated abroad, and who were neither future political elites nor graduates of the leading economic programs, were also significantly influenced by their educational experience. These cultural leaders came away from the United States as recipients of two primary influences, one complementary to that of the technocrats, and the other diametrically opposed: the acceptance of the importance of a sophisticated nationalism and an appreciation for political pluralism.

Sergio Aguayo, who studied at Johns Hopkins University, illustrates just how significant these influences can be. He is a particularly noteworthy example because he was strongly predisposed against the United States, viewing it as a manipulative, imperial power. He grew up in Guadalajara in a traditional, conservative, regional ambience in the 1950s and 1960s. His father had studied for the priesthood and his family sympathized with the Cristero rebellion. Like so many members of his generation, in 1968 he became a student leader in Guadalajara. The lives of most of his friends, who were also student leaders, were destroyed by their

71. Pamela Starr, "Monetary Mismanagement and Inadvertent Democratization in Technocratic Mexico," *Studies in Comparative International Development,* 33, no. 4 (winter 1999), 35–65.

72. Little evidence exists on the impact schooling has on promoting acceptance of or support for democracy. We do know that if students are not encouraged to take an active interest in politics they are unlikely to participate fully in democratic processes as adults. We also know that tolerance of freedom and nonconformity are essential ingredients for this sort of democratic political change. Philo C. Washburn, "The Public School as an Agent of Political Socialization," *Quarterly Journal of Ideology,* 10, no. 2 (1986), 26–28.

73. Lourdes Melgar argues that the Monterrey capitalists were fearful of the left coming to power in a democratic environment, and instead, opted for a semi-authoritarian state to firmly establish the basis for a free economy. Nevertheless, even among capitalists as early as the mid-1980s, dissenting points of view existed. "The Monterrey Industrial Elite," 18. For those opposing sentiments, see my *Entrepreneurs and the State in Twentieth Century Mexico.*

experiences in the student movement. Aguayo offers several penetrating insights about those experiences:

> One of the most important tenets I learned from my studies is that I could transform my nationalism, and that of Mexico, into a more mature form. In other words, I could work with other countries without giving up my nationalistic sentiments. . . . Being educated abroad, in large part, helped to break up the monopoly which the Mexican government had on relations with the U.S.—dispersing those connections among other types of leaders and organizations. I believe my degree from Johns Hopkins opened up this type of connection.[74]

Like the técnicos, this Mexican intellectual learned that he could accept and make use of "foreign" methodologies and ideas in Mexico without giving up his Mexican identity. But an equally important point, basic to understanding existing structural patterns in Mexico and between Mexico and the United States, is that intellectuals, or political opponents of the state, opened up their own, separate channels of communication to the United States. Aguayo, who is an influential independent voice in Mexico, to this day is heavily involved in Mexico-related activities at Johns Hopkins's Strategic and International Studies (SAIS) center in Washington, D.C., which reaches a broad community of government policymakers and academics through its Latin American program.

Given the oppression he suffered as a student leader in 1968, it is natural that Aguayo would seek out experiences and techniques in the United States that might be put to good use in Mexico to bring about the pluralism he dreamed of in his youth. After returning to Mexico he helped to found the opposition paper *La Jornada*, served as a leader in the incipient human rights movement, and directed the broadest civic umbrella organization in the country, Alianza Cívica, which played a crucial role in moving the country forward on electoral democracy.[75]

> I am still very Mexican, but I now understand the complexities of the relationship between the U.S. and Mexico, and the political complexities in Mexico. So, I have become an agent of a new dialogue. The whole experience contributed to producing these consequences for me personally, and I learned a lot about the Mexican political system studying abroad, especially about external influences. This is why I studied external factors. I sharpened my democratic values abroad, and

74. Personal interview with Sergio Aguayo, Chicago, September 25, 1998.
75. Roderic Ai Camp, *Politics in Mexico: The Decline of Authoritarianism*, 3rd ed. (New York: Oxford University Press, 1999), 149.

not just in the United States. . . . In the U.S. I studied and was influenced by the non-violent civil rights movement, and therefore, I transferred that experience to Mexico in terms of what I tried to do with the NGOs. I started the NGO strategy in 1979—to me this was a logical consequence of my experiences in the U.S. after I returned in 1977. This was a confluence of my experiences as a student in 1968 and my examination of the civil rights movement in the U.S.[76]

These personal experiences, and those of many other members of the power elite, clearly suggest the importance of foreign education in both the United States and Europe. Each individual's experience abroad is a product of many other intervening personal experiences, including familial upbringing, place of residence, student and career activities, all of which, as Aguayo lucidly demonstrates, meld together and mold the formative influences which occur outside of Mexico.

As a group, military officers are particularly likely to have been strongly affected by educational experiences in the United States. Educational statistics for Mexico's power elite demonstrate that a higher percentage of the officer corps has studied in the United States than any other specific group. But as the following analysis suggests, their classroom experiences, and not their numbers, determine actual socialization influences. Nevertheless, military officers learned one central value complementary to intellectuals and technocrats, the exploration of differing viewpoints.

This high percentage contradicts the overall relationship between the United States and the Mexican military, which is one of suspicion on the part of Mexico.[77] The Mexican military is so suspicious of contacts between U.S. military personnel and its own officers that it requires prior, formal authorization for social contacts with U.S. officers, or for that matter, civilian foreigners. The Mexican government has expelled U.S. military attachés for gathering "information too aggressively and has imposed early

76. Ibid.
77. A former U.S. member of the Inter-American Defense Board in the 1990s described the meetings of the Joint Mexico-U.S. Defense Commission as follows: "[it] was a bilateral forum which accomplished little in the eyes of the U.S. delegates. We held meetings every three months and exchanged briefings on topics of each delegation's choosing. So while we used these meetings as a vehicle to promote a better understanding of U.S. interests and programs in Latin America or on doctrinal issues, such as training, the Mexicans tended to brief us on topics such as their role in 'civil defense' of Mexico City during intense pollution, i.e., support to civilian authorities. They never briefed us on topics such as operations in Chiapas, for example." Personal letter to the author, March 25, 1997.

retirement on senior [Mexican] officers who had become too friendly with the U.S. mission."[78]

Among all Mexican officers of general rank, two-fifths were known to have trained abroad and all but a handful received their education in the United States. Military power elites acquire even more extensive foreign training than the average general officer, since four-fifths studied abroad, three-quarters of them in the United States. Despite the well-documented tensions between U.S. and Mexican military personnel over the years, Mexico has accepted monies from the United States International Military Education and Training Program. Between 1950 and 1993, when most of the top officers in the power elite sample studied abroad, that program allocated $6.7 million for 2,061 students (primarily officers) to receive professional instruction or technical training in the United States.[79]

Officer corps experiences, with the exception of the School of the Americas, have received little attention in the media compared to graduates of elite universities in the United States. The type of officers selected for this training abroad are typically staff officers. Higher percentages of naval and air force officers, compared to army officers, study in the United States. The Mexican navy has had an officer in every U.S. Navy Command College class since 1960, and "the high quality of these naval officers can be seen in the fact that thirty-three graduates have risen to flag rank, and six have gone on to lead the navy." Most important, Mexican officers have both studied and taught at the U.S. Army School of the Americas and attended all senior service war colleges.[80]

There is no question that the United States has exerted the major external influence on Mexican military doctrine.[81] It acquired that influence in two ways: first through curricular materials used in Mexican military academies, and second, by administrative design. When many of the contemporary Mexican specialty arms programs were modernized in the late 1960s and early 1970s, a significant percentage of Mexican officers trained

78. John A. Cope, "In Search of Convergence: U.S.-Mexican Military Relations into the Twenty-First Century," in *Strategy and Security in U.S.-Mexican Relations beyond the Cold War* (La Jolla: Center for U.S.-Mexican Studies, University of California, San Diego, 1996), 191.

79. Ibid., 194.

80. Ibid., 193.

81. Edward J. Williams, "The Mexican Military and Foreign Policy: The Evolution of Influence," in David Ronfeldt, ed., *The Modern Mexican Military: A Reassessment* (La Jolla: Center for U.S.-Mexican Studies, University of California, San Diego, 1984), 196.

in the United States from 1964 to 1968 received training in how to establish military schools. They repeated this pattern again from 1971 to 1976.[82]

Prior to the 1980s, the Mexican military never followed a coherent general policy of sending its officers to study in the United States. A division general explains that in the mid-1960s, when he took the general staff and command course at Ft. Leavenworth, the procedure was that the secretariat of national defense would announce an available scholarship or position abroad in the *Revista de Ejército y Fuerza Aérea*. Any interested officer could then take an examination, competing with anyone else desiring the assignment. The most difficult requirement was meeting a certain level of language fluency.[83] In 1976, the new secretary of defense completely reorganized the training abroad program, giving it greater focus and purpose.[84]

Mexican officers have trained at dozens of United States military schools and bases since World War II, but the most influential schools have been each service's war college, the Army School of the Americas at Fort Benning, Georgia, the Inter-American Air Force Academy at Lackland Air Force Base, Texas, and the Naval Small Craft Instruction and Technical Training School at Rodman Naval Base, Panama.[85] "These three institutions all present, in Spanish, professional courses that use U.S. curriculum models filtered through the platform delivery of a sophisticated inter-

82. José Piñyero, "The Modernization of the Mexican Armed Forces," in Augusto Varas, ed., *Democracy under Siege: New Military Power in Latin America* (Westport: Greenwood, 1989), 116.

83. Personal interview with General Luis Garfías Magaña, Mexico City, August 24, 1990.

84. Personal interview with General Gerardo de la Vega García, commandant of the Colegio de Defensa Nacional, Mexico City, August 19, 1990. De la Vega also suggested that since the reforms took effect in the early 1980s, sending officers to study abroad has been part of the military's overall educational goals, and that the secretariat of national defense has given considerable thought to increasing its general officers' technical training. He is likely to pursue that goal as Fox's secretary of national defense.

85. Among the leading Mexican officers who have studied in the United States, 10 percent completed the U.S. Army Staff and Command School course at Ft. Leavenworth, Kansas. Nine were army officers, and the tenth officer, Héctor Berthier Aguiluz, eventually served as head of the air force. Nine officers have completed courses at the U.S. Army Caribbean School, Ft. Gulick, Panama (forerunner of the School of the Americas) or at Ft. Benning, Georgia. All of them took special courses, not the lengthy staff and command course. There are no records of any members of the military power elite completing the staff and command course at the School of the Americas. A number of other Mexican officers have taken the course, and in the 1995 and 1996 classes, they doubled and tripled their numbers.

American faculty. Since the early 1960s the Inter-American Defense Board has operated the Inter-American Defense College (IADC), at Ft. McNair, in Washington, D.C."[86]

The staff and command course offered by the Inter-American Defense College in Washington, D.C., is the program most frequently taken by the military power elite. Between 1952 and 1975, sixteen navy and army officers completed this course. Two of those officers became navy secretaries.[87] Five naval officers also graduated from the U.S. Naval War College in Newport, Rhode Island; three out of the five became navy secretaries.

The Inter-American Defense College, which opened its doors in October 1962, operates on the same post as the U.S. National Defense University (formerly the Army National War College) and shares similarities with the NATO Defense College in Rome. It is fundamentally an inter-American institution offering a war college diploma. Faculty are employed by the Inter-American Defense Board, not by the U.S. Department of Defense.[88]

The course consists of a nine-month curriculum which is very similar in scope to that of the U.S. National War College, focusing on political, social, economic, and military theories. Officers enroll at the rank of lieutenant colonel or colonel, and some civilians take the course. A major theme in the curriculum is the internal threat posed by poverty, disease, and social and economic injustices. Numerous speakers from U.S. universities and the government address the students, who work in small groups, focus on various problems, and write a short research thesis.[89]

Mexican graduates of the School of the Americas and its predecessor at the Canal Zone have taken classes in a variety of specialties, including infantry, airborne, naval intelligence, and counterinsurgency. The command and general staff course is forty weeks, patterned exactly after its sister course at Ft. Leavenworth, but is taught in Spanish.[90] Latin American

86. Russell W. Ramsey, "U.S. Strategy for Latin America," *Parameters: U.S. Army War College Quarterly,* 29, no. 3 (autumn 1994), 74–75.

87. Admirals Miguel A. Gómez and Luis C. Ruano Angulo.

88. Russell W. Ramsey, "U.S. Military Courses for Latin America Are a Low Budget Strategic Success," *North-South: The Magazine of the Americas,* 2 (February/March 1993), 39.

89. "Inter-American Defense College," *Military Review,* 50 (April 1970), 21–23. In the field of social study, topics include labor organizations, labor and social security, human communications, education, religion, housing, and health and nutrition in the hemisphere.

90. "U.S. Army School of the Americas," *Military Review,* 50 (April 1970), 89.

as well as American officers jointly attend classes. The School of the Americas has generated intense controversy for decades because some of its graduates from Latin America participated in notorious human rights violations, prompting its critics to assert that the U.S. training was responsible for those abuses.[91] Since 1990, it has incorporated human rights instruction into every course; the stated mission of this part of the curriculum is to promote democratic values and respect for human rights.[92] In recent years critics have focused on the argument that graduation from the program confers prestige and power on those officers upon returning to their home institutions.[93]

In spite of the extensive experience shared by top Mexican officers in the United States, it is doubtful that those experiences resulted in a cohesive, measurable influence on Mexican military policy or civil-military relations. The empirical evidence on this issue, just as is the case of international civilian student experiences, is ambiguous and sparse.[94]

Several factors may temper possible influences from such experiences

91. In response to these accusations, the U.S. Congress trimmed the school's budget, eliminating its recruitment funds in July 1999. In reality, however, there is little empirical evidence to support a connection between the school's training and its graduates' behavior. As John A. Cope notes, 59,000 students have graduated from the school since its inception, and most of these attended one- to two-week technical courses, allowing for little instructor influence. Fewer than .5% were known to be guilty of misconduct. Such influences are difficult to prove, but it is equally difficult to identify actual cases of human rights violations, which are underreported. *International Military Education and Training: An Assessment* (Washington, D.C.: Institute for National Strategic Studies, 1995), 22.

92. John T. Fishel and Kimbra L. Fishel, "The Impact of an Educational Institution on Host Nation Militaries: The U.S. Army School of the Americas as an Effective Instrument of Policy or Merely a Scapegoat," paper presented at the Latin American Studies Association meeting, Guadalajara, Mexico, April 1997, 4. In fact, the School of the Americas is the only U.S. army academic institution where human rights instruction is incorporated into every course. For a detailed discussion of the content of the human rights program, see Russell Ramsey, "Forty Years of Human Rights Training," *Journal of Low Intensity Conflict and Law Enforcement*, 4, no. 2 (autumn 1995), 254–70, and Russell W. Ramsey, "U.S. Strategy for Latin America," 78.

93. John A. Cope, *International Military Education and Training*, 22. This is a point I have made about the careers of Mexican officers. Yet a high-ranking general informed me that my assessment that training from or holding a post in the United States was beneficial to an officer's career was incorrect. Instead, he argued, these assignments were viewed by top staff as rewards for individual officers, not as credentials enhancing their upward mobility in the armed forces.

94. J. Samuel Fitch, "The Political Consequences of U.S. Military Aid to Latin America: Institutional and Individual Effects," *Armed Forces and Society*, 5, no. 3 (1979), 361.

abroad. First, most of the courses taken by Mexican officers are short in duration, one to two weeks, and they are technical in nature, allowing for little interaction with U.S. instructors. Second, officers who graduated from courses taught in the Panama Canal Zone, the case until 1984, received their instruction in Spanish and in a Latin American setting. These two conditions discourage the impact of new ideas from a different cultural and professional perspective.[95] Third, the existing preconditions in Mexico run counter to U.S. social and political ideas, and brief periods of training, especially in the case of mature adults, are not likely to displace existing beliefs about the role of the military in society or its relationship to the civilian population.[96] However, individual instructors, both inside and outside the classroom, can reinforce perceptions that encourage specific attitudes and behavior.[97]

A RAND Corporation evaluation of the effectiveness of international military training in the United States, the most comprehensive evaluation of actual socializing consequences, concludes that such training has "almost no influence over . . . civil-military relations," and exerts only marginal influence, positive or negative, on the officer's home nation's development.[98]

Despite factors which might diminish the potential impact of these socializing experiences from abroad, and the difficulty in identifying qualitatively what has been taught in the last four decades, careful analysts of these training programs suggest several possible influences. These may well have significant professional and political consequences, but because they are not direct, they are easily overlooked.

The greatest impact of U.S. military training may well be due to the exposure of these officers to an environment which encourages exploring and discussing opposing views. Learning strategies used in U.S. military academies are totally new to Mexican officers. Openly exploring alterna-

95. John A. Cope, *International Military Education and Training*, 23.

96. J. Samuel Fitch, "The Decline of U.S. Military Influence on Latin America," *Journal of Inter-American Studies and World Affairs*, 35 (summer 1993), 22.

97. For example, the author once heard an American officer going through an orientation program for managing U.S. military assistance in Latin American countries assert unequivocally that all Maryknoll nuns were communists.

98. Jennifer M. Taw, "The Effectiveness of Training International Military Students in Internal Defense and Development" (Santa Monica: RAND, 1993), 7, 15. A much earlier study by Ernest W. Lefever found little effect one way or the other of U.S. training on the political role of the armed forces. "The Military Assistance Training Program," *Annals of the American Academy of Political and Social Science*, no. 424 (March 1976), 90.

tive ways to solve operational and strategic problems is completely counter to the rote memorization characteristic of the Heroico Colegio Militar and the Escuela Superior de Guerra.[99]

Until 1995, no evidence of such an approach existed at Mexican military academies below the National Defense College level, yet the CDN's own approach might well be the product of officer experiences in the United States. It is worth noting that the defense secretary who created this school served as assistant military attaché in Washington, D.C., and lectured frequently at the Inter-American Defense College.[100] The IADC shares many similarities in its approach with Mexico's National Defense College.

Because the National Defense College produces the cream of the crop among recent officers reaching general rank, it legitimizes methodological approaches and curricular orientations in Mexican military academies. There is strong evidence of significant changes occurring at the Escuela Superior de Guerra, for example, since the publication of an internal national defense document in the summer of 1995 which specifically criticized severe failures in domestic military education and called for increased training in the United States.[101] Recent directors at the ESG have begun to emulate the CDN approach, bringing distinguished civilian speakers, including nationally prominent politicians, to lecture to the student officers. These presentations raise serious criticisms about civilian leadership among these officers, and in turn encourage potentially critical thinking about civil-military relations.

The second potential source of influence is through personal contact with U.S. military personnel as students or instructors in these training programs, or with foreign military attachés in their own country. Sam Fitch, a noted expert on the Latin American military, suggests that these contacts provide "myriad opportunities for the U.S. to communicate its policy preferences and its view of local politics"[102]

In the 1950s and 1960s, the years most Mexican officers studied abroad, the dominant U.S. ideological message was opposition to local and global communism, consistent with the Mexican military's own perception of communism as anti-national, anti-Catholic, anti-Western, and anti-

99. John A. Cope, *International Military Education and Training,* 15.

100. General Félix Galván López.

101. Roderic Ai Camp, "Militarizing Mexico: Where Is the Officer Corps Going?" *Policy Paper on the Americas,* Center for Strategic and International Studies, Washington, D.C., January 15, 1999.

102. J. Samuel Fitch, "The Decline of U.S. Military Influence in Latin America," 16.

military. In the 1980s and 1990s, the U.S. concentrated on the strategy of engaging in low-intensity conflicts, focusing on domestic threats to national security, including drug trafficking, terrorism, and guerrillas, and on the need to win the "hearts and minds" of the non-combatant population, providing a new and important argument for promoting democracy and respect for human rights.[103]

Third, the requirement to speak English in order for Mexican officers to come to the United States is an indirect means through which educational participants expose themselves to external intellectual influences going well beyond strictly military topics. Officers whose second language becomes English can read other types of literature that are unavailable in Spanish.[104] A revealing example of this is my own book on the Mexican military, which for political reasons was never published in Mexico. National defense headquarters widely circulated an unpublished version throughout the general staff.[105]

There is little question that selected Mexican officers are affected by their experiences in the United States. It is evident that they have carried back some intellectual currents which slowly filter down through the armed forces. Those influences appear most strongly in domestic educational programs, primarily at the National Defense College.

As the larger political context in Mexico became increasingly open, these influences reinforced the methodological shift favoring pluralism, paralleling that trend in the body politic.[106] Attitudes toward mission and civil-military relations largely remain determined by professional training at home.

The clergy's professional training shares certain similarities with the military and with politicians educated in economics. It also features important differences. Just as a large number of Mexican military elites study in the United States, so half of Mexico's leading bishops studied in Rome at the Gregorian University. The priests who were chosen for this oppor-

103. Ibid., 24–26.
104. H. Amos et al., *U.S. Training of Foreign Military Personnel*, 1 (McLean: General Research Corporation, March 1979), 2.
105. Personal interview with a member of the presidential staff, Mexico City, July 17, 1992. I also received, equally mysteriously, a twenty-page single-spaced commentary with suggestions and criticisms from an unidentified high-ranking general.
106. For example, the high command has insisted on learning American techniques from U.S. public affairs officers in order to present its own story to the Mexican public and to enhance its image in the media.

tunity, a highly selective group, were handpicked by their mentors and approved by their local bishop, often one and the same individual.

Although the Gregorian University is run by the Catholic Church, it is truly an international institution. As one of its historians and graduates has noted, Jesuits were summoned from all over the world to teach there. This meant that future bishops were exposed to theological points of view from many countries in Europe as well as from the United States. Most of the clergy in the power elite sample attended the "Greg" in the 1940s, 1950s, and 1960s.

The other major difference between Mexican clergy who go to Rome, Mexican politicians who study at Ivy League universities, and officers who train at United States bases is that clergy reside abroad for much longer periods, typically five or more years, and most of them complete part of their undergraduate as well as their graduate studies abroad.[107] This means that bishops, more than any other Mexican power elite member, go abroad at younger ages, typically starting at seventeen or eighteen. Most politicians, intellectuals, and capitalists do not travel abroad until their mid-twenties. Military officers rarely are sent abroad until their thirties. The younger the individual, the greater the potential socializing influence of the experience.

In the 1960s, the curriculum taken by Mexican bishops involved three years of philosophy and four years of theology.[108] The textbooks and lectures, according to former students, followed a common, well-defined format, and the material in the 1940s, 1950s, and 1960s was divided into thesis statements, not chapters.[109] Father Francis A. Sullivan, a long-time instructor in theology at the Gregorian University, offers insightful recollections about the curriculum:

> I began teaching at the Gregorian in the fall semester of 1956. My subject was ecclesiology. This was one of the major courses of "fundamental theology," which the students were required to take in their first year of theology. Almost all of the courses were required, hardly any were elective. Thus, I began lecturing to all the students

107. Some bishops in the power elite have studied in Rome for periods of ten years, such as Ricardo Guízar Díaz. Adolfo Suárez Rivera, author of an influential pastoral letter on civic responsibility, lived in New Mexico for three years, followed by five more years in Rome.

108. Anthony Kenney, *Path from Rome: An Autobiography* (London: Sidgwick, 1985), 50, notes that the syllabus and method were laid down in Pius XI's encyclical *Deus Scientiarum Dominus*.

109. Ibid., 45–47.

enrolled in the first year of theology: at that time there were about 350 in each year. My textbook was the two-volume treatise of ecclesiology written by my older colleague, Fr. Timothy Zapelena, SJ. I continued to use his book for several years, until I had written my own, the first volume of which was published at the Gregorian in 1963, *De Ecclesia: Quaestiones Theologiae Fundamentalis.* The second volume *(Quaestiones Theologiae Dogmaticae)* was made available to the students in mimeographed form, but never published, since by the time it was ready (after Vatican II) the students were no longer using Latin texts.

In those years, each professor was expected to write a textbook for the course or courses that he was teaching. As the lectures were given in Latin, and examinations were conducted in Latin, the books were also in Latin. These constituted the major reading required for the course. . . . It was difficult to assign reading in modern languages, since there was no one modern language that all the students could be expected to know. However, suggestions were given in the bibliography which followed each thesis in my textbook.[110]

The philosophy tract, which potentially might expose priests to "secular" as well as religious thinking, has been described in detail:

The philosophy course was divided into three years, and its subjects had to be taken in a prescribed order, beginning with minor and major logic and metaphysics. Minor logic was the "Aristotelian" formal logic which had been on the curriculum of most European universities since the Renaissance; it owed little first-hand to Aristotle's own logic, or to the developments of that logic in the Middle Ages, but was a truncated torso of the genuine medieval logic . . .

The difficulty was that both the ancient wisdom and the contemporary problems were brought to our acquaintance in a derivative and second-hand manner. . . . We were supposed to be learning Aristotelian philosophy. . . . according to the mind of St Thomas; but we never opened a book of St Thomas until our third year of philosophy. . . . Similarly, it was only in the third year that we met anything of Aristotle at first hand.[111]

At the end of the year, examinations corresponded to this thesis method of presentation. The principal examinations were oral and were conducted in Latin.

The critical impact of education on the elite mentoring process and the impact of individual professors on specific students was nonexistent among

---

110. Personal letter from Francis A. Sullivan, March 7, 1997.
111. Anthony Kenney, *Path from Rome,* 47–48.

priests at the Gregorian University. As Archbishop John R. Quinn explains, the teaching was done strictly via lectures, and no exchange between students and professors occurred. Not only were the theology and philosophy classes taught in Latin, but so too were Hebrew, biblical Greek, and all other courses.[112]

There are two points of view among bishops about the impact of the classroom experiences at the Greg. In addition to the exclusive use of Latin and class size, these courses involved no discussion. As Kenney suggests, philosophy, and I would argue theology as well, are not subjects which can be taught through lecture alone. Pupils need discussion and extensive writing and criticism to learn to think philosophically rather than solely mastering the jargon.[113]

Other bishops, including John R. Quinn, respond to this criticism: "While the system employed in the Gregorian University has been criticized by some, I believe that it was very beneficial in that the student had no real props to fall back on, but was forced to learn how to study independently and how to tackle issues based on his own resources, using original sources in the original languages. I have always felt this to have been a lifelong benefit."[114] According to Quinn, his professors were thorough and he felt well prepared for the changes which occurred after the Second Vatican Council.

Many bishops responded quite negatively to the Greg's "classroom learning." Kenney explains why:

> But many us for a long time, and all of us for some time, found the Latin of the lectures incomprehensible. It was quite common to see students, like jurors at the Pétain trial, or delegates at a dull political conference, whiling away their time by openly reading newspapers, or playing "battleships" with their neighbors. The course information could be made up by buying, from more diligent students, cyclostyled copies of the notes they had taken.[115]

The most important learning for the majority of future bishops at the Gregorian University and other colleges in Rome occurred outside the

---

112. The only exception to this was as part of the examinations for graduation, where all students had to complete a short thesis which could be written in their own language, and they were encouraged to write about authors in their own national tradition. Letter to the author from Archbishop John R. Quinn, March 17, 1997.

113. Anthony Kenney, *Path from Rome*, 50.

114. Letter to the author from Archbishop John R. Quinn.

115. Anthony Kenney, *Path from Rome*, 45.

classroom. For Mexican bishops, this included peer influence, the international flavor of the Gregorian university, and exposure to historic Rome.[116] It is apparent, therefore, that foreign educational mentors were not significant in forming the clerical elite. Several bishops among the Mexican elites describe the influential learning process of the larger setting in detail. For a future bishop who attended the Pontifical Athenaeum Angelicum (St. Thomas University) from 1945 to 1949, who later lived in the Mary Brothers seminary (1949–52), and who was in constant contact with Mexican priests at the Gregorian University, Rome

> opened a vision of the World Church and in my case, in the same international seminary of Mary brothers, I lived with brothers from diverse parts of the world, and I learned to love the different people and be inclined to serve them. For me it signified living in a deep communion in becoming a priest and in the possibility of service. . . . helped introduce me to other social currents and thoughts. . . . gave me the opportunity to know priests and laity through personal contacts and involved me in their writings and personal experiences. For me those were years of searching, of filling my heart with uncertainty. It was a time of discovery and assimilation of ecclesiastical process. . . . It helped me become the priest-bishop I have been and I am: searching, restless, faithful to my Church which I love and with which I have sometimes suffered deeply.[117]

Another bishop recalls similar influences from attending the Gregorian University in the critical years of the war, from 1936 to 1942:

> In the Colegio Pio Latino Americano, I lived with students from twenty Latin American countries, and in the Gregorian University, I came in contact with students from fifty-seven countries, which from necessity a person becomes universal and escapes from a narrow mentality. One aspect of what is achieved in Rome is fulfilling a deep

116. Rome, as the center of ancient Christianity, obviously would exercise a unique cultural influence on potential priests. As Bishop Manuel Talamás Camandari reveals, "To study in Rome, for its history of nearly 3,000 years, as well as its having been the capital of one of the great, ancient empires, with its great failures as well, demonstrates on a grand scale many elements which continue to impact on the world, and especially on those who live there. Its presence creates in an audible manner from St. Peter to John Paul II, the center of Christian faith, were Popes, artists, philosophers, theologians and many other contributors to culture have flourished in those corresponding centuries. Whoever lives and studies there feels through diverse means all of this cultural and religious influence infiltrating the mind and heart in an overwhelmingly enriching manner." Letter to the author, January 4, 1997.

117. Letter to the author from Bishop José Rovalo Azcué, May 13, 1997.

sense of humanism and faith. . . . In Rome you experience fully the sentiment . . . "I am a human being, and nothing human is foreign to me." Also from Rome I perceived the good and bad of many movements and social battles, which evidently prepared us to evaluate and form mature judgments over their significance and goals, producing much restlessness which comes out during the years of priesthood. Because of this, we could form more balanced and objective opinions of the social aspects presented by the people's struggles, in such a manner that far from affecting us negatively, it prepared us to act always in a positive manner, trying to achieve what Pope Pius XII said at the end of World War II: "It is the entire world that has to be remade, to transform the savage into a human being, and a human being into the divine." . . . It is certain that we returned with many social themes which in time produced a seed from which human development and Christian evangelization were initiated.

But, apart from those who helped our perceptions and affected our values, they helped mature our evaluations, because the Aristotelian-St. Thomas philosophy and Christian theology we studied formed us, nurtured us not in passing ideologies or what was in vogue, but rather in unchanging principles of human reason and evangelism.[118]

One important intellectual influence to which future bishops were exposed, equal in magnitude to the impact of economic neoliberalism on foreign-educated political elites, emanated from the progressive consequences of Vatican II. The Concilium was held in Rome beginning in 1962, and the students who attended the Gregorian University during these years (1962–65) were deeply affected by the experience. One of the members whose education straddled the previous decade describes the Gregorian University as passing from a pre- to a postconcilium era.[119] But among religious power elites, only three bishops actually witnessed the Concilium firsthand, and all others, with one exception, studied in Rome prior to Vatican II.

Vatican II's pronouncements did produce a group of bishops who took its most progressive components to heart, but they never dominated the theology and pastoral mission of the Mexican Catholic church. Mexican bishops agree, however, that the Church's activist role in the 1980s and

118. Letter to the author from Bishop Manuel Talamás Camandari, January 4, 1997. One reader suggested that these recollections might be contrasted with Rome's deplorable record on Nazi and Fascist anti-Semitism. It is doubtful, however, that seminary students would have been well informed on the Vatican's posture during those years.

119. Personal interview with Bishop Ricardo Guízar Díaz, Atlacomulco Diocese, Atlacomulco, México, June 28, 1994.

1990s would have been impossible without Vatican II.[120] Thus Vatican II can be viewed as a precursor of political liberalism among Mexican clergy.[121]

The influence of Vatican II, regardless of its limitations, cannot be overstated. The Catholic clergy became an active voice in promoting increased political participation among the laity. Since priests as individual actors are associated with one of Mexico's most highly respected institutions, the Catholic Church, their attitudes toward politics, civic responsibility, and political participation were fundamental in laying the groundwork for much of the grass-roots movements supporting electoral choice and competitiveness, especially in the provinces. These specific democratic convictions are repeated in influential pastoral documents, right up through the 2000 presidential race.[122]

This brief case study of the Gregorian University suggests the importance of a single foreign experience on the formation and attitudes of Mexico's religious power elite despite the noted structural limitations of the classroom. Mentors were largely responsible for sending priests to the Gregorian University, but Gregorian professors did not provide a significant socializing influence. Instead, future Catholic elites were influenced by the intellectual currents flavoring that educational experience, particularly the younger generation.[123]

The discussion and debates about Vatican II in the 1960s paved the way for a strong pro-democratic pastoral message in the 1980s and 1990s, significantly undergirding Mexico's shift to electoral competition. There is every reason to believe that secular institutions in the United States and

120. Roderic Ai Camp, *Crossing Swords: Politics and Religion in Mexico* (New York: Oxford University Press, 1997), 87.

121. Some Mexican elites outside the clergy also were influenced by Vatican II. Cecilia Soto, the presidential candidate of the Workers Party in 1994, who surprised most analysts in garnering more than 1 million votes, was greatly influenced by Vatican II and her Catholic education at the Colegio Vallarta, which sparked her interest in politics. *Líderes*, 6 (1994), 138.

122. See, for example, Conferencia del Episcopado Mexicano, "Mensaje del episcopado mexicano al pueblo de México: La democracia no se puede dar sin ti, elecciones del 2000," May 2000. Seven of the bishops in the power elite are among the authors of this document. For the most influential pastoral document preceding the 1988 presidential elections, see Adolfo Suárez Rivera, "Instrucción pastoral sobre la dimensión política de la fe," Archdiocese of Monterrey, Nuevo León, March, 1987, 6, 9, 17, 23.

123. Some of the older generation, who spent World War II trapped in Rome, were equally influenced by the Fascist and anti-Fascist currents there in the late 1930s.

Europe conveyed equally important social and economic ideas to other Mexican students.

It is impossible to assert that foreign student experiences alone determined significant economic and political changes occurring in Mexico in the last two decades, or even that it was the most influential of the many potential socializing forces. What can be said with assurance, however, is that many power elite Mexicans shared these experiences abroad and many were exposed to a methodological approach which was empirically oriented and strongly analytical.

A small but ultimately influential group shared a core of cultural, political, and economic influences from abroad. Their exposure to these differing views, specifically to the legitimacy of pluralism in practice and in intellectual discourse, and to the credibility of international concepts and development, laid the groundwork for, and in some cases initiated and supported, the changes in Mexico's political and economic landscape.

One of the fascinating distinctions which emerges from this educational experience abroad is the differing emphasis among power elites on the two primary ideological shifts in Mexico in the 1980s and 1990s. In the first place, Mexican technocrats make little mention of being influenced in the direction of political liberalism. An important explanation for this is that they were going abroad to hone their skills in macroeconomic policy-making, not to alter the path of Mexico's *political* development.

Mexican technocrats, on the whole, saw little that was wrong with the political model. Indeed, they wanted to retain control because they believed that they had found the solution to Mexico's economic failures, that is, a rational, logical, pragmatic approach which encouraged growth through competition domestically and globally. They were made aware of social inequalities in some economics courses, and in their electives in history and the social sciences, but their focus was on more effective economic policy tools, not liberal politics.

Political power elites' emphasis on neoliberal economic solutions to the neglect of democratization also was the result of their benefiting from the existing political model. In other words, they were a product of those authoritarian institutions, and instead of rejecting them outright, they hoped to enhance their effectiveness through better-managed economic solutions.

The political technocrats were complemented by a capitalist power elite whose educational focus was even narrower, often concentrated in the fields of engineering and business administration. Absolutely no evidence exists of leading capitalists expressing any liberal tendencies within their own business organizations in the 1980s, which they controlled in an authoritarian manner. It is quite evident that pluralist representation within influential Mexican business organizations was exceptional.

The Mexican technocratic pattern did not follow the extreme authoritarian Chilean ideological example for several reasons, of which the most important were the nature of their educational experience abroad and the ideological setting from which these leaders emerged. In the Chilean case, the technocrats grew out of one of the most repressive authoritarian periods in Latin American political history, representing an extreme ideological alternative in a highly divided society politically and economically.[124] A large percentage of the influential figures in Chile were graduates of a single school, the University of Chicago, whereas their Mexican counterparts came from several leading Ivy League institutions.[125]

Unlike the political power elite, intellectuals and clergy were receptive to fresh political currents. As suggested, they were exposed to a much broader curriculum in the humanities and social sciences, a curriculum which naturally encouraged them to discuss political alternatives. Moreover, their institutional setting at home was quite different from that of Mexican political and capitalist elites. Clergy and intellectuals were not the primary beneficiaries of the Mexican political model.

Among clergy, even the relatively modest influence of Vatican II in Mexico, which eventually became incorporated into general Catholic teachings, pushed Church leadership to acquire a greater sensitivity to the social and economic inequalities experienced by most of their parishioners. Many clergy viewed the state, and its policies, as responsible for these conditions. Therefore, their natural inclination was to stress political pluralism as a means for ultimately changing government policies which would benefit the ordinary Mexican's interests. Clergy could be viewed as being formed in an institutional setting similar to that of opposition politicians, that is, operating in a completely restrictive environment dominated by a semi-authoritarian state.

It is not surprising, given their posture on civic responsibility and political pluralism, as well as the influences of Vatican II, that many Catholic

124. Louis Goodman, "Chilean Citizens and Chilean Democracy," in Roderic Ai Camp, ed., *Citizen Views of Democracy in Latin America* (Pittsburgh: University of Pittsburgh Press, 2001).

125. See Anil Hira, *Ideas and Economic Policy in Latin America: Regional, National, and Organizational Case Studies* (Westport: Praeger, 1998), especially 134 ff.

leaders who were otherwise not found within the "progressive" religious camp were strongly opposed to economic neoliberalism, viewing it as perpetuating the laity's poverty. It is often forgotten that the Catholic leadership, with the help of influential allies in the United States hierarchy, played a crucial role in renegotiating Mexico's foreign debt, arguing that ordinary Mexicans were bearing this economic burden unfairly.[126]

Unlike their political, clerical, and military counterparts, Mexican intellectuals, of course, don't share a cohesive institutional setting. By nature, they are dispersed among many cultural institutions, and their educational experiences abroad, comparatively speaking, are quite diverse. They, like the clergy, have operated in a controlled environment, and especially since 1968 have pursued an independent, critical posture against an authoritarian model, actively supporting political pluralization. Some power elite intellectuals, like Sergio Aguayo, experienced state repression firsthand, and therefore were inclined to seek out political remedies to open up the system.

Educated Mexicans have long been influenced by American and European ideas, and these influences were strongly ingrained into the curriculums of many university professional programs as early as the 1920s. But two dramatic changes occurred in the origins of foreign educational influences among Mexican power elites in the last third of the twentieth century. First, a younger generation of these power elites began placing a stronger emphasis on postgraduate education. Their focus on those higher levels of professional and academic education increased the potential influence of ideas from abroad. Second, most members of the power elite who initially sought postgraduate studies abroad chose to obtain their degrees in England and France, but a dramatic shift occurred among younger power elites, who, with the exception of priests, who studied in Rome, ignored the established patterns and traveled to the United States.

As the exploration of the educational experiences of técnicos, clergy, and the officer corps makes clear, leaders within specific institutions made

126. In their joint statement, Mexican and U.S. bishops, in a letter to President Bush, argued: "as pastors we are deeply anguished by the devastating effects of the debt on real people, especially the world's poor, who had no voice in creating the debt and received minimal benefits from it." The Mexican signatories of this letter, and individuals who participated in later efforts, all were members of the religious power elite. United States National Conference of Catholic Bishops, "Relieving Third World Debt: A Call for Co-Responsibility, Justice, and Solidarity," September 27, 1989, 4. See my discussion of their efforts on the debt and their opposition to NAFTA in my *Crossing Swords*, 245–46.

critical choices which channeled the vast majority of the younger political, clerical, and military power elite, with institutional or government financial support, to foreign institutions. Those choices were frequently made by influential mentors in their professions, oftentimes by individuals who had studied abroad, whether they were bishops, top public officials, or high-ranking officers.

Obviously, differences in elite attitudes are also the product of different professional and institutional interests. This chapter clearly illustrates that educational experiences abroad may enhance, moderate, or alter those differences. The analysis of these foreign educational experiences also suggests significant differences in the socialization process which can be attributed to qualitative distinctions in education, the level of education experienced, or the length of time abroad.

Among Mexican political elites, nearly all of whom studied at the graduate school level, mostly in the United States, individual professors were specifically identified as intellectual mentors, in the same way that Mexicans had served as socializing mentors in their undergraduate education. These American mentors also became part of an more extensive international networking system, complementary to and linked with their own domestic career network, patterns which Anil Hira found in numerous countries.[127]

In other educational experiences, such as those by future bishops, students alluded to the broader intellectual currents found inside and outside of the classroom, rather than specific mentors. These influences were just as important as those conveyed more directly by a classroom teacher. For Mexican officers, however, it was neither a classroom mentor nor the larger residential setting, but the actual classroom environment, where American-style teaching, which encourages class discussion, opened the officer corps to the concept of debating opposing points of view. This unique experience, especially in the longer staff and command courses, legitimized their desire to question their instructors and to educate themselves about opposing viewpoints. These new methodological tools encouraged influential officers to change the style of military training in Mexico in the 1990s, exposing the officer corps to the same social and political currents infecting Mexican society generally.

127. He refers to these as "economic knowledge networks." See his excellent *Ideas and Economic Policy in Latin America,* 133.

Part III

POWER ELITES, NETWORKING, AND DECISION MAKING

9 Decision Making, Networking, and Organizations

The first two parts of this book set forth an argument about the existence and influence of power elites in Mexico, analyzing in detail the means by which influential Mexicans are linked to each other within and across power elite circles and further developing the crucial role mentors have played in the recruitment, networking, and socialization process. Part 2 identifies the significance of various agents of socialization which have contributed to important power elite values and provides substantial evidence demonstrating the impact of elite educational experiences both at home and abroad. Part 3 explores the connection between networking and decision making, the emergence of certain elite prototypes, and the consequences of power elite leadership in the recent past and into the future.

This chapter attempts to incorporate the special characteristics of power elite networking to demonstrate how influential Mexicans use their informal associations in formal institutional settings to influence major policy decisions. In the case of public officials, it argues that informal networking linkages clearly reinforced the ability of economic policymakers in the executive branch to implement their macroeconomic philosophy, including ideas and techniques learned in the United States.

Networking occurs in many contexts and through numerous sources. In postindustrial societies, as suggested earlier, the theoretical focus characterizing networking literature is biased toward organizations. This institutional emphasis, which is natural in such countries, also has a place, however atypical, in Latin American countries. In Mexico, even if organizations are not always paramount in the networking process, they provide significant links.

Two important points are worth keeping in mind about the extent to which organizational linkages serve as primary vehicles for connecting elites or as channels for potential elite influence on decision making. First, institutions are underdeveloped in Mexico compared to the United States. Not only are institutions fewer in number, but the numbers of independent policy organizations and foundations which have provided critical linkages among elite groups in the United States and Europe are less common in Mexico. However, certain types of research institutions are very much on the increase in Latin America.[1]

A second issue, one which has remained fundamentally unexplored in previous studies, is that organizational scholarship assumes that when two elites are linked together on the basis of their shared organization positions, those positions determine their personal linkage. I would argue that in the United States, and more so in Mexico, the possibility exists that these individuals are connected in some important way *before* they sit together on the same board or serve in the same organization.

One of the assumptions in the networking literature is that organizations often operate in dynamic and unpredictable settings.[2] Such settings not only encourage organizations to acquire control over resources which determine their operations environment, but also provide an additional incentive for influential members within these organizations to collaborate.

In the United States, the growth of the public bureaucracy and private sector companies led to the increasing influence of organizations and individuals who controlled their resources, human and financial. In the corporate world, as the dispersion of ownership increased, managerial staffs and their executives typically replaced individual capitalists as influential actors.[3] Analysts predicted that the same pattern would occur in Mexico. With the advent of neoliberalism and global economics in the 1990s came

1. See Daniel Levy, *Building the Third Sector: Latin America's Private Research Center and Nonprofit Development* (Pittsburgh: University of Pittsburgh Press, 1996), 17–22.

2. Mark S. Mizruchi and Joseph Galaskiewicz, "Networks of Interorganizational Relations," *Sociological Methods and Research*, 22, no. 1 (August 1993), 47.

3. In Suzanne Keller's classic study comparing the careers of top business leaders from 1870 through 1950, she illustrates these dramatic statistical trends in the careers of corporate executives. Self-made men accounted for 36 percent of top businessmen in 1870, but only 6 percent in 1950. Family-made executives in the same period declined from 32 to 11 percent. In contrast, bureaucratically made individuals (managerial types) rose from a mere 18 to 68 percent. *The Social Origins and Career Lines of Three Generations of American Business Leaders* (New York: Arno Press, 1980), 82.

the "creation of transcorporate networks of ownership and directorships."[4] In the last decade more foreign corporate executives, primarily from the United States, have taken seats on Mexican boards than previously, but control of its most influential corporations remains largely in the hands of Mexicans, specifically capitalists—not the managerial class.

Organizations play two potentially influential roles among power elites. They may act to link together the career experiences of an influential group of individuals. While performing this function, they may also serve as a focal point in promoting the careers of future power elites.

As political systems grow in size and complexity, the argument can be made that organizational imperatives surpass family and class interests as the primary source of influence, and that organizations, not individuals, become the principal political actors.[5] Nevertheless, individual power elites as agency heads set the tone and direction of their respective organizations, even if they may not actually significantly alter organizational interests and behavior.

NETWORKING AND DECISION MAKING
IN THE PUBLIC SECTOR

Institutions play significant roles in the transmission of ideas once those ideas become embedded in an organizational culture.[6] One of the most influential examples of organizational networking in Mexico during the last three decades, which produced significant personnel linkages and policy consequences, is the institutional interconnection between the presidency (programming and budget), treasury, and the Bank of Mexico. A key figure who set this pattern in motion was former president José López Portillo. Similar patterns can be found elsewhere in Latin America, for example, Argentina.[7]

4. Michael Useem, *The Inner Circle* (New York: Oxford University Press, 1984), 178.

5. David Knoke, "Networks of Elite Structure and Decision Making," in Stanley Wasserman and Joseph Galaskiewicz, eds., *Advances in Social Network Analysis* (Thousand Oaks: Sage, 1994), 290.

6. Ideas embedded in organizations can have an impact for decades, extending well beyond the rationale for their existence. This definitely appeared to be the case in Mexico, when the technocrats battled traditional state economic policy preferences. See Judith Goldstein and Robert O. Keohane, "Ideas and Foreign Policy: An Analytical Framework," in Judith Goldstein and Robert O. Keohane, eds., *Ideas and Foreign Policy: Beliefs, Institutions, and Political Change* (Ithaca: Cornell University Press, 1993), 20.

7. See Judith Teichman, "Mexico and Argentina: Economic Reform and Tech-

John Bailey, who carefully explored the inner workings of the Mexican federal bureaucracy and the impact of administrative changes on policy making, describes López Portillo in the following terms:

> José López Portillo pioneered the Ph.D. program in administrative science at the Instituto Politécnico. He was a leader in the administrative reform efforts of the national government in the mid-1960s and fashioned a career as a high-level administrator through posts in Sepanal, Presidency, the Federal Electric Commission (CFE), and Treasury. He is, then, a sophisticated student of administrative theory and practice.[8]

Although he was a lawyer, not an economist, López Portillo anticipated the technocratic revolution by emphasizing the importance of public administration theory as a vehicle for streamlining and coordinating decision making, making it more responsive to objective, universal criteria, a fundamental ingredient in the ideology of the next generation of economist-technocrats. He carried out these activities in the presidency, a governmental agency which was the antecedent to programming and budget, the central institutional source of leading political technocrats in the 1980s.

After leaving an academic career as director of the department of legal counsel to the presidency in 1965, López Portillo formed the Committee on Public Administration. He appointed seven individuals to that committee; six served in his presidential administration from 1976 to 1982, four of them at the cabinet level. Three of the committee members, in addition to the president, are members of the power elite.[9] This committee did not produce influential legislation or affect public policy in any significant way, but it attracted a group of individuals who saw the value of administrative reform and exposed their talents to López Portillo, whose favorable impression of their abilities led to their first cabinet-level appointments.

---

nocratic Policy-Making," *Studies in Comparative International Development*, 32, no. 1 (spring 1997), 47.

8. John Bailey, "Presidency, Bureaucracy, and Administrative Reform in Mexico: The Secretariat of Programming and Budget," *Journal of Inter-American Economic Affairs*, 34 (1980), 42.

9. The original members were José López Portillo, president; Emilio Mújica, secretary of commerce; Julio Rodolfo Moctezuma, secretary of the treasury; Carlos Tello Macías, secretary of programming and budget; Fernando Solana, secretary of public education; Miguel Duahlt, *oficial mayor* of commerce; Enrique Loaeza, director of airports and auxiliary services; and Gustavo Martínez Cabañas, President Salinas's first political mentor.

During the 1970s, the planning and budget secretariat became more influential than the treasury secretariat in furthering the careers of Mexico's future technocrats. According to Miguel Centeno, these technocrats were younger, had more training in the quantitative techniques required for econometric planning, and were more willing to accept a powerful public role in economic development compared to their economist counterparts in treasury.[10]

They also boasted other advantages as a group, including their social, educational, and professional homogeneity, which helped foster their more unified view of the way to solve Mexico's problems. At the same time, this level of unity permitted them to avoid the internal ideological battles that weakened other contenders for power. As observers elsewhere in the region (including Chile) have noted, the crucial explanation for the technocrats' success in reaching the apex of state power was their ability to capture the commanding heights of the economic policy-making bureaucracy.[11] Their unity and control of the policy process also led to a special air of arrogance, labeled *technocratic elitism* by some observers, an attitude reflected in their view that they actually had the right to rule, and that they alone could determine the course of social change.[12]

Members of the technocratic generation in Mexican public life used their informal linkages from family, friends, and school to establish a formal organizational structure within which they could expand their personal ties and extend their ideological and bureaucratic influence. The Bank of Mexico, treasury, and programming and budget served this goal. Shortly after López Portillo took office in 1976, he formally converted the old secretariat of the presidency into the new programming and budget agency. It was an organizational means of taking budget decisions away from treasury and placing them in a separate agency under close presidential scrutiny.

During Miguel de la Madrid's administration (1982–88), the president formalized economic decision making in the hands of an "economic cabinet." In addition to the three agencies which exerted such an impact on the flowering of technocrats and neoliberal ideas, the secretariats of energy,

10. Miguel A. Centeno, *Democracy within Reason: Technocratic Revolution in Mexico* (University Park: Penn State University Press, 1994), 90–91.

11. Eduardo Silva, *State and Capital in Chile: Business Elites, Technocrats, and Market Economies* (Boulder: Westview, 1996), 108.

12. To some extent this pattern was occurring in all countries, including the United States and Canada. For the latter case, see Dennis Olsen, *The State Elite* (Toronto: McClelland and Stewart, 1980), 82–83.

mines, and para-statal industries, as well as commerce and industry, were involved in macroeconomic policy discussions. However, the most influential voices in the policy process were from the programming and budget office, the treasury, and the office of economic advisers to the president, headed by Leopoldo Solís, magnet mentor to the most influential generation of economist-technocrats, including President Zedillo.[13]

Under de la Madrid's successor, the agencies and individuals involved in macroeconomic policy making narrowed further. According to Teichman, not only were agencies such as energy and mines excluded, but only cabinet secretaries, not their representatives, were included in meetings where these policy decisions were made.[14] The popularity of economist-technocrats reached a high point during this era for the same reasons that held elsewhere in Latin America. The constant economic crises, and the difficulty of economic decision making, especially as it related to foreign debt, strengthened the demand for well-trained and qualified individuals in the highest governmental circles.[15]

The younger generation of economists' control over influential cabinet posts contributed significantly to continuity in economic policy, a pattern also found in Brazil and Argentina.[16] As these individuals acquired a strong foothold at all levels of their respective agencies, the neoliberal predisposition of treasury and the Bank of Mexico was

> reinforced by a process of institutional socialization that has created a homogeneity of views. The common outlook of middle- and upper-level technocrats in the Ministry of Finance and the Central Bank has been traced to an in-house training program developed by the bank. Cohesiveness and attitudinal homogeneity are further reinforced in the Finance Ministry and the Central Bank by a high level of personnel continuity and a tight network measured by exchange of personnel.[17]

13. Judith A. Teichman, *Privatization and Political Change in Mexico* (Pittsburgh: University of Pittsburgh Press, 1995), 75.

14. Ibid., 75–77.

15. Patricio Silva, "Technocrats and Politics in Chile: From the Chicago Boys to the CIEPLAN Monks," *Journal of Latin American Studies*, 23, no. 2 (1991), 387.

16. In her comparative study of Argentina and Brazil, Kathryn Sikkink concludes that "ideas held by powerful individuals are the key to understanding the adoption of policies," and that "the accumulation of intellectual talent" explains why one country implemented its developmental policies differently. *Ideas and Institutions: Developmentalism in Brazil and Argentina* (Ithaca: Cornell University Press, 1991), 26–27.

17. Barbara Teichman, *Privatization and Political Change in Mexico*, 73.

Programming and budget similarly became a "center of learning for a small group inculcated in a new terminology, a new vision of the world, and a new *ethos*."[18]

If we examine these three public agencies from 1970 to 2000, considering only the individuals who achieved status in the power elite, their influence becomes apparent.[19] A careful analysis of these organizations suggests that they were crucial actors in the formation and evolution of Mexican macroeconomic policies, and that they provided a formative environment in the molding of public figures' professional values and attitudes, but they were not necessarily the basis of the linkage between mentors and disciples or between influential public figures.

Even if we consider only those Mexicans who have held positions at the director general level, equivalent to a division head, and confine our position-holders to those who reached power elite status, the interchange among the three agencies is remarkable. Seventeen individuals held policy-making positions within the treasury secretariat during the thirty-year period of this study (1970–2000), including three presidents and a presidential candidate.[20] If we examine the overlap with the programming and

18. Isabelle Rousseau, "La SPP y la dinámica de constitución de un equipo: 1982–1988," *Foro Internacional* (April/September 1998), 339.

19. By far the best explanation of institutional networking, and its consequences for policy making and politics, is Eduardo Torres Espinosa's insightful work on the secretariat of programming and budget. His conclusions support the arguments developed here. *Bureaucracy and Politics in Mexico: The Case of the Secretariat of Programming and Budgeting* (Brookfield: Ashgate, 1999), 101.

20. They were Ramón Aguirre Velázquez, subsecretary and director general, 1971–76 (disciple of Hugo B. Margáin and Miguel de la Madrid; network source: treasury); Pedro Carlos Aspe, secretary, 1982–88 (disciple of Carlos Salinas; network source: MIT); Mario Ramón Beteta, subsecretary and secretary, 1970–76 (disciple of Rodrigo Gómez; network source: family [uncle]); Herminio Blanco Mendoza, adviser to the secretary, 1978–80; Miguel de la Madrid, director general and subsecretary, 1972–79 (disciple of Mario Ramón Beteta and José López Portillo; network source: Bank of Mexico and UNAM); Héctor Hernández Cervantes, director general, 1970–76 (disciple of Raúl Salinas Lozano and Hugo B. Margáin; network source: UNAM); David Ibarra Muñóz, secretary, 1977–82 (disciple of Manuel Gómez Morín); Francisco Labastida Ochoa, director general, 1976–79 (disciple of Miguel de la Madrid and Fernando Hiriart Balderrama; network source: treasury); José López Portillo, secretary, 1973–75 (disciple of Luis Echeverría; network source: preparatory school); Hugo B. Margáin, director general and secretary, 1947–59, 1970–73 (disciple of Ramón Beteta and Antonio Carrillo Flores; network source: UNAM); Emilio Mújica Montoya, adviser to secretary, 1973–75 (disciple of José López Portillo; network source: presidency); Guillermo Ortiz Martínez, subsecretary and secretary, 1988–98 (disciple of Pedro Aspe and Leopoldo Solís; network source: ITAM and presidency); Gustavo Petricioli, director general, subsecretary, and secretary, 1965–74, 1986–88 (disciple of Miguel Mancera; network

budget secretariat, which eventually was incorporated back into treasury at the end of the Salinas administration, of those seventeen individuals, five obtained top posts in that agency.[21] Finally, five of the seven principal figures in the Bank of Mexico, the Mexican equivalent of the American Federal Reserve, held positions in at least one of the other two agencies, including President Zedillo.

One of the advantages of institutional networking is its potential to bring together large numbers of individuals over short periods of time. Many technocrats associated with Salinas and Zedillo came together as research economists working for magnet mentor Leopoldo Solís in the division of economic and social planning of the secretariat of the presidency. For example, Zedillo and Jaime Serra Puche were employed in this agency together.[22] But scholars have mistakenly attributed their positions together as the source of an influential networking linkage which produced personal and professional consequences for both men. While that is true for some prominent economists-politicians, it is not the origin of their personal networking ties.

An examination of the actual source of networking ties between a prominent individual and the person for whom he or she works, often a significant mentor in his or her career, typically is not the agency. In short, these individuals are linked together *before* they become colleagues, whether indirectly or directly. Of the seventeen Mexicans who held top posts in the treasury secretariat, thirteen have known multiple networking ties. Of those, fewer than half established a connection with an influential mentor

---

source: ITAM); Carlos Salinas de Gortari, director general, 1978–79 (disciple of Hugo B. Margáin and Miguel de la Madrid; network source: family and UNAM); Bernardo Sepúlveda Amor, adviser to the secretary and director general, 1971–81 (disciple of Julio Moctezuma Cid; network source: presidency); Jaime Serra Puche, adviser to the secretary, subsecretary and secretary, 1979–88, 1994 (disciple of Leopoldo Solís and Ernesto Zedillo; network source: presidency and Yale); Jesús Silva Herzog Flores, director general, subsecretary, and secretary, 1970–72, 1979–86 (disciple of Rodrigo Gómez and Jesús Silva Herzog; network source: Bank of Mexico and family). Some fascinating parallels exist with New Zealand. See Shaun Goldfinch, "Remaking New Zealand's Economic Policy: Institutional Elites as Radical Innovators, 1984–1993," *Governance*, 11 (April 1998), 177–207.

21. Although it may seem strange, many individuals become career disciples of their peers. In public life, this is often explained by the fact that one individual's upward career trajectory is more rapid, or as in the case of presidents José López Portillo and Luis Echeverría, boyhood friends, López Portillo did not even pursue a serious governmental career until late in his professional life.

22. Other influential figures in the power elite who worked for Solís during those years include Esteban Moctezuma Barragán, Guillermo Ortiz Martínez, and Manuel Camacho Solís.

or peer through the actual agency position. Nine, or nearly three-quarters, of these prominent figures established their initial contact in an educational setting, either as fellow students, such as presidents José López Portillo and Luis Echeverría, or in a professor-student relationship. The networking pattern among these technocrats mirrors the known networking contacts among political power elites generally, among whom two-thirds established their friendships at school, and only a fourth through organizational settings. (See table 6.)[23] The third source of networking is completely non-institutional: ties through family friendships.

I have detailed these networking ties as they relate to the creation and evolution of President Carlos Salinas's "group." My description of Salinas's early career indisputably establishes the indirect influence of his father on his early formation and rise up the economic bureaucracy ladder.

> When he completed his economics degree in 1969, he sought out the help of Hugo Margáin, one of his father's old political disciples [Margáin held his first influential post under Salinas senior in the 1950s]. Margáin assisted Salinas in getting started with a career in the treasury secretariat, giving him a post as adviser to Miguel de la Madrid. . . . de la Madrid helped him with a scholarship to Harvard. . . . Salinas' first administrative post in 1974 as a department head was under his father's old disciple, Hernández Cervantes, who was directing the division of international studies at the time. Hernández Cervantes also gave him a second fellowship to complete another degree at Harvard.[24]

The networking pattern in programming and budget is similar. Of the nine individuals about whom multiple networking information is available, seven established connections through school or college, three through the agencies themselves, and one through family. Only in the case of the Bank of Mexico does it appear that personal linkages are established through organizational positions in the presidency or the bank itself, although two of the five known sources also include contacts made at school.

I would argue that it is difficult to attribute with certainty a networking tie based on linkages established through shared organizational positions. In Mexico, an individual, especially early in a career, establishes a crucial contact with a mentor through the intervention of a third party—that person's original mentor, a professor, or a family member. These informal

---

23. Based on 510 known networking contacts among the 100 leading politicians in the power elite.

24. Roderic Ai Camp, *Political Recruitment across Two Centuries: Mexico, 1884–1991* (Austin: University of Texas Press, 1995), 252.

linkages are extremely difficult to trace in any culture, leading researchers to attribute connections to individuals on the basis of published information which establishes that individual A simultaneously served in the same department or on the same board as individual B. This fact may well contribute to deepening the ties between individuals A and B, but it may not be the original source of their friendship.

The consequences of these assertions for networking theorists and scholars in the United States are significant. Their research has led them to conclude that organizations exercise the greatest influence on networking ties, and consequently that organizational linkages are crucial to decision making. Instead, the organizational linkage may be secondary to some antecedent source, and institutional networking may not be the primary vehicle for understanding how initial mentoring takes place, especially in other societies.

NETWORKING AND DECISION MAKING IN THE PRIVATE SECTOR

Some of the same features which characterize networking in Mexican public organizations can be found in private sector organizations. The private sector institution having the greatest potential to influence the government's macroeconomic decision making is the Mexican Council of Businessmen (Consejo Mexicano de Hombres de Negocio). The council consists of Mexico's leading capitalists, the majority of whom are members of the capitalist power elite.

In 1957, president-elect Adolfo López Mateos asked a group of prominent businessmen to promote national companies abroad after a *Life* magazine article misrepresented Mexican industry. All of the original group consisted of members of the capitalist power elite.[25] They called themselves the Association of Public Relations, and soon added several other leading capitalists.[26] In 1962, they changed their name to the Mexican Council of Businessmen (CMHN), redefined their mission as the promotion of foreign investment, and expanded their membership to thirty of their peers.[27] According to one of its original members, they came "together with the

25. They were Carlos Trouyet, Bruno Pagliai, Miguel Alemán Valdes, Manuel Senderos Irigoyen, Jorge Larrea, and Rómulo O'Farrill.
26. Agustín Legorreta and Eugenio Garza Sada. See *Reforma*, June 20, 1997.
27. Miguel Basáñez, *La lucha por la hegemonía en México, 1968–1990*, 9th ed. (Mexico City: Siglo XXI, 1991), 269.

purpose of trying to unite elements in the private sector."[28] In order to join, you needed to receive the unanimous vote of all other members.

Some scholars have argued that, ironically, this newly organized approach emerged in response to policies encouraged by Adolfo López Mateos's own administration (1958–64), which included limitations on foreign capital investment in petrochemicals, the restructuring of the automobile industry, support for Fidel Castro's government in Cuba, and the nationalization of the electric industry.[29]

During its initial years, some CMHN members were what North American business analysts describe as professional managers, individuals who emerged through the ranks from corporate careers, but who were not from capitalist families and who did not control major financial resources. These members contributed a different flavor to council views. One such individual, Ernesto Robles León, presided over Bacardi for nearly twenty-five years; he resigned from the council in the 1970s because he sensed that the other members "no longer wanted people on the council with managerial experience to express themselves and vote, but were only interested in members who represented an important economic force in the country. The position of [Eugenio] Garza Sada was that only those who represent large economic consortiums should be members of the council."[30]

Robles León explains why professional managers added a different perspective to council positions, and their potential influence on government macroeconomic policy making.

> I think we need people with experience and expertise, and not just people with large capital. I think also that a person with my type of experience can deal with the government because I do not have a personal financial interest in the outcome. Members of the council criticize the government, but they do so timidly. When people who are members speak, they speak as individuals and not as council members as a whole. They did not criticize the last two presidents' [Echeverría and López Portillo] bureaucratic growth because of their timidity and fear that there might be government reprisals.[31]

Council members have largely been leading capitalists, not professional managers, and granting membership is tantamount to providing special

28. Personal interview with Cresencio Ballesteros, Mexico City, July 26, 1984.
29. Ricardo Tirado Segura, *Las organizaciones empresariales mexicanas: Pérfil y control durante los sesentas* (Mexico City: Instituto de Investigaciones Sociales, UNAM, 1979), 6.
30. Personal interview with Ernesto Robles León, Mexico City, May 21, 1985.
31. Ibid.

access to government decision makers, including the president. Those capitalists who have relied heavily on state contracts, or who have close ties to the state, have remained members well beyond retirement age.[32]

Of all the major business organizations in Mexico, this group is the most selective in its composition. It remains semi-secret in terms of its actual functions, but interviews with present and past members have provided some insights into its behavior. No entrepreneurs representing the interests of small and medium size business groups have ever been invited into the organization, and its private rules prohibit foreign members.[33] The council has certain similarities to Japan's Keidanren, a sort of super-business organization. The Keidanren's members, however, include top executives of the most powerful Japanese corporations, not exclusively capitalists.[34]

The council meets regularly. The core activity is a monthly luncheon, almost always including a guest politician or government official responsible for financial and economic policies. This might be an official from commerce, the Bank of Mexico, or treasury. The meeting is closed and generally lasts most of the afternoon. The government invitee makes a brief presentation and several hours of discussion follow. Since the mid 1970s, the president of Mexico has met with CMHN about once a year.[35] In an economic crisis, however, the council consults more frequently with

32. An example of such an individual is Rómulo O'Farril, one of the few founding members who remained active into the late 1990s. Fernando Ortega Pizarro, "Como empresario político: Claudio X. González vive en una simbiosis inaceptable," *Proceso*, November 9, 1997.

33. Ricardo Tirado Segura, *Las organizaciones empresariales mexicanas*, 90.

34. Harold R. Kerbo and John A. McKinstry, *Who Rules Japan? The Inner Circles of Economic and Political Power* (Westport: Praeger, 1995), 121.

35. Ben Ross Schneider, "Why Is Mexican Business So Organized?" unpublished paper, Northwestern University, March 1999, 14. The only other organization, even more informal than the council, which seems to have had similar access to the president, is the "Grupo de los Díez," ten presidents or directors general of the most powerful holding companies in Monterrey. According to Lourdes Melgar, they met with Miguel de la Madrid every two months. De la Madrid actually asked them to reduce their financial support to the National Action Party after it defeated the PRI in many local and state elections in 1985. Members during the 1980s were Bernardo Garza Sada, Eugenio Garza Laguera, Adrían G. Sada Treviño, Andrés Marcelo Sada Zambrano, Eugenio Clariond Reyes-Retana, Alberto Santos de Hoyos, Lorenzo H. Zambrano Treviño, Humberto Lobo, Gregorio Ramírez, and Jorge Garza. All but one are members of the capitalist power elite, and six are or were Consejo members. "The Monterrey Industrial Elite: Ideological Contradictions, Political Alliances and Economic Practices," paper presented at the National Latin American Studies Association meeting, Los Angeles, September 1992, 10, 15.

a sitting president. In the three-week span prior to Zedillo taking over the presidency, characterized by drastic capital flight and a liquidity crisis, the council met twice with Zedillo and once with President Salinas. These meetings are typically held in a council member's home.[36]

The council also has a "senate" composed of former members who opt to stay with the organization as active members after retiring at age seventy-five, and of former council presidents. According to members, the ex-presidents are the actual heart of the senate.[37]

Members and leading businessmen view the council as a small, private club. Structurally it differs from national governmental agencies in two significant ways. First, careers in and control over influential government economic agencies have been crucial to the success of top political power elites. Capitalists, however, achieve their influence without membership in the Mexican Council of Businessmen. Indeed, they can become members only *after* achieving national prominence.[38] Second, because they achieve membership only after they are at the apex of their careers, it does not produce successful capitalists, nor does it function organizationally in molding successful entrepreneurial careers. Studies of North American elites confirm that the most important contribution personal wealth makes to networking and to policy influence is the access it provides to exclusive clubs and nonprofit foundation boards, and the council may be seen in that light.[39]

In the case of the council, members do not benefit from the typical policy influences associated with an exclusive organization. Former members explain why.

> Look, I will tell you something else about the Mexican Council of Businessmen. I have found from luncheons with the president that

---

36. Lucy Congor, "Power to the Plutocrats," *Institutional Investor,* February 1995, n.p. According to Congor, Zedillo came to know a number of Mexico's leading capitalists as a young technocrat in the Bank of Mexico, where he directed FICORCA, a foreign exchange risk coverage program that aided strapped conglomerates in managing their foreign debt. In the first days of his administration, Zedillo met individually with several top capitalists, including Roberto Hernández and Jorge Martínez Guitrón.

37. Fernando Ortega Pizarro, "Como empresario político."

38. Many of Mexico's most influential capitalists never become members. Such is the case of the late television magnate Emilio Azcárraga Milmo, whose fortune topped $3 billion.

39. Gwen Moore and Richard D. Alba, "Class and Prestige Origins in the American Elite," in Peter Marsden and Nan Lin, eds., *Social Structure and Network Analysis* (Beverly Hills: Sage, 1982), 52.

each member of the council will use that as an opportunity to ask the president for an individual meeting. In other words, what the council has become is a channel for individuals to make contact with the president rather than to represent the interests of the private sector as a whole. Now, when they talk to the government about something, they never talk as a group. To me, this is like committing suicide, because when you are isolated as an individual, you weaken your impact on the government. . . . I think this kind of behavior represents a myopic attitude on the part of the private sector.[40]

Academic analysts agree with this criticism, suggesting that this type of informal personal behavior defeats institutional goals.

Members of the council view it as providing something beyond access to cabinet figures and even to the president, however. They also believe access to powerful peers is a source of information, which is considered a priceless product in Mexico because it is not widely shared. As a leading capitalist told Lucy Congor, "you need the most information possible." Another member, who had joined the council only two months prior to her interview, found it to be an influential forum for seeing what was going on in other regions of the country.[41]

It is apparent that the council does attempt to have a broad influence on government macroeconomic philosophy, if only indirectly. Sánchez Navarro, a long-time member who has been outspoken about what goes on inside the council, claimed that in early meetings with President Zedillo, the members expressed the hope that he would continue Salinas's economic program, but with the proviso that Zedillo would "give greater attention to the distribution of wealth and solving poverty." Sánchez Navarro suggests Zedillo agreed with that view.[42]

It is abundantly clear that this same pattern will continue under President Vicente Fox. Less than three weeks after his victory in July 2000, Fox met with members of the council at the Bankers Club. The meeting was arranged by Roberto Hernández, a power elite member who was Fox's school companion at the Ibero-American University.[43] Hernández, as president of Banamex, previously arranged a successful credit card program

40. Personal interview with Ernesto Robles León.
41. Lucy Congor, "Power to the Plutocrats," n.p.
42. Ibid.
43. Fox and Hernández are also close friends of another fellow student, José Madariaga Lomelín, a prominent banker who is co-owner of Probursa with Eugenio Clariond Reyes Retana, president of the Council of Mexican Businessmen in 1998. *Reforma*, June 10, 1996, A1.

with Fox to allow migrant workers in the United States to send money safely back to their families in Guanajuato. One percent of the profits was donated to social programs in Fox's home state.[44]

Even the most complete analysis of the Mexican Council of Businessmen concentrates on capitalists' access to government decision making, especially to the president. These analyses, however, pay little attention to the impact this small but powerful organization has on personal and business relationships *among* Mexico's leading capitalists.[45]

Given the council's size—currently it has thirty-nine active members—the argument can be made that after being a member for several years, one would come to know most other members, at least socially if not professionally, from meeting once a month. It is difficult to ascertain the relationships among power elites who are members, but it is apparent that many of them were connected to each other *prior* to council membership. Among all leading capitalists, family mentors provided the most important networking sources, followed by corporate boards, which were responsible for a third of such contacts. (See table 5.)[46] Among council members, the prevailing networking ties *before* they became members were through family, partnerships, and board membership, with family accounting for more than half of those friendships.[47]

Membership in the council reinforces other networking ties while opening up the possibility of new ties with a highly selective, influential group, without question the most important group of capitalists in Mexico. There is no doubt that the small size of this specific organization would lead to permanent business and social relationships among leading capitalists, but numerous relationships occurred previously through other venues, formal and informal.

Ben Schneider makes the point that in the last twenty years there has been a considerable amount of turnover on the council.[48] That is technically accurate, but a survey of the organization's membership from 1962 to 2000 also reveals another important pattern. Only fifty-seven individuals have

44. "Roberto Hernández reafirma su amistad con Fox," *Diario de Yucatán,* July 25, 2000, www.yucatan.com.mx.

45. Alicia Ortiz Rivera, "Consejo Mexicano de Hombres de Negocios," M.A. thesis, Instituto Mora, Mexico City, 1998, is an excellent evaluation of this group, the best to date.

46. Based on 299 known ties among the 100 capitalist power elites in this study.

47. Based on sixty-two known ties of council members *prior* to joining the organization.

48. Ben Schneider, "Why Is Mexican Business So Organized?" 14.

ever been a member of this group in forty years of existence. The turnover argument is substantially countered by the fact that more than a fifth of the new members are the children or nephews of original members, and an even larger percentage are related by marriage to older members.[49]

In the private sector, the most influential organizations are not company bureaucracies but corporate boards and the Mexican Council of Businessmen. The advantage of boards is that they are small and, as demonstrated earlier, overlapping. The advantage of the council is that it is small, has overlapping membership from various economic sectors, has direct access to top government officials and the president, and provides its members with direct access to thirty-nine of Mexico's top capitalists.

A comparison between the governmental financial bureaucracy and these two private sector organizations (the council and corporate boards) reveals several distinguishing characteristics of Mexican networking and decision making. In the first place, government agencies are much more likely to perform socializing functions typically associated with organizations. In this sense, Mexican government agencies share characteristics with Latin American, North American, and European public agencies.

It is apparent that individual Mexican agencies evolved their own organizational cultures, and that these cultures contributed to a dramatic change in government macroeconomic policy and to producing the leadership which engineered those new directions. These agencies also reinforced each other, socializing a new generation of economists-politicians who initially began their careers in their lower echelons.

Most younger technocrats were mentored by individuals who led these agencies during the crucial, formative years of the technocratic transition

---

49. The classic example is Eugenio Garza Laguera, an original member in 1962. Four other members of his extended family have since become Consejo members: Alejandro Garza Laguera, his brother and father-in-law of Alfonso Romo Garza, who joined in 1998; Bernardo Garza Sada, who joined in 1975 and who is the nephew of Eugenio; and Dionisio Garza Medina, who joined in 1994 and who is the nephew of Bernardo Garza Sada and the cousin of Eugenio Garza Laguera. He is also related by marriage to the Creel Terrazas family, who are directly related to Federico Terrazas Torres, who joined in 1997. Other family relationships include Roberto Hernández Ramírez and Carlos Slim, who are cousins, and three father and son ties: Adrián G. Sada Treviño and Adrián Sada González Jr., Manuel Senderos Irigoyen and Fernando Senderos Mestre, and José Represas and Carlos Eduardo Represas. Juan Cortina Portilla, also an original member, is the father-in-law of Agustín F. Legorreta Chauvet, who joined in 1970.

in Mexican government leadership. These individuals often taught their younger disciples and were engaged simultaneously in altering academic programs and government attitudes.

It is equally apparent that the Bank of Mexico provided a permanent anchor in the exchange among the other leading financial agencies and that its own in-house training program, along with its decision to send future leaders to Ivy League universities in the United States, collectively reinforced views favorable to economic neoliberalism.

The networking sources of prominent political power elites in the three economic agencies are varied, reflecting the patterns found among all political power elites. But they also demonstrate the influence of career contacts among politicians, as well as the importance of specific government agencies in providing those contacts. In political life, organizations have exerted a greater influence than is true among capitalists, because future politicians are concentrated in a handful of agencies. Capitalists, on the other hand, rarely work with other capitalists within specific companies; rather, they work in their own companies. Typically, their only contact with other leading capitalists, at the beginning of their careers, is with family members, many of whom have served as their mentors.[50]

Capitalists' shared organizational experiences are delayed until they have acquired prestige, recognition and control of major financial resources. Once that level of influence is reached, they may be incorporated into two important organizational settings: the corporate board and the Mexican Council of Businessmen. Corporate board membership is the most common shared organizational setting among leading capitalists. All have served on other capitalists' boards. Among capitalist power elites, however, only half have ever belonged to the Mexican Council of Businessmen, because of its exclusive membership.

Unlike public agencies, within which influential politicians are formed after years of service, capitalists spend only a few days a year in their two organizational settings. Although Mexican capitalists are molded and socialized within a corporate culture, that culture is typically different for each individual.

The Mexican Council of Businessmen provides an opportunity for an

---

50. There is recent evidence from France and England that business-related family backgrounds have increased in importance, rather than declining, with the rise of big business and the managerial class. Michael Mayer and Richard Whittington, "Euro-elites: Top British, French and German Managers in the 1980s and 1990s," *European Management Journal*, 17, no. 4 (August 1999), 405.

intellectual exchange among capitalists and between capitalists and leading political figures, including the president. While the relationship between the two groups could be seen from an educational perspective, each socializing the other to their respective views of the broader changes occurring in the Mexican economy, testimony from various members suggests that the council never provided a cohesive, reinforcing environment among capitalists; nor did it function as an institutional locus for mentor–disciple relations. The members of this organization, like the members of the major Mexican holding company boards, can be viewed most accurately as peers. Thus, while both organizational settings provide for some learning, their primary function is one of intelligence (access to information).

In the public governmental setting, a seemingly low-level, insignificant organization such as a committee, research group, or small department within a larger agency, when directed by an energetic, well-placed, and ambitious official, can produce strong networks which ultimately may alter the texture and direction of government economic policy. Power elite capitalists, while they obviously share many interests, tend to act individually or in concert with their affiliated partners, not as a collective group.

Only the most careful research could draw out the actual depth of informal ties which crisscross all of the power elite connections established formally through positional interlocks in small and large organizations. Furthermore, we know almost nothing about the extent to which informal ties, including within families, impact decisions reached by individuals who share organizational positions. To what degree does one influence the other? The question requires careful research, without which we cannot draw all-encompassing conclusions about organizational networks.

10 Power Elite Prototypes in the Twentieth Century
The Old and the New

The formation of Mexican leaders over the last half of the twentieth century followed numerous paths. The present examination of these patterns among various leadership groups demonstrates significant changes in the agents likely to exercise an influence on elite values and beliefs in the next millennium. These altered patterns in turn will affect how leaders are recruited and the mentors who will reinforce their credentialing process, career experiences, and ideological direction.

This chapter divides Mexico's power elite into two major generations, those born between 1910 and 1940, and those born after 1940. The first generation was responsible for continuing a well-established pattern of behavior across power elite circles. It was also responsible for producing selected mentors who identified, groomed, and educated a younger generation of power elites, many of whom contributed significantly to the political, economic, and religious currents dominating Mexico in the 1990s, and who are likely to continue their influence in this century. A subgroup within that older generation also laid the groundwork for the initial transitions characterizing influential institutions at the end of the 1980s.

THE GENERATIONAL GUIDEPOST

The most striking variable across Mexican power elite groups, one that highlights changing patterns, is a leader's age. An examination of the power elite sample by generation reveals sharp delineations in many characteristics. Scholars have known for decades that an individual's age often correlates closely with the level of influence exercised by differing socializing agents.[1] Patterns among Mexican power elites from 1970 to 2000 show sweeping changes across leadership categories, the kind of change that produces significant structural and attitudinal differences.

Generational patterns are significant not only for what they reveal about Mexican leadership generally, but for what they say about differences *within* the power elite. If distinct age groups share somewhat differing values or attitudes, this may affect the relationship between one group of leaders and another—for example, between the officer corps and politicians.

A breakdown of Mexico's power elite according to their dates of birth leads to several important findings. A single decade, the 1920s, dominates the birth dates among Mexican leaders since 1970. In fact, nearly a third of all prominent figures were born in the 1920s. Second in importance is the preceding decade, which accounts for one out of five leaders. Combined, the years 1910 through 1929 produced half of Mexico's influential leaders during the period under study. (See table 18.) This generational dominance is symbolized by the fact that it produced three consecutive presidents from 1970 through 1988, Echeverría, López Portillo, and de la Madrid.[2]

The historical setting in Mexico during those two decades can be summed up as an unstable postrevolutionary era following ten difficult years of intense conflict.[3] It was a politically unsettled period in which influential institutions of government evolved, and unresolved conflicts of the revolution, personal and ideological, were settled in a sometimes violent, unpredictable fashion. Among the most influential experiences affecting the youthful formation of some members of the generation raised during those years was the Cristero rebellion, 1926–29, an intense confrontation between the state and religiously motivated peasants which devastated Mexico's West Central region and affected church–state relations for decades thereafter. It was formative for an entire generation of bishops, molding their attitudes toward the state, Mexican society, and political peers.[4]

1. Allan Kornberg and Norman Thomas, "The Political Socialization of National Legislative Elites in the United States and Canada," *Journal of Politics*, 27 (November 1965), 765.

2. That same period also produced two other presidents, Adolfo López Mateos (1958–64) and Gustavo Díaz Ordaz (1964–70).

3. These events are captured in John W. F. Dulles, *Yesterday in Mexico* (Austin: University of Texas Press, 1961).

4. Roderic Ai Camp, *Crossing Swords: Politics and Religion in Mexico* (New York: Oxford University Press, 1997), 146–48.

Table 18. Significant Generations among Mexican Power Elites

	Date of Birth				
Power Elite Group	Pre-1900 (%)	1900–09 (%)	1910–29 (%)	1930–40 (%)	1941– (%)
Politician	0	1	11	7	7
Intellectual	1	0	8	3	2
Capitalist	2	4	11	4	4
Military	0	4	17	5	0
Clergy	1	1	6	3	0
Totals	4	10	53	22	11

NOTE: $N = 398$.

The nationalization of the petroleum industry by President Cárdenas in 1938 also served as a landmark political decision which had a tremendous influence on the views of most Mexicans toward national sovereignty and the role of the state. The recollections of many politicians, including President José López Portillo, demonstrate its impact on students from the era. The last, short-lived organized rebellion against the Mexican government occurred in 1939, bringing the era of open violence to a close and reinforcing the state's dominant power.[5] Finally, the fast-approaching world war, which ultimately involved Mexico as an ally of the United States, forced this generation to look beyond Mexico and the western hemisphere, introducing the threads of internationalism so prevalent in the 1990s.

What is extraordinary about Mexican leadership generationally is that younger elites, those born after 1945, have produced two presidents, Salinas and Zedillo, yet this Mexican baby boomer group accounts for only a minuscule 8 percent of all power elite leadership since 1970. The political influence wielded by its small numbers is suggested by the fact that politicians alone account for nearly two-thirds of power elite baby boomers.

This distortion in the generational patterns *among* Mexican power elites points to several significant conclusions. First, politics has offered ambitious Mexicans a channel for the most rapid upward mobility of any leadership group in the last third of the twentieth century.[6] A power elite

5. This period is effectively captured in Luis González, *Los días del presidente Cárdenas* (Mexico City: El Colegio de México, 1981), and Alicia Hernández Chávez, *La mecánica cardenista* (Mexico City: El Colegio de México, 1979).
6. For the importance of generational patterns on upward mobility and their structural consequences among Mexican politicians, see my *Political Recruitment*

politician could, on average, achieve an influential policy-making post ten years earlier than his peers in other leadership categories. Second, politicians, especially the dominant group since 1988, are out of sync generationally speaking with most other elites, notably capitalists, the officer corps, and Catholic bishops.

Most important, not a single power elite in the military or clergy was born after 1941. If generational experiences play any role at all in the formation of leadership, it is fair to conclude that these two elite groups share a vision which reflects generational differences from other peer groups.

Mexico's baby boomers, born between 1946 and 1966, grew up in a societal setting dramatically different from their older peers. In the years after 1966, Mexico witnessed strong novel domestic and international influences. Internationally, the Cold War provided the most influential impact, brought closer to Mexicans by the United States' difficult relationship with Fidel Castro's Cuba after 1960, and later its involvement in Nicaragua's and El Salvador's civil conflicts in the 1980s.[7] For a generation of priests, including many Mexicans, the ideological influences of Vatican Encyclicals altered Latin American Catholic theology and pastoral orientation.[8]

Domestically, state growth continued unabated, and Mexicans began to experience the consequences of the industrialization policies introduced under the administrations of Miguel Alemán (1946–52) and Adolfo Ruiz Cortines (1952–58). Consistent economic growth prevailed during the era of Mexico's "economic miracle," but, as was true of subsequent periods, without substantial improvement in the working class's purchasing power.[9]

---

across Two Centuries, Mexico: 1884–1991 (Austin: University of Texas Press, 1995), 37 ff.

7. A summary of these issues, from a Mexican viewpoint, can be found in Adolfo Aguilar Zinser, "Mexico and the United States: The Lost Path," in Susan Kaufman Purcell, ed., *Mexico in Transition: Implications for U.S. Policy* (New York: Council on Foreign Relations, 1988), 120–35. Aguilar Zinser is a member of the intellectual power elite and a close foreign policy adviser to Vicente Fox.

8. Michael Tangeman traces these currents in Mexico in his *Mexico at the Crossroads: Politics, the Church, and the Poor* (Maryknoll: Orbis Books, 1995), 46 ff.

9. Real purchasing power declined 65 percent from 1939 to 1957. Roberto Newell and Luis Rubio, *Mexico's Dilemma: The Political Origins of Economic Crisis* (Boulder: Westview, 1984), 96. Income distribution also deteriorated from 1950 to 1963, with the lowest quintile declining from 4.5 to 3.5 percent of the total national income. Daniel Levy and Gabriel Székely, *Mexico: Paradoxes of Stability and Change*, 2d ed. (Boulder: Westview, 1987), 148.

The Institutional Revolutionary Party's dominance and institutionalization paralleled civilian control over post-revolutionary military leadership. As students, the oldest members of the post-1945 generation witnessed Mexico's most serious breakdown in political leadership with the 1968 massacre of students and bystanders in Tlatelolco Plaza.[10] They also experienced a series of financial crises, in 1976, 1982, 1986, and 1994–95.

These generational data also reveal that a leader's longevity, and therefore his or her potential ability to exercise influence over society, varies considerably according to power elite category. Capitalists stay active much longer than do politicians. For example, nearly half of the influential capitalists in the last three decades were born prior to 1920. This difference in longevity is equally apparent among capitalists and military officers.

Generational longevity also creates possible repercussions on mentor and recruitment patterns. As demonstrated in chapter 2, the simultaneous presence of mentors and disciples within the power elite is determined, in part, by the fact that an elite mentor born in the 1910s could still be functioning in elite circles in the 1980s. Structurally, capitalists and intellectuals have the ability to do this most frequently because they are not constrained by artificial, institutional, or informal restrictions on their age.[11] They can continue to function as long as they are productive. In contrast, Catholic bishops and military officers have mandatory retirement ages of seventy-five and sixty-five, respectively.

Bishops actually benefit from their structured tenure, given the fact that their mandatory retirement age is well beyond the average age at which most of their peers in politics and the military have retired. Thus bishops, who reach the apex of their careers by their early fifties, typically have twenty-five years during which they might have an influential voice among Catholic leadership. Influential officers, on the other hand, rarely reach two-star rank before their late fifties, and therefore the span of years they may influence their institution is considerably reduced, typically between ten and fifteen.

A generational portrait of Mexico's power elite reveals how overall re-

10. Zedillo, for example, was injured in one of the antecedent conflicts as a student at the National Polytechnic's Vocational School No. 5. *Proceso,* January 13, 1992, 13.

11. Of course, institutional restrictions are easily evaded on the local level by prominent regional bosses such as Gonzalo Santos in San Luis Potosí, or in the labor movement at the national or regional levels. Two classic cases are Fidel Velázquez's dominance of the largest labor federation for five decades, and Heliodoro Hernández Loza's control of a regional union in Jalisco for many decades.

cruitment patterns are changing. The three most important sources responsible for elite recruitment, as suggested in chapter 2, are peers in the individual's professional field, relatives, and teachers or students. Table 19 demonstrates that a sharp demarcation occurs among those members of the power elite born prior to and after 1920. The older generation was, as might be expected, more influenced than their younger peers by familial linkages. In fact, family members recruited slightly more than two-thirds of power elites born prior to 1920.

Recruitment sources appear to have stabilized among the post-1920s power elite groups, with approximately half of all elites the subject of family recruitment linkages, and the remainder evenly divided between professional peer or educational recruitment. Further analysis of the youngest power elites born after 1945 does suggest the possible beginnings of a decline in family influence; only 42 percent were recruited by family members.

We may be witnessing a change in recruitment sources among elite baby boomers as we enter the twenty-first century, but a stronger and more remarkable pattern is that family has remained, in spite of all the institutional changes and maturation, the dominant entry gate to an elite's respective profession or career. Family connections were still responsible for the recruitment of one out of two individuals through the end of the twentieth century.

What explains the dominance of family linkages into the new millennium? One might suspect that children often choose to follow in their parents' footsteps, providing an opportunity for assertive, successful parents to use their personal connections to advance their children's careers. This pattern is clearly illustrated among capitalists: four out of five capitalists in the present sample followed in their father's footsteps. This is an extraordinary figure and explains why Mexico's most successful capitalists typically have "inherited" their positions. Family, not surprisingly, exerts an overwhelming influence on recruiting future capitalists, 91 percent of whom began their careers at the urging of a father, uncle, or grandfather.

Only a third of all Mexican power elites pursued their parents' careers; these figures are reduced by the fact that none of the clergy, under normal circumstances, can be the prodigy of priests and nuns. A second linkage to family, which may explain its importance, goes beyond the confines of the nuclear circle. If power elites are examined on the basis of their extended family ties to prominent figures, we find that nearly half of all politicians are related to influential Mexicans, as are a third of intellectuals and a fourth of top officers in the armed forces. Extended family, therefore, has

Table 19. Recruitment Patterns by Power Elite Generations

Recruitment source	*Date of Birth*					
	Pre-1900 (%)	*1900–9 (%)*	*1910–19 (%)*	*1920–29 (%)*	*1930–40 (%)*	*1941– (%)*
Peer in Field	13	19	14	29	21	28
Relative	50	81	61	46	52	49
Teacher/Student	37	0	25	25	27	23

NOTE: The figures for the Pre-1900 column should not be viewed as representative of that generation since they account for a tiny, exceptional group among Mexican power elites after 1970.

played and continues to perform an important role in recruiting and mentoring power elites.

A second explanation for the overriding importance of family in recruiting and mentoring power elites is, of course, the comparative lack of institutional development in Mexico, which perpetuates a reliance on informal patterns developed over centuries.[12] The strongest institutional force in elite recruitment and mentoring remains education—typically higher education, as illustrated in chapter 6. Proportionately, the group most influenced by this institutional locus are intellectuals, two-thirds of whom are protégés of instructors or occasionally a student. This is not surprising given the fact that many intellectuals pursue careers in academia.

The most pronounced generational division within Mexico's power elite, which explains many of the patterns contributing to the extraordinary ideological shift occurring in Mexico in the 1980s, is the dramatic difference between power elites born before or after 1940. Nineteen-forty is a natural demarcation explaining significant background variables affecting the present power elite's choices.

Two crucial background variables are generationally linked in significant ways. The first of these variables is the social class from which Mexican leaders are drawn. Studies of individual groups of leaders have long demonstrated the importance of middle-class families. Parents of Mexican elites with professional occupations have persisted across generations from

12. By institutionalization, I refer primarily to the degree to which an organization has its own identity, has developed its own institutional culture and processes, and functions without a dominating, individual leader.

1900 through the present, accounting almost consistently for half of elite parental backgrounds, as demonstrated in chapter 3.

There has been an extraordinary social change, however, in the dwindling number of elites from working-class families, who had accounted for more than a fourth of all power elite parents in the first few decades of the century. This pattern ends abruptly in 1940, when blue-collar parents (including peasants) suddenly began to produce only 4 percent of power elite families.[13] This radical decline in the number of blue-collar parents is countered by a concomitant rise in the number of wealthy parents, exceeding for the first time Mexican power elite families from professional, middle-class socioeconomic circumstances. (See table 20.)

The dramatic change in the socioeconomic background of Mexico's top leadership is paralleled by an equally dramatic regional shift in elite residence. Prior to 1910, a third of Mexican power elites resided outside of the three largest metropolitan centers, Mexico City, Guadalajara, and Monterrey. In the years between 1910 and 1940, Mexico City continued to grow as the preferred residence of influential Mexicans. Most of the decline elsewhere occurred in Guadalajara and Monterrey. After 1940, however, Mexico City, which during that same period became the home to slightly fewer than one out of five ordinary Mexicans, served as the primary residence to four out of five leaders. Guadalajara disappeared altogether as a residence of younger influential Mexicans.

Many hypotheses can be offered about the influence of class background and place of residence in the formation of a leader's values. Because there are so many other influences that come to bear on an individual's socialization, the literature is by no means conclusive or convincing. What can be argued convincingly is that the pool of Mexicans who are recruited into power elite circles, and those who become influential mentors, has narrowed sharply over the last half-century. This narrowing process has contributed importantly to the continued impact of family mentors among

13. One would expect a gradual decline in blue-collar backgrounds among power elite parents as their proportion in the general population declined. But the decline in the general population has been gradual, not dramatic. One would also expect, as a counterpoint to this trend, that larger numbers of children from blue-collar families would have access to higher education in the 1970s compared to the 1930s and 1940s. What David Lorey demonstrates, however, is that while access to public education increased, students from lower socioeconomic backgrounds rarely completed their degree programs. Thus, as he suggests, they acquired some "social status" but not upward social mobility. See his discussion in *The University System and Economic Development in Mexico since 1929* (Stanford: Stanford University Press, 1993), 158 ff.

Table 20. Social Class Background of Power Elite Generations

	Date of Birth					
Parents' Class	Pre-1900 (%)	1900–09 (%)	1910–19 (%)	1920–29 (%)	1930–40 (%)	1941– (%)
Working	0	29	24	24	30	4
Professional	67	54	50	57	52	45
Wealthy	33	17	26	19	18	51

NOTE: The figures for the pre-1900 column should not be viewed as representative of that generation since they account for a tiny, exceptional group among Mexican power elites after 1970. (N = 398)

power elites. Higher socioeconomic backgrounds, as shown previously, substantially increase the importance of families as sources of recruitment, mentoring, networking, and socialization.

A demonstrated link can be established between residence, income, and access to education, determining to a significant degree a Mexican power elite's educational level, location, and even discipline. The obvious change which any student of education expects to see over time is a gradual increase in educational levels. This pattern is nicely demonstrated by the present data. Among power elites born prior to 1910, nearly a third received at most a preparatory education. That proportion drops by half among elites born in the next three decades, while university graduates remain stable at approximately half of all elites and graduate training more than doubles.

Two educational patterns appear in the data which go well beyond expectations. The most dramatic change is the complete disappearance of non-college graduates from Mexican power elites since 1940. This pattern is directly related to the equally remarkable decline in working-class backgrounds and increased residence in Mexico City, where higher educational access is more widespread.

The changing socioeconomic background in power elite families is equally significant and is linked to the dramatic increase in advanced education beyond traditional professional or undergraduate degrees. Two-thirds of the power elite born after 1940 completed some level of graduate work, a figure nearly double that of the previous generation. More important, half of the post-1940 generation actually acquired Ph.D.'s.

One of the fundamental arguments made in this study is that education performed a crucial task in influencing several generations of leaders' economic and political values. Expanded interest in graduate-level education from a generational perspective would not have been possible without all power elites being college-educated, and this in turn would be less likely to happen among individuals from working-class socioeconomic backgrounds. As noted in chapter 7, many of these students sought advanced training in newer, technical fields with the support of mentors who also had completed advanced degrees.

Suddenly, within a single generation, Mexicans seeking graduate education outside of Mexico doubled. At the same time, their preferred location for that education changed in equally dramatic terms, with more than twice as many power elite Mexicans compared to those born in the previous generation choosing the United States. The most popular degree choice of this younger group, of course, was economics. Mexican mentors educated in the United States played a fundamental role in this shift.

The crux of the generational data is that the power elite that has influenced Mexican decisions in the last third of the twentieth century is divided sharply into two distinct groups whose background characteristics, credentials, and experiences differ sharply. The generational demarcation falls between those born from 1910 to 1940 and those born from 1941 to the present.

Using broad generational criteria in combination with specific characteristics which emerge from the present analysis of networking and socialization patterns, it is possible to generate some prototypes among influential leaders who illustrate 1910–40 leadership, post-1940 leadership, and where appropriate, future leadership in the first two decades of the twentieth-first century.

It is possible, of course, for a transition to occur generationally at this very moment, with a birth date in the 1970s or 1980s becoming an equivalent benchmark for the twenty-first century that 1941 became in the last century. But children born during those decades are still teenagers and young adults today, and have not yet entered power elite circles. Therefore, such lines of demarcation cannot yet be determined with certainty.

PROTOTYPICAL ELITES FROM THE TWENTIETH CENTURY

The Mexican power elites who experienced the most extensive changes from 1970 to 2000 are without question politicians. In fact, this group instigated many of the changes it underwent during this period. Until very recently, prototypical politicians could be divided into two influential categories, *traditional politicos* and upstart *technocrats*. The technocrats upstaged Mexico's traditional politicians in the 1980s and, with the advent of the Salinas administration, seemed to be deeply entrenched for the foreseeable future.

Two important alterations in the political landscape in the 1990s derailed the technocrats' dominance over public policy making: the increasing strength of political opposition, and the failures of government economic decision making, which was accompanied by the devastating popular decline of their preeminent advocate and symbol, Carlos Salinas de Gortari.

No better example exists of the traditional politico during the thirty-year period under study than Arsenio Farell Cubillas. Farell represents the dominant generation among all elite leaders, having been born in the 1920s. A peer and close friend of two presidents, Luis Echeverría and José López Portillo, Farell attended public school with both men in the capital, including their secondary years at the Heroes de Chapultepec high school.[14] Educated entirely in Mexico, as is typical of his generation, he completed his law degree at the National University in 1945. Like so many members of his generation, Farell taught at UNAM for three decades, putting himself in a position to mentor a younger generation of students. A practicing lawyer for many years, he held his first government post in his classmate's cabinet in 1973. Farell has the distinction of being the only politician in the power elite to have served in all five presidential cabinets from 1970 to 2000.

A new-style politician began replacing the traditional politico by the early 1980s, the political-technocrat. The typical political-technocrats share some characteristics in common with their older peers. As the chapters on networking illustrate, they too come from the Federal District in large numbers, they too have little or no experience in the governing party, and they have also typically confined their public careers to national political office, typically the federal bureaucracy.

Technocrats, most of whom were born after 1946, also introduce many new features rarely found among their older predecessors. They were educated in Mexico City, but often at private schools. The technocrats attended undergraduate school in the capital, but increasingly have graduated from distinguished private, not public, universities. They have sought advanced training abroad, almost always in the United States, and the typical technocrat graduated with a degree in economics from an Ivy League institution. Finally, their careers are confined to the federal bu-

---

14. An excellent interview with ex-president Luis Echeverría about Farell appears in *Excélsior*, March 17, 1997.

reaucracy, but they have rarely held positions outside of economically related agencies.[15] These characteristics make them one of the few prototypical groups in Mexico with important similarities to leaders elsewhere in Latin America and the Third World.[16]

All the typical qualities of the technocrat are present in the career of Pedro Aspe, the cabinet member who symbolized the high point of U.S. neoliberal economic influence during the Salinas administration. Aspe also epitomizes many of the other changes revealed in the present analysis of the pre- and post-1940 generations.

Like most of the younger generation, Aspe comes from a wealthy and distinguished Mexican family, as does his wife, the daughter of a renowned anthropologist and diplomat.[17] His own father directed El Palacio de Hierro, one of Mexico's oldest, most chic department stores. Unlike Farell and his political generation, most of whom were part-time university instructors, Aspe became a full-time academic, establishing a reputation in the economics program at the Autonomous Technological Institute.[18]

The older political power elite is not the only group that is linked strongly to public universities, education in Mexico, and residence in the capital. A Mexican leadership group which in the past shared many characteristics with its political counterpart is the intellectual power elite. Changes taking place in Mexico since 1970 affected patterns in the intellectual community, but the pace of those changes has been slower and their direction less clear than in the political world. Among the most important of these structural changes, one that has contributed to the emergence of a different type of cultural power elite, is the decreased importance of the link between the intellectual and the state. The growth of private institutions, especially in higher education, and the increased competition in

15. For a detailed discussion of their characteristics and consequences, see my "Technocracy *a la Mexicana:* Antecedent to Democracy," in Miguel A. Centeno and Patricio Silva, eds., *The Politics of Expertise in Latin America* (New York: St Martin's, 1998), 196–213.

16. See Jorge I. Domínguez, ed., *Technopols: Freeing Politics and Markets in Latin America in the 1990s* (University Park: Pennsylvania State University Press, 1997).

17. His wife's father is Dr. Ignacio Bernal y García. For family background, see *Proceso,* August 31, 1992, 15.

18. For his impact on academia, see Stephanie Golob's excellent "Making Possible What Is Necessary: Pedro Aspe, the Salinas Team, and the Next Mexican 'Miracle,'" in Jorge I. Domínguez, ed., *Technopols: Freeing Politics and Markets in Latin America in the 1990s* (University Park: Pennsylvania State University Press, 1997), 95–143.

the media, generated economic opportunities for prominent cultural figures, which have substantially contributed to greater intellectual autonomy.

Basically, three types of Mexican intellectuals appeared in the second half of the twentieth century. The most traditional is the *public intellectual*, who for the most part has followed a well-hewn path characterizing the Mexican intellectual power elites for generations.[19] This type of intellectual dominated cultural life during most of this century. These kinds of intellectuals are found in other countries as well and have been described in similar terms in Edward Shils's work on India.[20]

The public intellectual has traveled a career path between the public sector, in educational-cultural institutions, and the publishing sector. Most of these individuals, like the older political leaders, grew up and resided in the capital. They graduated from Mexico City universities, and typically received their formal education in Mexico, as suggested in chapter 7. The baby boomer public intellectual is exemplified by Héctor Aguilar Camín's career.

Aguilar Camín was born in Chetumal, Quintana Roo but went to Mexico City as a child. From modest economic circumstances, he attended the Jesuit-operated Instituto Patria, the alma mater of other leading intellectuals and politicians; his mother ran a boarding house in the capital.[21] A disciple of Daniel Cosío Villegas, an influential mentor to numerous leading intellectuals, Aguilar Camín joined a circle of distinguished historians and future intellectual figures, including Enrique Krauze, as a Ph.D. student at the Colegio de México in the early 1970s.[22] Following the completion of his doctorate, he became a columnist and editor of *Uno Más Uno*, a leading Mexican daily, and co-founded the intellectual journal *Nexos*, one of the two most important cultural magazines in Mexico in the 1980s and 1990s.

Other power elite intellectuals of Aguilar Camín's generation are pursuing different tracks. The two most discernible new types are the *private*

19. For evidence of this since the 1920s, see my *Intellectuals and the State in Twentieth Century Mexico* (Austin: University of Texas Press, 1985).

20. Edward Shils, *The Intellectual between Tradition and Modernity: The Indian Situation* (The Hague: Mouton, 1961).

21. For example, Carlos Monsiváis and Enrique Florescano Mayet.

22. For background on his friendships and teenage years, see Pilar Jiménez Trejo and Alejandro Toledo's chapter on Aguilar Camín in *Creación y poder: Nueve retratos de intelectuales* (Mexico City: Contrapuntos, 1994).

intellectual and the *international intellectual,* both of whom are likely to exercise more influence in the twenty-first century. These two types are analyzed in chapter 11.

Mexican elite culture is most influenced by secular intellectuals, but members of Mexico's power elite intellectual community have exerted very little influence on ordinary Mexicans. Instead, religious elites have exercised a greater cultural influence on the masses. On the other hand, Catholic bishops, who form the most significant core of religious influentials, have little impact on the intellectual community or their publicly aired ideological debates. Catholic bishops not only convey spiritual values to 85 percent or more of the population, but have taken active positions on major secular issues, notably human rights abuses, the maldistribution of wealth, and democratization.[23] These positions have become increasingly pronounced, and offer an alternative vision from others in the military, capitalist, and political arenas.[24]

The most influential Catholic bishops are *Catholic insiders,* who operate within institutional structures. The Mexican episcopate is not much larger than the United States Senate, and despite some serious policy differences among its members, it operates very much like an elite religious club.[25]

Catholic bishops, young or old, are born and raised in the provinces, having received early religious training from seminary institutions in their local diocese. Nearly all of the priests from the older generation acquired their higher education in Rome, typically from the Gregorian University, while residing in the Colegio Pio Latino América, a residence for Latin American priests.[26] Most return to their dioceses of origin, after which they serve as parish priests and seminary instructors.

23. For a discussion of church attendance and the potential role clergy play in the formation of mass social, political, and economic values, see my "The Cross and the Polling Booth: Religion, Politics and the Laity in Mexico," *Latin American Research Review,* 29, no. 3 (winter 1994), 69–100. The Tijuana diocese also conducted an insightful survey of how laity respond to their priests: *Plan pastoral, 1989–1994: Hacia una iglesia nueva* (Tijuana, 1989), based on a survey of 22,000 Catholics.

24. See the Conferencia del Episcopado Mexicano, *Carta pastoral del encuentro con Jesucristo a la solidaridad con todos* (Mexico City: CEM, 2000).

25. For example, in 1994 there were only ninety-four members of the Mexican episcopate. Conferencia del Episcopado Mexicano, *Directorio, 1992–1994* (Mexico City: CEM, 1994).

26. This level of contact will not be maintained in the future since Mexican priests who have attended the Gregorian University since 1963 are housed exclusively in the Colegio México, removing them from direct residential contacts with other Latin American priests.

Catholic insiders are bishops who are actively involved in the Episcopate leadership and committees, contributing prominently to episcopal declarations expressing nonbinding positions on a variety of pressing issues, spiritual and pastoral. As suggested earlier in this chapter, the most influential bishops today are much older than their intellectual and political counterparts, generally a full generation's difference (approximately twenty years).

One priest who typifies the institutional Catholic insider is Cardinal Adolfo Suárez Rivera. One of the most influential bishops of his generation, Suárez Rivera was born in San Cristóbal de las Casas in the late 1920s; he attended seminary in Chiapas, and then in Jalapa, Veracruz, after which he studied in the interdiocesan seminary in Montezuma, New Mexico. He traveled to Rome in 1948, and was ordained there in 1952. After returning to San Cristóbal de las Casas in 1952, he held a number of posts as a parish priest, rising to vicar general under Bishop Samuel Ruiz in 1971. The pope appointed him bishop of Tepic, Nayarit in 1971, and nine years later, bishop of Tlanepantla, México. He joined the archdiocese of Monterrey in 1984.

Suárez Rivera served on numerous episcopate committees, and his colleagues selected him as their president in 1988 and again in 1991. He has been equally active in the Conference of the Latin American Episcopate (CELAM). His pastoral letter on civic responsibility, written while he was serving as archbishop, emerged as an episcopate-wide reference point for the official Catholic position on the democratic political transition in Mexico.[27] Suárez Rivera is respected by his colleagues for his independence and his moderate positions.[28]

The Catholic Church is topped only by the armed forces as the most institutionalized source of Mexican leadership. It allows for much greater diversity in attitudes and behavior than the officer corps. Indeed, the Vatican encyclicals of the 1960s promoted diversity by introducing numerous fresh structural and processual patterns, which were much more broadly implemented in other areas of the world than in Mexico.[29] Nevertheless,

---

27. Adolfo Suárez Rivera, "Instrucción pastoral sobre la dimensión política de la fe," Archdioceses of Monterrey, Monterrey, Nuevo León, March 1987.

28. *Cambio,* May 15, 1989, 38; Conferencia de Episcopado Mexicano, *Directorio* (Mexico: CEM, 1989), 20–22; and *Punto,* September 8, 1986, 17.

29. Daniel H. Levine, "Assessing the Impacts of Liberation Theology in Latin America," *Review of Politics,* 50 (1988), 244. In his recent work on Latin America, Paul Sigmund argues that Catholicism supports democracy and has contributed to a democratic consensus among ordinary citizens. See his "Christian Democracy,

many Mexican priests and bishops were influenced by these ideals, and the autonomy of individual dioceses and their respective bishops allowed progressive positions to found their way into many parishes throughout the country. Liberation theology even provided a grass-roots foundation for many moderate and traditional bishops who took a proactive posture on democratization and human rights in the 1980s and 1990s.[30]

No Mexican bishop in recent years has provoked as much controversy as Samuel Ruiz García, who presided over the diocese of San Cristóbal de las Casas for forty years. A product of the strongly Catholic state of Guanajuato, Ruiz came, like so many of his peers, from a practicing Catholic family, and his father, who almost joined the Cristero rebellion, was a local leader of Catholic Action, active in the Knights of Columbus, and a militant Sinarquista. But Ruiz, who accompanied his parents to work the vineyards in Colton, California, grew up in modest circumstances.[31]

After studying under the firm hand of the Sisters of the Sacred Heart in his hometown in Guanajuato, Ruiz entered the León Seminary at the age of twelve. He spent nearly ten years there, in one of Mexico's most conservative seminaries, and in 1947 was selected to accompany eleven priests to the Gregorian University in Rome. Four of those dozen students became bishops. Ruiz's formative educational experiences occurred not at the Gregorian University, but at the Pontifical Biblical Institute, where he studied sacred scripture for three years after his ordination in 1949.[32]

Returning to his home diocese in 1952, Ruiz rose from a confessor of nuns and seminary instructor to rector of the León Seminary, his alma mater, in just three years. He was appointed bishop only six years later, at the remarkably young age of thirty-six. He attended the opening session and the closure three years later of the Vatican II encyclical gatherings in Rome, which greatly influenced his thinking.[33]

Ruiz attained international prominence after the Zapatista uprising

---

Liberation Theology, and Political Culture in Latin America," in *Political Culture and Democracy in Developing Countries* (Boulder: Lynne Rienner, 1993), 329–46.

30. For background on some of these patterns, see Michael Tangeman, *Mexico at the Crossroads: Politics, the Church, and the Poor* (Maryknoll: Orbis Books, 1995).

31. Personal interview with Samuel Ruiz García, Lago de Guadalupe, Cuautitlán, Mexico, April 30, 1992.

32. Carlos Fazio, *Samuel Ruiz: El caminante* (Mexico City: Espasa, 1994).

33. *Letras Libres*, January 1999. See www:letraslibres.com.

broke out in his diocese on January 1, 1994, both as a protector of indigenous interests and as a mediator between the Ejercito Zapatista de Liberación Nacional (EZLN) and the government. As President López Portillo remarked, Ruiz (then at the midpoint of his career) would have "made a good leader of PRI."[34] Ruiz's professional trajectory as a *Catholic innovator* is similar to a new political prototype, the *provincial outsider*, represented by Vicente Fox, which will be analyzed in the next chapter. Both men demonstrate the increasing importance of the provinces as an agent of national policy debates and a source of national power elite leadership.[35] Ruiz stirred up major conflicts within the Church hierarchy and the Mexican episcopate in the same way that Vicente Fox, as a provincial outsider, stirred up divisions within the National Action Party. The Catholic renovator and the provincial outsider also have a shared ability to develop new modes of institutional action which confront the state and its relationship to the Catholic Church and political parties.

Future Catholic power elites will continue to stress their local and regional origins—this, after all, has been a pattern for decades among leading Mexican clergy. If anything, younger Mexican power elites as a whole are now moving in this direction.

Other power elite groups, most notably the military, share certain characteristics with the religious elites. The strong institutional structures, and the reinforcing organizational cultures they create, explain certain similarities. Ideological patterns in the military take less radical directions than those found within the Catholic Church, but moderate institutional reforms are producing a different set of leaders, and some of their characteristics parallel those found among other Mexican power elite groups.

Of all the power elite-producing institutions, the Mexican military has undergone the least pronounced changes in structure and leadership during the years studied here. The typical career officer during the 1970s was the *field officer*, an individual who achieved influential positions in the national defense secretariat hierarchy through field commands. No better example exists of an influential officer with these roots than division general Marcelino García Barragán, who actually fought in the revolution as an enlisted soldier before being promoted to second lieutenant in 1915. Barragán, like

34. *Cambio*, May 15, 1989, 43.
35. A point recognized in the work of Peter Ward and Victoria Rodríguez, *New Federalism and State Government in Mexico: "Bringing the States Back In"* (Austin: LBJ School of Public Affairs, University of Texas, 1999).

many of his peers who converted to the professional army after 1920, fought once again during internecine rebellions against the federal government in the mid-1920s. During the 1930s, he commanded a number of cavalry regiments. He was forced out of the army for political reasons in the 1950s, but was reinstated by President Adolfo López Mateos in 1958, after which he commanded two military zones, taking on the most influential field command in the Mexican army. The changing political situation in Mexico, the disappearance of disaffected active revolutionary officers through death and retirement, combined with increased professionalization after 1920, began to produce a new type of officer, one whose experience was largely confined to staff positions in the secretariat of national defense and at the military universities.[36]

Prominent officers who dominated the military power elite at the end of the century are *staff generals*. Most were born in the 1930s, and their parents were Mexicans of modest means. Enrique Cervantes Aguirre, Zedillo's secretary of defense, typifies this type of officer. His father was a laborer, and he began school late, when he was eight years old. He attended primary and high school, and joined the army as a cadet in 1951, at age sixteen. After graduating as a second lieutenant, he was assigned sequentially to several small units in the provinces, the typical career pattern of his generation.

Unlike García Barragán, few contemporary generals have experienced combat. Some officers (such as division general Cervantes Aquirre) began, in the 1970s and 1980s, to acquire brief combat experience in skirmishes with rural guerrillas, and more commonly during anti–drug trafficking missions.[37] A generation of younger officers has experienced short periods of combat with the EZLN and the Popular Revolutionary Army, the more active of the two leading guerrilla movements in the 1990s.

Cervantes Aguirre has spent most of his years in staff positions at the secretariat of national defense headquarters, abroad on military attaché staffs, in the military academies as an instructor and administrator, and as a department head. He held no significant field commands until he was appointed commander-in-chief of the Seventh Military Zone in Monterrey, Nuevo León, the most important northern regional command.

36. Roderic Ai Camp, *Generals in the Palacio: The Military in Modern Mexico* (New York: Oxford University Press, 1992), 196.
37. He served as chief of staff of the military zone in Guerrero during the years Lucio Cabañas was an active guerrilla fighting against the army.

The new generation of political, military, and clerical power elites are products of institutional careers, suggesting the increasing importance of organizational cultures. It is evident that while these organizations con- tributed to distinctive features among power elite groups, those same lead- ers will put their stamp on altering their organizational cultures in the future. One group of power elites who are subject to few organizational influences are capitalists; as we have seen, these elites function outside shared organizational settings. However, they do share one characteristic with highly institutionalized military elites: they remain products of sig- nificant familial influences. A father's occupational background strongly flavored the choices of these two groups, and this trend shows no sign of abating among future power elite capitalists and officers into the next mil- lennium.

Mexican capitalist power elites fall into two distinct categories: the *boot- strap* and the *global* capitalist. The older generation of Mexican capitalists came from business-oriented families but, unlike their younger peers, they started out as low-ranking employees, paying their dues until they ac- quired the capital and opportunity to create their own businesses, which they eventually turned into the leading corporations of the 1960s and 1970s. Such was the case of Cresencio Ballesteros Ibarra, whose father founded the National Irrigation Commission and was dean of the School of Engineering at the University of Guadalajara.[38]

Ballesteros Ibarra began his career as a topographical engineer for the secretariat of hydraulic resources in 1935, after graduating from his father's university. He worked on major public works projects, including the Madero Dam in the state of Hidalgo. Six years later, he and his brother founded Constructora Ballesteros, which eventually proliferated into a number of construction firms, eventually becoming the Grupo Mexicano de Desarrollo, a family-owned holding company. Ballesteros Ibarra, already a leading capitalist in 1962, helped co-found the influential Council of Mexican Businessmen. He served as president of the boards of John Deere, Union Carbide, and Mexicana Airlines, and as a board member of other leading firms, including Kimberly Clark and Industrias Luismín.[39]

Mexico's global or baby boomer capitalist is typically a child or a grand-

38. Personal interview with Cresencio Ballesteros Ibarra, Mexico City, July 26, 1984.
39. For some background, see *Expansión*, April 26, 1995, 18, 20.

child of the bootstrap capitalist. Like the staff general in the armed forces, he is a corporate insider, a person who rises up the ladder via a series of increasingly influential management positions. Unlike many self-made Mexican capitalists, this younger global capitalist is well-educated, with advanced degrees in business and engineering. The global capitalist shares this level of education abroad with members of other power elite groups. Many of these younger capitalists, similar to the technocratic prototype in the political power elite, have studied at American universities, typically at Ivy League schools. Their graduate studies in these academic programs, and their residence in the United States, contributed to some shared networking and socialization experiences.

This new generation recognized the globalization of the economy and capitalized on their linkages with North American and European firms.[40] That has affected the structure of corporate organizations, especially among influential holding companies in Monterrey. Capitalist owners have handed over the direct management of these firms to professional management while retaining control over corporate boards. "The cumulative effect of these multiple changes within the Mexican private sector was the emergence and consolidation of a corporate, northern-oriented, outward-looking, multinationally linked, big business elite."[41]

No individual better represents this generation than Dioniso Garza Medina, great-grandson of the leading scion of the Monterrey industrial families. He was raised in Monterrey, and his father was the long-time general manager of Empaques de Cartón Titán, one of the Monterrey Group's original flagship companies. Dionisio Garza Medina went abroad to obtain a B.A. and M.A. in industrial engineering from Stanford University, followed by an M.B.A. from Harvard University.

In 1979, he began his career as projects subdirector at ALFA, one of Mexico's most influential holding companies, which was directed by his uncle. He gradually rose up the corporate ladder in ALFA, departing in 1987 to take over from his father as director general of Empaques de Cartón Titán. Seven years later, he replaced his uncle as CEO of ALFA, in 1994 the second largest industrial corporation in Mexico. In the

40. Many global capitalists are purchasing shares in major U.S. companies. Carlos Slim Helú, a capitalist power elite, bought 6 percent of Circuit City Stores, Inc., in March 2001. Martha McNeil Hamilton, "Mexico's Slim Buys Stake in Circuit City," *Washington Post*, March 13, 2001, www.washingtonpost.com.

41. Strom C. Thacker, *Big Business, the State, and Free Trade* (Cambridge: Cambridge University Press, 2000), 99–100.

1990s, he entered into joint ventures with ATT, Shaw Industries, and Payless Cashways.[42]

Each sector in Mexican society has produced, and will continue producing, leaders with distinctive qualities, molded by their own unique professional settings and reinforced through residential, familial, and educational experiences at home and abroad. Despite the distinctive qualities that set each leadership group apart, Mexicans who guided their society through the last decades of the twentieth century shared certain features.

The centralization of Mexican politics, culture, and economic infrastructure reinforced the importance of a small, select number of urban centers as the residence, and to a lesser degree, the birthplace, of that century's leadership. The rapid demographic shift during the past century, and the concentration of cultural, economic, and institutional resources in a few urban centers, facilitated and reinforced a tendency favoring power elites. The concentration of these power elite prototypes in Mexico City, Monterrey, and Guadalajara contributed to the importance and continuation of informal networking processes, accentuating the impact of mentors, many of whom were members of the older generation of power elites.

Changing residential patterns among power elites was complemented by an even more striking change, the disappearance of leaders from working-class backgrounds. Two characteristics help to explain this pattern. First, as I have demonstrated, higher socioeconomic family backgrounds increase the potential for access to influential mentors, either through the family itself, as is the case for capitalists, or through their professional contacts, as in the intellectual and political worlds. Children from working-class families have less access to potentially influential mentors.

Second, as each of these power elite circles raised the bar of formal credentials necessary for successful achievement in their respective areas, they decreased the likelihood that children from working-class families would be able to meet those requirements. The clearest measure of those achievements in Mexico is formal education, and advanced levels of education crosses all power elite circles. The officer corps and the clergy provided greater access than other groups to children of families from modest

---

42. *El Financiero* (international edition), January 2, 1995, 14–15; *Mexico Business*, September, 1996, 37, and *Forbes*, July 18, 1994, 195.

circumstances because they automatically incorporated living expenses and education into their core structures. Among all groups, however, the overall trend favored the middle and upper-middle classes.

The continued importance of family as a source of mentors and recruitment for Mexico's power elite is remarkable, given the growing trend toward institutionalization. As several of the case studies illustrate, organizational cultures do not automatically exclude the influence of non-institutional mentors. The narrowness of the pool from which future Mexican power elites are drawn, and the fact that mentors and future elites often emerge from the same pools, helps to explain the integration between informal and formal sources of networking, recruitment, and socialization.

The generational divide between power elites who maintained the incremental features of Mexican political and economic development in the 1960s and 1970s and those who began fomenting change by the mid-1980s is dramatic. The older generation of power elites was exposed to historical experiences incorporating civil violence, political instability, and economic nationalism. The socializing influences of those experiences produced leaders who were afraid of significantly changing the political and economic model. It also produced leaders who were suspicious of the United States and unreceptive to its political development strategies. Relatively few members of this older generation shared educational experiences abroad, which might have exposed them to alternative economic and political institutions.

The younger generation of power elites, as I have suggested, came of age in an entirely different set of historical circumstances. In Mexico, they witnessed the declining efficacy of the political model, represented most notably by the events of 1968, as well as repeated economic crises. Some of their knowledge of these events was acquired outside Mexico.

Ironically, the importance of social inequalities was brought home in the strongest terms to religious elites, as Catholic theology, even within the confines of a relatively unprogressive episcopate by region-wide standards, absorbed the influence of Vatican II encyclicals and incorporated elements into mainstream Catholicism. At the same time, the failures of the Mexican state to achieve consistent economic growth after 1970, and its antagonistic treatment of the private sector, alienated individuals within the capitalist class, prompting them to redefine their relationship to the government.

The older generation of political elites sought to maintain the status quo by introducing modest electoral changes beginning in the 1960s, allowing opposition parties limited representation in the political system. As support for incumbent leadership slowly waned, they continued to expand political participation in increasingly sophisticated ways, developing formulas for the presence of those forces, but structuring them to favor PRI's dominance. Nevertheless, they opened the door to greater opposition and legitimized political pluralization.

Those incremental changes led to an important shift in elite attitudes. A significant minority within the incumbent political power elite, a vocal group of opposition party leaders, an increasingly proactive and vociferous group of bishops, and numerous leading intellectuals all engaged in an active campaign in support of clean elections. These younger elites favored democratization from within and outside the political model. A smaller, less influential group of businessmen, often related by family ties to Mexico's most powerful capitalists, also joined this battle for increased participation, and began supporting opposition parties financially, typically the PAN.[43]

The youngest generation among the officer corps, many of whom had also witnessed the events of 1968 and had fought in the anti-guerrilla campaigns in the 1970s, also began questioning the government's competence, but did so privately. Historically subordinated to civilian authority, they expressed their dissatisfaction with the political leadership in the decision-making process, where they demanded and received a larger voice and increased visibility in national security.[44] They made it clear after 1988 that they would support the popular vote in a fair election for a presidential candidate from any of the leading parties, thus legitimizing the evolving electoral system.

A narrower group of power elites from a younger generation were also responsible for the changing economic strategy which characterized Mexican policy after 1982. These Mexicans, represented by the technocrats in the political leadership, and by the younger global capitalists in the capitalist power elite, chose to decentralize state economic control, to increase competition, and to pursue global strategies.[45] Almost without exception,

43. Yemile Mizrahi, "La nueva relación entre los empresarios y el gobierno: El surgimiento de los empresarios panistas," *Estudios Sociológicos*, 14 (1996), 493–515.

44. Eric L. Olson, "The Evolving Role of Mexico's Military in Public Security and Antinarcotics Programs," Washington, D.C., Washington Office on Latin America, May 1996, 4.

45. For detailed evidence and their international alliances, see Angelina Gutiérrez Arriola, "Reflexiones sobre la reestructuración del capital y del trabajo en México," *Problemas del Desarrollo*, 26, no. 101 (April/June 1995), 173–204.

every individual in the political and economic leadership who advocated such a global economic strategy completed graduate training in the United States. That economic philosophy predominated in the economics and business administration departments of the prestigious universities they attended.

It is apparent that a confluence of experiences contributed to these profound generational changes in Mexican political and economic policies. Power elites played an essential role in facilitating these changes and, in the case of economic policy, these elites contributed to the speed with which they occurred. On the political liberalization front, young power elites were more strongly divided, with the majority of incumbent political leadership adamantly opposed to rapid pluralization. President Zedillo, even though he came from the technocratic wing, helped to break down that barrier, frequently shifting the balance of power to a younger group of incumbent reformers.

In spite of these extraordinary changes, the younger generation of leaders lost sight of a fundamental issue in Mexico: social and economic inequality. A careful examination of the public statements of Mexican leadership, with the exception of the clergy, demonstrates that power elites placed inequality on a back burner. Indeed, a strong case can be made that the older generation spoke to this issue much more directly, as represented by Luis Echeverría Alvarez, who believed the state and state economic control were the most effective tools for achieving greater economic and social equality and increasing the distribution of wealth. Echeverría even publicly associated himself with leading progressive Mexican clergy, such as Bishop Sergio Méndez Arceo, who introduced the principles of liberation theology, with its emphasis on the poor and on human rights, in his diocese and elsewhere in Mexico. Outside of the clergy, the visible spokesperson among the power elite on this issue was Cuauhtémoc Cárdenas, but he is from an older generation.

A significant question remains: Why did a younger generation, attuned to the need for reforms in the Mexican economic and political arenas, ignore this issue? Advocates of neoliberal economic policies focused on the issue of economic growth, not on redistribution.[46] They assumed that gaps

46. Miguel Szekely notes that neoliberal economic policies, at least through 1992, produced both progressive and regressive consequences. Overall, however, the results have led to a decline in income distribution and an increase in concentration of control over resources. See his "Aspectos de la desigualdad en México," *El Trimestre Económico*, 62, no. 246 (April/June 1995), 201–43.

in the distribution of wealth would be closed through natural, trickle-down effects resulting from sustained economic growth.[47] In their search for stable economic growth, they set aside an emphasis on resolving economic inequalities. Politicians had traditionally viewed the Mexican state as an arbiter among class social and economic interests. But younger generations viewed the state as the fundamental obstacle to growth, and economic policymakers did not provide a structural substitute, even in the form of an extensive progressive fiscal system which would complement their economic growth strategies. Leading capitalists contributed little to altering this view, having rarely incorporated a concept of social responsibility toward economically active Mexicans into their entrepreneurial mission.[48]

There are three possible explanations for this lack of attention to inequality. The under-representation of humble social origins among Mexico's power elite, especially among younger generations of intellectuals and politicians, who typically would be the most influential advocates of social policies, may be a contributing factor. As suggested earlier, no empirical evidence exists to support the notion that social class background directly determines elite policy preferences. But it is difficult to argue that personal experiences have not sensitized future elites to emphasize specific social issues. Interviews with Mexican bishops from modest circumstances, and bishops who eventually lived in the poorest dioceses, demonstrate unequivocally that those experiences influenced their social views on poverty. It is also apparent among Mexico's political and intellectual leadership that those who emphasize this issue in their ideology and writings, especially rural poverty, often come from modest circumstances.

The second explanation is that a younger generation, typically without any firsthand experiences with poverty, obtained their theoretical views of economic development from academic settings in the United States.

47. In a series of essays, Diana Alarcón González and Terry McKinley have shown that absolute poverty increased in Mexico from 1984 to 1989. See, for example, their "A Poverty Profile of Mexico in 1989," *Frontera Norte*, 6 (1994), 141–54. Very little change has occurred since 1994. According to Banamex, as of 2000, the poorest 20 percent of Mexico's households accounted for 4 percent of generated income (4.4 percent in 1994, 3.8 percent in 1996, and 4.2 percent in 1998), while the richest 20 percent of households account for more than 50 percent of the total (54.5 percent in 1994, 52.4 percent in 1996, and 54.1 percent in 1998). *Review of the Economic Situation of Mexico*, 76 (October 2000), 418.

48. In a survey sponsored by the Inter-American Development Bank, that task ranked last on a list of potential goals. See Jorge Camerena and Pablo Lasso, *Hacia un estilo propio de dirección de empresas: Proyecto piloto, Guadalajara, México* (Washington, D.C.: IADB, 1984), 60.

Though it has serious problems with poverty, the United States is characterized by less inequality than Mexico, by a substantially larger middle class, and by a progressive fiscal system. Many influential Mexicans accepted the underlying theoretical explanations for increasing the role of capitalism without giving the same degree of consideration to the impact on this strategy of the general setting in the United States and its more progressive taxation system.

The final explanation is that, at the high point of their influence, the technocrats– especially under President Salinas–decreased the number of actors participating in the decision-making process. As Sidney Weintraub recently concluded from a detailed analysis of Mexico's economic crisis in 1994–95, government economists had formed "a habit of *top-down decision-making*," had automatically kept "the group small," had consciously excluded dissenters, and had arrogantly believed little need existed for national debates on economic policy.[49] Influential Mexicans who stressed the necessity of redistributive goals were not given the opportunity to express their criticisms within power elite policy circles.

49. Sidney Weintraub, *Financial Decision-Making in Mexico: To Bet a Nation* (Pittsburgh: University of Pittsburgh Press, 2000), 167–68.

11 Power Elites in the Twenty-First Century
Consequences of New Leadership

The end of the year 2000, and the inauguration of Vicente Fox, marked the culmination of the political and economic trends in Mexico since the mid-1980s. The beginning of a new century does not promise the creation of a different leadership from the end of the last century; rather it suggests that certain types of power elites who achieved prominence in the last two decades are likely to expand their numbers in the first decades of the present century.

Power elites enjoy a healthy and vigorous influence as Mexico welcomes the twenty-first century. They have not declined in importance. In fact, as the preceding chapters illustrate, they were crucial actors in transforming Mexico politically and economically. Not all of these groups were equally active, but all five played an essential role in the process, each responding to different constituencies.

These five power elite groups played their respective roles because of the existing structures of society, the characteristics of the political model, and the qualities of the institutional cultures, all of which determined many other relationships. The Mexican state's semi-authoritarian qualities, and its relationship to such power elite groups as intellectuals, clergy, and capitalists, affected their behavior in transforming Mexican society in the 1990s. It also affected the hidden role of the armed forces, which could have vetoed incumbent leadership or altered its new-found directions during times of crisis.

There is no question but that limited pluralism in many facets of Mexican society has accentuated the importance of elites. What is changing in the 2000s is not the influence of power elites but the composition thereof, as societal influences which elites themselves set into motion alter the pools from which power elites are drawn. Different social and political patterns will also alter the nature of the influence they exercise.

The second fundamental theme which this book has addressed is the unique role of mentors among power elites, and their impact on major transformations in Mexican society. What little research that exists on mentors elsewhere has largely viewed them as gatekeepers and recruiters in their respective professions. That, indeed, is a crucial task. But mentors have exerted far greater influence on the Mexican political and economic landscape.

Mexican mentors' longer-term influence is evident in their molding of disciples' attitudes and professional values. Even more interesting, they have crafted the organizational cultures in which various power elites operate, and will continue to function in this way in subsequent decades. Mentors have been fundamental in steering their disciples toward certain institutions. These institutions often were educational, whether they functioned inside the elite group's institutional structure, such as the clergy, or operated outside of the elite's organizational apparatus.

Informal networking is a way of life in Mexico, and it is an ingrained behavior among elites. The fact that a huge majority of Mexico's influential decision makers have been mentored by other influential decision makers contributes an incestuous quality to Mexican leadership, providing additional sources of homogeneity.

What this book demonstrates, however, is that mentors are crucial actors in traditional networking activities, and as they encounter important niches within organizations, they often use their positions to advance the credentials, values, and career possibilities of their disciples. They achieve long-term influences on other elites through their contributions to imbuing certain values within their respective organizational settings.

This chapter highlights those representative prototypes of the power elite who will dominate in the immediate future and who will mentor the next generation. I will describe what they represent and, most importantly, suggest their consequences for Mexico's future. Drawing comparisons across each of the power elite groups indicates that some groups represent a well-defined shift in elite leadership, while others can claim only modest differences from their predecessors.

It is logical to explore political leadership first. Political power elites deserve this attention because incumbent politicians, and their opponents, whatever their overriding characteristics, have initiated recent dramatic economic and political transformations, even though these changes would not have occurred without the other four leadership groups' participation.

Contrary to the expectations of most analysts, who only recently viewed the technocrat as the dominant Mexican political figure for years to come, a hybrid politician emerged from the new and the old in the late 1990s: a pragmatic political-technocrat of the future. This *hybrid politico* shares characteristics with the traditional politician born before 1941 and also with the technocrat from the younger power elite. The hybrid politico too comes from an urban environment, more often than not from the Federal District, but increasingly from the provinces. The parents of this hybrid politician, who have produced most politicians in the last century, are still likely to be part of Mexico's professional middle class.

The hybrid politico, however, reintroduces five important features that characterized Mexican politicians prior to 1970: they were born in the provinces; they have career experience at the state level; they have experience in the party; they have held elective office; and they are bureaucratic generalists, having directed political and economic agencies.

The PRI's presidential candidate for 2000, Francisco Labastida Ochoa, epitomizes this new hybrid politician. Born in the port town of Los Mochis, Sinaloa, on Mexico's northwest coast, Labastida came to Mexico City with his parents, attending private primary school at the Colegio Madrid. Labastida, like most technocrats, obtained a college degree in economics, but he attended the National University, not a private undergraduate institution.

Labastida joined the PRI in 1960, while still a student at UNAM; he took his first government job in the treasury secretariat as an analyst before graduating. Labastida worked in five different federal agencies before reaching cabinet rank in 1982. In 1976, he established a close professional relationship with Miguel de la Madrid. His government career from 1964 to 1982 —with the exception of the 1975–76 presidential campaign, during which he served in a party post—follows a typical technocratic pattern, with posts primarily in economic agencies.

Unlike Pedro Aspe and his technocratic peers, Labastida emulated a pattern more typical of politicians in the 1960s and 1970s, who used their national posts to achieve elective office as state governors, and then used their gubernatorial experiences to return to cabinet positions. Labastida left the cabinet in 1986, serving as governor of his home state for six years.

Younger hybrid politicos in the twenty-first century are also likely to have been born outside the capital. Governorships will become increasingly important among all political power elites, as they are currently in the United States as stepping stones to national political office. Mexico's three leading presidential contenders in 2000 were governors, and two of them resigned their positions to become their party's candidate. In Spain, which underwent an earlier democratic transformation, large provincial cities also have begun producing important national figures.[1]

The competitiveness of the political system in Mexico since 1988 ensures that the dominant and opposition parties will produce candidates who have electoral experience, either in Congress or as state governors, have campaign experience with their parties, and come increasingly outside of Mexico City, even if they have lived in the capital as adults.

The hybrid politico also alters the technocratic pattern found among the post-1941 political elite of careers concentrated in executive branch agencies responsible for economic policy. He replicates the generalist qualities found among older politicians, but combines those qualities with educational and professional credentials in economics. Labastida, for example, spent fourteen years as governor of Sinaloa and director of three unrelated cabinet-level agencies, one of which was the most influential political post, secretary of government.

The hybrid politico prototype, however, represents a generational change in the last three decades among only those power elite politicians who have come from the PRI. A different type of political power elite, one who might well become the most influential figure in the 2000s, is the new provincial politician representing other leading parties, including the new incumbent party, PAN. This individual too shares certain characteristics with the hybrid politicos from the PRI, and is taking over national, executive branch posts.

These *provincial outsiders*, as their name implies, were born in the provinces. But unlike so many of the hybrid politicos, they have never lived in the Federal District. Their socializing experiences, networking sources, and mentors, therefore, are strongly shaped by regional geography and provincial institutions. They too are college graduates and, like many of their national government peers, they are increasingly products

1. They were Labastida, Vicente Fox, who served as governor of Guanajuato, and Cuauhtémoc Cárdenas, who became the first elected head of the Federal District. This position is often referred to as mayor by U.S. analysts, but that is not an accurate translation. The elected head of the Federal District is a region which encompasses more than Mexico City proper. Also, it is second only to México state as the most populous entity in Mexico, thus having the second largest number of congressional districts. For patterns in Spain see Irene Delgado, "Las elites políticas en España: Adecuación representativa en los niveles de gobierno," *Perfiles Latinoamericanos*, 6 (December 1997), 133–34.

of private schools, but more typically schools located outside the national capital.

The provincial outsiders can also be distinguished from their national government colleagues in that they are not career politicians, having earned their living in a professional occupation or in business. They join political parties as mature adults, becoming involved in local politics, typically in city government. These individuals, after successful stints as mayors, often compete successfully as gubernatorial candidates.

This new breed of politician, and possibly also a new kind of PRI politico, are products of a sea change in the Mexican polity. As Alonso Lujambio demonstrated in a recent study, in just ten years—from 1988 through 1998—the percentage of the Mexican population living under non-PRI-controlled municipal governments increased fifteen-fold, from only 3 to 50 percent.[2] The importance of party competition and pluralism at the local and state levels created a logical demand for a new type of political figure, one whose characteristics are gradually extending to political power elites at the national level.

Like the hybrid politicos, these outsiders are changing the face of non-PRI political leadership (which has traditionally come from Mexico City), using the national Congress and national party bureaucracies as their source of political influence. The rise of the provincial outsider suggests the importance of grass-roots politics and the revival of political influence among Mexican states, which have become more politically and financially autonomous since 1994.[3] The success of Vicente Fox in defeating orthodox opposition politicians for the National Action Party presidential nomination, and his success as a presidential candidate, highlights the importance of these qualities and ensures their continuation after 2000.

Illustrative of this power elite prototype is the career of Ernesto Ruffo Appel, the first member of an opposition party to win a governorship in Mexico since the PRI's founding in 1929. The descendant of Italian, Irish, and German immigrants, Ruffo's family lived for generations on the Baja California peninsula, and his father moved to Ensenada in 1940 to work in the fish packing industry. Ruffo attended school in Ensenada and, like

2. It doubled from 1995 to 1997, from 24 to 49 percent. See *Diario de Yucatán*, November 22, 1999, at www:yucatan.com.mx.
3. For evidence of this, see the most comprehensive study on the consequences of federalism in the 1990s: Peter M. Ward and Victoria E. Rodríguez, *New Federalism and State Government in Mexico: Bringing the States Back In* (Austin: LBJ School of Public Affairs, University of Texas, 1999).

many border children whose parents want them to learn English, studied for a year in San Diego, California, before attending preparatory school and college.[4] He graduated in accounting and business administration from the Higher Technological Institute of Monterrey—the institution, as demonstrated in chapter 7, that has produced many of Mexico's leading capitalists. He followed his father into the fishing industry, and held several management posts before joining the PAN in 1983.

After heading the local chapter of COPARMEX, a leading politically active business organization, he captured the mayor's office of Ensenada on the PAN ticket in 1986. His successful term as governor of his home state provided PAN with the opportunity to elect its second consecutive governor of Baja California, a nationwide first in the twentieth century. Fox appointed him to head border affairs in his cabinet.

It is interesting that intellectuals, the other group of power elites deeply involved in political liberalization, should also be characterized by two new prototypes who are likely to dominate the secular cultural world in the twenty-first century. This is not surprising, since political and economic changes have produced an environment in which intellectuals can extract themselves from their traditional dependence on the state, increasing the possibilities for different intellectual prototypes.

The newer, younger intellectual prototype with the greatest potential influence in the first decades of this century is the *private intellectual*. This private intellectual can trace its roots to members of the previous generation like Daniel Cosío Villegas; while he never actually held public office (he served briefly as an economic adviser to treasury in the 1920s), Cosío Villegas directed numerous publicly supported cultural institutions. He was a cultural entrepreneur who believed in the importance of creating cultural enterprises to employ intellectuals and to support their activities.[5] In the 1930s he co-founded the Fondo de Cultura Económica, a leading publishing firm, *El Trimestre Económico*, the first significant economics journal, and El Colegio de México, an elite college in the social sciences.

One of Cosío Villegas' protégés, Enrique Krauze, extended certain aspects of his mentor's agenda, but linked his career more closely to the private, not the public, sector. Krauze, a graduate of the Colegio de México's Ph.D. program whose ancestors were Polish Jews who emigrated to

4. Letter to the author from Ernesto Ruffo Appel, May 14, 1997.
5. Enrique Krauze, "Daniel Cosío Villegas: El empresario cultural," *Plural*, 5, no. 55 (April 1976), 7–17.

Mexico, was born and raised in the capital, attending a Jewish school until he enrolled in the National Preparatory School with a generation of other important intellectuals and politicians in the early 1960s. His grandfather, a successful tailor, included Maximino Avila Camacho, the president's brother, as a regular client.[6] Unlike most of his intellectual peers, he graduated from the National University with a degree in engineering, preparing him technically for his father's business in commercial printing.

Throughout his career, Krauze operated his own business, which gave him a degree of financial and intellectual independence atypical of his cultural peers. After Cosío Villegas's death in 1976, Krauze became a protégé of Nobel prize–winning poet and essayist Octavio Paz; he became managing editor of Paz's *Vuelta*, which established itself as a leading Mexican intellectual journal, alongside *Nexos*.[7] Krauze, who has mixed his intellectual endeavors with commercial success, used the publishing world and the electronic media, namely Televisa, to broaden the reach of his historical interpretations, a strategy that offended some of his peers. The private intellectuals of the twenty-first century will not necessarily run their own businesses, as has Krauze, but they will be increasingly employed by, and have stronger ties to, the private rather than the public sector.

The private intellectual shares some characteristics with members of other power elite circles. The political provincial outsider and the private intellectual both suggest the importance of decentralizing influences in the political and cultural worlds in the 1990s and 2000s. The wresting of political control from a single party and its elite, and the declining control of the state over cultural life have all engendered the emergence of increasingly autonomous actors in the political and intellectual worlds. These shifts have had similar—although not as well delineated—consequences for capitalist, military, and religious power elites.

Intellectuals—both public and private—share some qualities with a third type of cultural power elite, the *international intellectual*. This cultural leader has developed a special hybrid quality differing from his typical Mexican peers. A number of leading Mexican intellectuals in recent decades have bridged the distance between Mexico and the United States and

6. Personal interview with Enrique Krauze, Mexico City, June 19, 1989. Krauze describes his grandfather's encounter with the general, in the tailor's own words, in his *Mexico: Biography of Power, A History of Modern Mexico, 1810–1996* (New York: HarperCollins, 1997), 498.

7. Pilar Jiménez Trejo and Alejandro Toledo, *Creación y poder: Nueve retratos de intelectuales* (Mexico City: Contrapuntos, 1994), 39 ff.

have established many academic and NGO networks in the United States, frequently writing for audiences in leading American newspapers and in academia.

Most international intellectuals live in Mexico, but a few have lived abroad for extended periods. Carlos Fuentes, an early example of this type, not only received much of his education abroad but spent a large part of his life in the United States and Europe—to such an extent, in fact, that his absence from Mexico has estranged some of his colleagues. A younger version of Fuentes is Jorge G. Castañeda, who has known Fuentes for many years. Castañeda combines many of the traditional qualities of leading Mexican intellectuals, but with the added element of being an international figure. Like most leading intellectuals, he is the product, in part, of an upbringing in Mexico City, and has dabbled directly in politics, first as an active member of the Communist Party in 1978 and then as an adviser to the secretariat of foreign relations on Central American and Caribbean affairs in 1980.

Unlike his colleagues, most of whom live in Mexico and maintain strong ties to various communities in the United States, Castañeda has spent much of his life outside Mexico, beginning with his elementary schooling in New York and Egypt, then an undergraduate degree from Princeton, and then five years of study at the Sorbonne. Even when he completed his secondary and preparatory studies in Mexico City in the late 1960s, it was at the French Lycee, subsidized by the French government.[8] Castañeda obtained an appointment as a political science professor at UNAM in 1982, but he has held numerous positions on fellowships and as a visiting professor at U.S. institutions, and since 1998 has held a permanent position at New York University.[9] He engaged in public affairs directly by frequently testifying before the U.S. Senate and by writing editorials in leading American magazines and newspapers. Cognizant of the importance of contemporary mediums of communication, Castañeda is one of the few members of the Mexican power elite to have a personal website.

It is difficult to say whether or not Castañeda's example will be followed by subsequent generations. Most international intellectuals remain in Mexico and conduct their primary activities in Mexico; some leave Mexico altogether, taking up permanent academic posts in the United States. It is not likely that future intellectuals will be able to live abroad while remaining influential in their own societies.

8. Personal letter from Jorge G. Castañeda, January 26, 2000.
9. *Contemporary Authors*, 144, 69–70.

Intellectuals like Castañeda also suggest another potential trend among leading cultural figures: political activism. In the past, many Mexican intellectuals were employed by the state. In the 1990s, some intellectuals interested in promoting democratization were at the forefront of opposition to the incumbent party, either through affiliations with other political parties or through non-governmental civic organizations.[10] Castañeda, for example, was a close adviser to Vicente Fox during his campaign, and Fox appointed him to his cabinet as secretary of foreign relations.

The new era of electoral competition that signaled Vicente Fox's victory may steer a new generation of intellectuals into the private arena because the need for direct political involvement may seem less urgent. Or, the new pluralism may result in the spread of politically ambitious intellectuals among many parties, several of which have realistic possibilities for achieving national political offices.

Among leading bishops, the religious counterparts of Mexico's secular intellectuals, there is no such clear a demarcation between older and younger elites. This lack of clarity can be explained, in part, by Catholic structures, which impose institutional values on their members, in contrast to the autonomy which secular intellectuals enjoy. While it is difficult to identify a new Catholic power elite prototype, certain trends are emerging.

What may well distinguish leading clergy in the future is a decline in the numbers of younger priests who have studied in Rome or who have completed only their undergraduate degrees abroad, complemented by an increased emphasis on Mexican regional diocesan seminaries and training. If regional Mexican seminary education becomes an established, exclusive pattern among power elite bishops as distinct from all bishops, it could produce several interesting trends.

First, regional education reinforces a generally conservative socialization found in most existing Mexican seminaries. Second, it reduces contacts between Mexican and other future bishops from Latin America and the United States, which has often been the source of progressive Catholic theological and pastoral interpretations. Third, it raises the potential for greater ideological divergence within the elite Catholic clergy, since future bishops are not as likely to undergo a shared theological training abroad. Such a development would mirror a similar trend among an influential group of Mexican political power elites in the 2000s.

The youngest member of the religious power elite, Norberto Rivera

10. For example, Sergio Aguayo, long-time human rights leader, ran as a congressional candidate of one of the smaller parties in 2000.

Carrera, who as the prelate of Mexico City's archdiocese is the youngest cardinal in Latin America, embodies some of these potential trends. Born in the village of La Purísima, Durango, Rivera Carrera completed his philosophy training at the Durango seminary, one of Mexico's most conservative, before obtaining his theology degree from the Gregorian University. Unlike most of his predecessors, he has no graduate training, but returned to his home diocese to teach and to serve as a parish priest. As bishop of Tehuacán, Puebla, he closed down the last liberation theology seminary in Mexico in 1990.[11] Since becoming archbishop of Mexico in 1995, Rivera Carrera became an outspoken critic of the government and an advocate of raising Catholicism's visibility in public life. He urged politicians to "express their faith openly" as a true sign of religious and political freedom.[12]

Because they view themselves as directly representing the Mexican laity, consisting of the vast majority of Mexicans, religious elites have increasingly stepped outside their internal institution roles and involved themselves in secular public affairs. Their closest institutional counterpart among the power elites, the armed forces, has not made a similar transition. One of the explanations for this important difference is that the officer corps represents the state, not individual Mexican citizens. Second, their organizational pattern is much more structured, hierarchical, and centralized in the national defense ministry than that of the individual bishop in his diocese. Third, given the military's modus vivendi with civilian political leaders, top officers essentially operate under a permanent gag order.

Vicente Fox's victory, and its reinforcement of the increasing pluralizing influences occurring at all levels of society, affected the closed nature of the Mexican armed forces at the end of the twentieth century. A younger generation of officers, born in the 1940s, will take command in the 2000s, building on the credentials favoring the *staff general* prototype. Almost universally they will have studied and trained in the United States, and furthered their own professional training with the equivalent of an M.A. in national security from a staff school in the United States, the Inter-

11. *Proceso*, June 19, 1995, 31–34. Ironically, among the founders of this seminary was his predecessor, Cardinal Ernesto Corripio Ahumada, and bishops Samuel Ruiz, Bartolomé Carrasco Briseño, and Arturo Lona Reyes, all members of the religious power elite.

12. "El Cardenal Norberto Rivera subraya que en una sociedad pluralista se necesita una verdadera libertad religiosa," *Diario de Yucatán*, November 6, 2000. www.yucatan.com.mx.

American Defense Board in Washington, D.C., or from the National Defense College in Mexico City.[13]

The staff general prototype shares important characteristics with Mexican religious and political power elites. The staff general has relied heavily on two institutional experiences: important positions inside the defense bureaucracy and teaching assignments in military academies. Top Catholic bishops, regardless of whether they represent the *Catholic insider*, the less common *Catholic innovator*, or a twenty-first-century version of the Catholic insider, will continue following well-established career paths inside the diocese, including many years as seminary instructors and administrators. The *technocrat*, a prototype in decline, also spent his entire career inside of the public bureaucracy and devoted considerable time to part- or full-time college teaching.

What qualities does this new power elite contribute to Mexico as it embarks on a new century? How will these qualities affect the continuation of power elites, and their mentoring, networking, recruitment, and socialization? And what consequences will these new leaders have on Mexican leadership and on significant policy issues? Some of the conditions which led to specific generational characteristics in the recent past will remain, whereas others are already in the midst of radical change.

One of the significant patterns in the last century which affected power elites and their mentors was the pace of Mexican urbanization. Demographic patterns favoring urbanization are not likely to change in the twenty-first century. What is changing, and what will have an impact on leadership, are the structural political and economic patterns introduced by members of the power elite. As pluralization gains a significant foothold in the Mexican political fabric and civil society, it shifts the focus of politics away from Mexico City to state and local governments, and from national to local organizations. It also shifts the focus of other policy issues away from the national government and, most specifically, away from the executive branch.

In the political arena, governorships have become the jumping-off point for national reputations as the major opposition parties have captured an increasing number of statehouses. The PAN and PRI have not been immune to these influences. For the party loyalist who has presidential political ambitions, holding an elective office is becoming essential. Congress-

13. The youngest military officer in the sample who reached three-star rank or its equivalent was born in 1937 (nearly fifteen years older than President Zedillo).

persons and governors who serve in the cabinet will be the likely source of their party's future leadership.

The importance of governors to the political power elite and to future political recruitment can only be carried so far. The mitigating structural condition limiting their influence now that their political autonomy from the center has been achieved is the fact that governors, and therefore states, remain heavily dependent on the revenue distributed by the federal government. Even with an increase in the state's share resulting from opposition pressure in the 1997–2000 Congress, states still receive less than 20 percent of the revenues. President Fox has made it clear that he will further revise this revenue distribution pattern in favor of states and local governments.[14]

If the Fox administration succeeds in reallocating federal revenues to state and local governments, this will have reverberations on producing future power elites and on reinforcing the importance of the provinces. The clearest change in leadership, because it is already symbolized by Fox himself, is among political power elites. But the allocation of financial resources has long-term implications for strengthening educational institutions in the provinces, thus increasing their role as sources of networking and socialization for future Mexican leaders, as well as for enhancing cultural institutions, providing a more supportive environment for independent intellectuals outside Mexico City.

A second political pattern which emerges after 2000 has to do with decentralizing decision-making authority at the national level, rather than between the national and local authorities. As Peter Ward and Victoria Rodríguez argue, the policy battles in the next decade will be fought between the federal legislative and executive branches.[15] The reason for this is that President Zedillo, and now President Fox, have increasingly transferred greater responsibilities to the legislative branch. Equally important, the executive branch does not control Congress, nor does any single party. As Mexican analysts have suggested, "the panorama in Congress represents formidable challenges for the new government and the PAN, including continuous negotiating aimed at building majorities, which will require a constant exchange of benefits and commitments with the opposition par-

14. Governors requested in late 2000 that the federal budget of 2001 transfer Mexico's poverty program funds, including Progresa, to state and local governments, and to increase the portion of federal revenues to the states to 23 percent. *Diario de Yucatán*, November 10, 2000, www.yucatan.com.mx.

15. Peter Ward and Victoria Rodríguez, *New Federalism and State Government in Mexico*, 169.

ties, mainly PRI and the PRD."[16] Thus, the give and take that is part of the ideal of democratic competition will characterize the culture of the national legislative branch, and its relationship with the executive, in the next few years. Committee chairs and party leaders in Congress will emerge as significant voices in the Mexican polity.

A complementary trend with equally significant consequences is the rapid growth in non-governmental organizations, especially on the local level. This phenomenal change since the mid-1980s creates a fertile ground for what Mike Mazaar identified as "new authorities."[17] Leaders of these organizations are found within the cultural and political power elites.[18] These new institutions generate opportunities for fresh actors who have developed their skills in the give-and-take environment typical of civic and interest group organizations emerging at the local and national levels. This is illustrated in a remarkable way by the Amigos de Fox, a hybrid political and civic organization which did not even exist before 1998, yet which helped Fox more than double PAN partisan support in his presidential victory two years later.[19]

The only group of power elites already focused on regional issues are the bishops, who have long been sensitive to issues in their immediate geographic constituency, the diocese. Although they are part of a larger centralized structure extending beyond Mexico's national boundaries, the central unit of their organizational life is the diocese, which is often molded by a bishop's personality and preferences. They also share a connection to local NGOs, since ordinary Mexican citizens are most likely to belong to a religious organization than any other type of group.[20]

---

16. *Review of the Economic Situation of Mexico,* 76 (October 2000), 414.

17. Michael J. Mazaar, *Mexico 2005: The Challenges of the New Millennium* (Washington, D.C.: CSIS, 1999), 95.

18. The most influential example in the 1990s is the San Angel group. As Vicente Fox recently admitted, during the meetings of the San Angel group in Mexico City, "I discovered that National Action alone was not fighting for a democratic advance in Mexico." Such figures as Adolfo Aguilar Zinser, Jorge Castañeda, Carlos Fuentes, Santiago Creel, and Alejandro Gertz belonged to this group. The first three are members of the intellectual power elite, and all but Fuentes held cabinet-level posts in 2001. "Tensiones, diferencias y recelos entre Fox y el PAN," *Proceso,* July 16, 2000, www.proceso.com.mx; and *Mexico Business,* January/February 2001, 38.

19. Roderic Ai Camp, "Citizen Attitudes toward Democracy and Fox's Victory in 2000," paper presented at Mexico's National Election Conference, Weatherhead Center for International Affairs, Harvard University, Cambridge, December 2000.

20. Hewlett Survey, Democracy through Mexican Lenses, September 2000, Mori of Mexico, Roderic Ai Camp, principal investigator. Over a third of Mexicans

The changing political context is complemented by the extraordinary developments in technology and their application to communications. The Internet, and the dissemination of ideas in general, is an equalizer, giving individuals access to volumes of new information within and outside of Mexico. It helps knowledge seekers in small communities which will never acquire adequate financial resources to house traditional print materials.

In 1999, 18 percent of Mexican families owned computers, compared to 69 percent of American families. Fifteen percent of Mexicans surf the Web each week. What is remarkable about ownership statistics is that 23 percent of non-users in Mexico plan to buy a computer by 2003. Computer shipments to Mexico increased by 30 percent in 1999, the highest increase in Latin America.[21] More important, the user rate among the 18-to-29 age group, which will provide much of Mexico's leadership from 2010 to 2030 and which voted overwhelmingly for political change symbolized by Fox, is 50 percent higher than among all other age groups combined.

Technology acts as a knowledge equalizer between Mexico City, Monterrey, and Guadalajara, and the rest of urban Mexico. It also furthers global linkages with the United States. Education generally, and foreign education specifically, has also been shown to be an influential source in the formation of Mexican power elites. Yet the potential influence of the Internet as a source of values and information in the future has no parallel, even when compared to the rapid rates of increase in study abroad. A huge percentage of Mexican power elites study in the United States, but the proportion of ordinary university students who have studied in the United States is less than .5 percent.[22]

Global household linkages wrought by technology are fortified in the private sector by structural linkages cemented through NAFTA and the altered behavior of younger Mexican capitalists. This philosophical and pragmatic sea change is nicely summed up by Lucy Congor:

> As the torch passes from founding fathers to sons and grandsons who studied abroad and grew up in the conglomerates, a new operating style is emerging. These youthful barons have a wider world of competition to contend with. The emphasis in Mexico's great family-held businesses today is on education, professionalism and international

---

belonged to religious groups. Sports organizations were the second most popular groups.

21. *Wall Street Journal Americas,* Mirror on the Americas, "The Challenge of Competing in the Digital Era," 1999.

22. David Lorey, "Mexican Professional Education in the United States and the Myth of 'Brain Drain,'" *Ensayos* (summer 1988), 59.

vision; the new generation needs to transform these coddled enterprises into global public companies with strong export operations and transnational strategic alliances. . . . [23]

The political and social pluralization patterns introduced into Mexico in the 1980s reinforced capitalists' changing perceptions of their political roles.[24] Francisco Valdés Ugalde has argued that it is no exaggeration to say that leading entrepreneurs formed an alliance with the technocrats "to effect a global reform of the relationship between state and society, and hence to redesign Mexico's insertion into the emerging neo-liberal global order," and that they were "central players in the institution of these changes."[25] Increasingly, capitalists have involved themselves in the political arena, providing support for parties and candidates espousing their beliefs, and in some cases, actually running for office. Eugenio Clariond Reyes Retana, president of the elite Mexican Council of Businessmen, 1998–2000, exemplifies the elite capitalist from a politically active family.[26]

Of course, the most prominent symbol of the changed relationship between the private sector and politics, and the role of the businessman in politics, is President Fox himself. Fox was not a prominent capitalist but an influential professional manager who directed the fortunes of Coca-Cola of Mexico—a firm owned by FEMSA, a leading holding company controlled by a prominent capitalist family.[27] Fox has further reinforced his own example by appointing eight cabinet-level ministers who come from extended management careers in the private sector.[28]

The longer-term impact of the private sector on public life will be or-

23. Lucy Congor, "Power to the Plutocrats," *Institutional Investor*, February 1995, n.p.

24. Rafael Montesinos Carrera, "Empresarios en el nuevo orden estatal," *El Cotidiano* 8, no. 50 (September/October 1992), 111.

25. Francisco Valdés Ugalde, "The Private Sector and Political Regime Change in Mexico," in Gerardo Otero, ed., *Neoliberalism Revisited: Economic Restructuring and Mexico's Political Future* (Boulder: Westview, 1996), 142.

26. Eugenio Clariond Reyes Retana is the brother and nephew, respectively, of Benjamín Clariond Reyes Retana, governor of Nuevo León from 1996 to 1997, and Fernando Canales Clariond, governor of Nuevo León from 1997 to 2000. *Excélsior*, June 20, 1997; *Reforma*, June 10, 1996, A1; *Expansión*, April 9, 1997, 37; *Integratec*, January/February 1995, 20–23; www:elector.com.mx/.

27. FEMSA is controlled by Eugenio Garza Laguera, a scion of one of Monterrey's leading capitalist families. His niece, the daughter of Alejandro Garza Laguera, is married to Alfonso Romo Garza, a prominent capitalist who served as a close adviser to Fox during the presidential race.

28. They include the secretaries of labor, communications, energy, environment, agriculture, tourism, and Pemex, the state-owned oil company.

ganizational in nature. In the first place, highly placed power elites in public life who have emerged from successful careers in the private sector bring their own networks with them. If they remain in public life for some time, and they function as mentors to a younger generation of capitalists willing to serve the state, these elites will create new channels, and potentially new magnet mentors, to sustain a continued linkage between the two power elite circles.

In addition to the recruitment function, a highly placed public servant whose life experiences have been in the private sector will introduce corporate culture into the public bureaucracy setting. As Fox has made clear on numerous occasions, he applied the techniques, methods, and approaches he learned at Coca-Cola to his presidential transition and to his executive management philosophy. Such private sector influences signal a decline in the orthodox public organizational culture, and the rise of a melded public-private organizational culture, perhaps most notably in economically oriented agencies.

Research has shown that Mexicans who work for multi-national corporations, most of which are based in the United States, gradually absorb those organizational and cultural values.[29] These changes in organizational culture will probably not be widespread because business types will head only a few agencies for long periods. Nevertheless, those agencies will provide institutional havens for a new public sector culture whose disciples might disseminate it throughout other bureaucracies in the same way the Bank of Mexico did in the 1970s and 1980s.

Fox's government has introduced a new dimension to the power elite, which has the same potential as the corporate culture: an international, public institutional culture. Some Mexican power elites have had short tenures in international agencies, but no figure has ever been a product of international institutions. Fox's new economic development secretary, who worked for the World Bank from 1983 to 1997, could be an early example of a new prototype. Power elites like Fox and his economic development secretary would introduce their own institutional cultures, and their own potential for mentoring and socialization.

The opening up of the specialized training of Mexico's leading military officers is breaking down another structural obstacle to networking among groups of power elites. The fact that nearly a fifth of the students in the

---

29. James Dull, "Effects of Multinational Corporations in Mexico on Attitudes of Mexican Executives," unpublished Ph.D. dissertation, Columbia University, 1981, 121.

National Defense College classes are now mid-level civilians in the executive branch provides a unique networking opportunity, through higher education, for future contacts between top generals and admirals and successful public figures. This is a smaller inroad than that between the private and public sectors, and its effects will not be known for at least a decade, until those graduates from the late 1990s reach influential posts in the public sector and the armed forces.

The most pronounced shared characteristics among several groups of future Mexican power elites will be their increased levels of education, their studies in the United States, and their focused professional specializations.[30] (The noteworthy exception is religious power elites.) These characteristics can logically be viewed as unifying, homogenizing influences, but the diversity of their familial backgrounds, personal experiences, and differing organizational origins often generate distinct socializing effects. Again, as some of these individuals become mentors, they can provide important networking links across elite circles.

The two most important shared characteristics among twenty-first-century Mexican power elites will be their openness to differing viewpoints and their use of analytically motivated (rather than purely ideologically focused) approaches to exploring an issue. These two features, regardless of which disciplines are studied, will flavor the values of returning Mexican graduates from abroad.[31] The plethora of foreign sources available through the Internet, the market economy, and even through domestic undergraduate and graduate programs will strengthen these qualities inside Mexico. Mexican power elites who remain in their country, however, are likely to be less influenced by such values.

In the public arena, the hybrid politico and the provincial outsider will replace the technocrat. In the realm of intellectual influences, especially

30. This functional specialization is found elsewhere. See Barbara Wake Carroll, "Bureaucratic Elites: Some Patterns in Career Paths over Time, *International Review of Administrative Sciences*, 62, no. 3 (September 1996), 394.

31. Howard Wiarda, a perceptive analyst who has long been interested in the exchange of cultural influence between the United States and Latin America, is convinced that few Latin Americans have converted to neoliberal economic ideas. He suggests that the North American experience "is always incomplete and gives rise to very mixed results, among both elites and the general population. Even those Latin Americans who get Ph.D.'s from U.S. universities tend to behave, when they go back to their own countries as cabinet ministers and tecnicos, as patronage politicians. They may have technical knowledge in economics but the political style is often caudillistic." Of course, the counterargument is that they may be "true believers," but they face a plethora of obstacles when confronted with their home country's political realities. Personal letter to the author, March 26, 1997.

from abroad, what may distinguish these twenty-first and late twentieth-century prototypes from their predecessors is an openness and connectedness to those they govern. Like the technocrat, the new political type will believe that reason can solve most problems, encouraging a pragmatic approach to public policy issues. But unlike the technocrats found in many societies at the end of the twentieth century, these new politicians in Mexico are not as likely to view the rest of the population as incompetent and uninformed.[32]

To govern successfully, power elite politicians will have to be strongly linked to the grass roots and be accountable to an increasingly well-informed Mexican voter.[33] Vicente Fox repeatedly stressed accountability in the transition process and promised to give the legislative branch legal responsibility for reviewing executive branch expenditures.

One structural change which facilitates accountability and transparency in Mexican society is a newly assertive media, which has begun to take on professional, investigative tasks attributable to the media in other democratic polities.[34] Power elite intellectuals, especially twenty-first-century prototypes, have published regular columns in the press or have edited and written for popular magazines.[35] As these patterns have taken hold in the national media, they are being replicated at the state and local levels.

32. David Lebedoff, *The New Elite: The Death of Democracy* (New York: Franklin Watts, 1981), 55, 67. Miguel Centeno used a similar description of Mexican technocrats in the 1980s, suggesting that "what characterized the new elite was an epistemological assumption that there was one truth and it was uniquely capable of interpreting it." *Democracy within Reason: Technocratic Revolution in Mexico* (University Park: Penn State University Press, 1994), 41.

33. There are a number of interesting parallels between the impact lawyers made on Mexico in the Alemán generation and that of technocrats under Salinas. But Salvador Azuela, son of the famous novelist, points out a significant difference: "Miguel Alemán was one of the friendliest people of my generation. He was a good student, not a great student. One of his outstanding qualities then was his friendship with all classes of people. He didn't have any moral prejudices. In the post-revolutionary period, lawyers were in positions inferior to that of generals. Psychologically, it was very important when Alemán brought many lawyers and professors into his ministries. This surprised us and had a serious impact, in fact, I would describe it as a political change of extraordinary proportions. Personal interview, Mexico City, October 24, 1976.

34. Chappell H. Lawson, *Building the Fourth Estate: Democratization and the Rise of a Free Press in Mexico* (Berkeley: University of California Press, 2002), develops the impact of media professionalization and competition on citizen perceptions of alternative political parties and democracy.

35. For example, Sergio Aguayo's, Jorge Castañeda's, and Lorenzo Meyer's col-

Another subtle but significant consequence of replacing the technocrat with the provincial outsider is a reduction in presidential power, a trend that was already under way in the Zedillo administration and has continued strongly under Fox.[36] When the president appoints bureaucratic specialists to top policy-making posts, he is able to wield greater personal control because these individuals are almost entirely dependent on the president for their influence. But when individuals who boast grass-roots support and the loyalties of affiliated groups reach office, they bring their own political assets with them. They can enhance presidential influence with these assets, but these politicians also can operate with greater independence from the president.[37]

Another significant change, also part of the trend toward greater plurality represented by Vicente Fox, is the recruitment of more diverse types of individuals into the political power elite. This may move the power elite in Mexico closer to the traditional definition—that is, individuals who have exercised a direct influence in two or more arenas. No influential capitalist since the administration of Miguel Alemán has ever served in a presidential cabinet. Fox, however, appointed two individuals with close ties to capitalists: the secretary of energy and the secretary of transportation.[38] Furthermore, the president surprised many observers by appointing a top general as his attorney general; this is the first time in three decades that a prominent military officer has held a non-defense cabinet post.

The most dramatic structural shift in the experiences of Mexico's power elite—the growth in the number of elites who have sought education abroad— corresponds with the most influential ideological shift in the last three decades, an emphasis on political and economic liberalization. The structural shift occurred as the generations born from 1920 to 1940, where

umns have appeared weekly in numerous newspapers, and each included an email address through which the author could be reached.

36. Only four of Fox's top appointees can be described as having the traditional national bureaucratic careers favored by technocrats.

37. This consequence is nicely developed in the American case by Margaret Jane Wyszomirski, "Presidential Personnel and Political Capital: From Roosevelt to Reagan," in Mattei Dogan, ed., *Pathways to Power: Selecting Rulers in Pluralist Democracies* (Boulder: Westview, 1988), 69.

38. They are Ernesto Martens Rebolledo and Pedro Cerisola y Weber. Martens Rebolledo was at Vitro, one of Mexico's top conglomerates, for two decades, rising to the position of CEO, and Cerisola held management positions at Telmex and Aeroméxico. Fox also appointed John McCarthy, president of Raintree Resorts International, as his head of national tourism development.

the educational pattern in study abroad essentially remained unchanged both in numbers and location, gave way to the group born after 1941, which witnessed a two-and-a-half-fold increase in those studying in the United States. (See table 15.)

The individuals who contributed most significantly to this shift were power elite mentors. As noted, many of these individuals were themselves educated abroad; they valued that experience and encouraged their disciples to pursue a similar experience. Some of these mentors, described as magnet mentors, provided government financial support to send their protégés abroad. Initially, as we have seen, many power elites, with the exception of capitalists and military officers, studied in Europe. Clergy were very much influenced by their exposure to Vatican II and to the intellectual atmosphere in Rome. Eventually, however, there was a dramatic shift in education abroad, with the exception of the clergy, from Europe to the United States, where most younger Mexican power elites completed some type of graduate training or studies.

As suggested in chapter 8, foreign education alone does not explain economic and political changes in the 1990s, but it did affect the intellectual openness of many leading Mexicans. Even military officers were not immune to this "methodological influence," which is just one element in what Peter Berger calls an international "faculty club culture."[39] Among those who sought out economic solutions to Mexico's long-term macroeconomic problems, the impact was more concrete, specific, and policy-oriented. Many of these Mexicans who studied abroad also encountered intellectual mentors, but these figures, however important, typically did not exert the same level of influence as magnet mentors in Mexico, because they did not perform all of the related mentoring tasks.

The precise point at which Mexican political change occurred, beginning in the mid-1960s and early 1970s, has been referred to by sociologists as the "tipping point." Malcolm Gladwell has explored this phenomenon from a variety of perspectives. He has tried to formulate a model which explains how perceptions, which translate into different behavior, suddenly shift. He discovered several interlinking patterns which correspond closely to those found among Mexican power elites.

In the first place, a sudden shift in perceptions can often be explained by an influential actor, designated as a *connector*. The connector shares many similarities with the magnet mentor—in other words, he or she

---

39. Peter L. Berger, "Four Faces of Global Culture," *The National Interest* (fall 1997), 25.

networks with large numbers of other individuals, often connected directly or indirectly to influential individuals from a variety of professions. It is apparent from interviews that Rodrigo Gómez, the longtime director of the Bank of Mexico, was such a person. He wanted to increase the technical skills of the bank's economists and chose to use graduate education in the United States to accomplish that goal.

Gómez created several generations of disciples who naturally were influenced by the substantive content of the economics they learned. As those economists moved up in the Bank of Mexico bureaucracy and other leading federal agencies responsible for macroeconomic policy making, their attitudes became inseparable from their organizational cultures. Those cultures, in turn, reinforced these attitudes among the next generation.

According to Gladwell's theory, Gómez's influence alone would not be sufficient to generate such a dramatic shift; context must also have played a role. What role did the larger environment play in encouraging such a change? Again, as I have suggested in this analysis, three broad contextual variables formed a larger confluence which flavored this ideological shift. Mexico itself, in the 1960s and 1970s, underwent a series of major political and economic crises, pushing power elites to consider alternative models. Second, the cold war came to a rapid and dramatic end in the 1980s, symbolizing the devaluation of statist economic models. And third, in seeking alternatives to the Marxist emphasis at Mexico's most prestigious economics program—an emphasis which was in direct contradiction to the needs of the bank and governmental financial agencies—prospective future government officials sought out economics training from private institutions in Mexico and from foreign economics programs, mostly in the United States.

Finally, Gladwell's work also reveals that small groups exercise a tremendous influence in conveying new attitudes and affecting behavior, whether in terms of retail buying patterns or social behavior. The research he cites suggests that groups which contain more than 150 people lose their cohesiveness and effectiveness. Most of the networking groups identified among Mexico's power elite would be even smaller, but their qualitative importance individually, and in combination with one another, gives them tremendous potential.[40]

The shared educational experiences and global perspectives which

40. Malcolm Gladwell, *The Tipping Point: How Little Things Can Make a Big Difference* (Boston: Little, Brown, 2000).

helped bring together Mexican capitalists and technocrats at the end of the twentieth century will continue in the twenty-first century.[41] What seemed to be a special profile among power elites will become more widely shared among other Mexicans.[42] The shared "language" of public debate will facilitate the discussion, but a greater diversity of views is likely to reach the policy arena.[43] The reason for this is that a wider range of power elites—intellectuals, priests, and military officers—will share in the knowledge of global economics. These three groups, who in so many ways differ from capitalists and politicians, will use their knowledge to challenge the existing debate and to offer differing policy alternatives. Bishops are already actively engaged in discussion about macroeconomic policies, a pattern found among leaders from the U.S. National Conference of Bishops.[44]

In authoritarian settings, foreign-influenced purveyors of knowledge and their representative domestic institutions might well operate unchecked. It is very unlikely in a democratic setting, however, that similar individuals or institutions could remain unopposed. The methodological influences borrowed from the United States, not specific substantive theories, will have a stronger long-term influence in Mexico and will increase the likelihood that any ideological alternative will face serious intellectual scrutiny. Ultimately, these influences will expand, not reduce, the range and depth of the ideological debate, at least in the short to medium term.

41. Centeno believed their "homogeneous profile" helped to prevent internal divisions among the ruling elite. See *Democracy within Reason*, 40.

42. For a discussion of these trends worldwide, and detailed evidence of their existence, see Ronald Inglehart, Miguel Basáñez, and Alejandro Moreno, *Human Values and Beliefs: A Cross-Cultural Sourcebook* (Ann Arbor: University of Michigan, 1998). For a fascinating comparison between Mexico, the United States and Canada, see Ronald F. Inglehart, Neil Nevitte, and Miguel Basáñez, *The North American Trajectory: Cultural, Economic, and Political Ties among the United States, Canada, and Mexico* (New York: Aldine, 1996).

43. Carlos Monsiváis expressed dismay at the linguistic impact of U.S. education on Mexicans. "It is producing an extraordinary change in Mexican life, on the language, even the diction of Mexicans. So many of these Mexicans are not only attending private schools, but they are going for advanced studies in the United States. Today, the products of these educational experiences no longer speak correct Spanish. And of course, their language or vocabulary, affects the substance of what they say. Really, it's a very disturbing trend." Personal interview, Claremont, California, November 18, 1998.

44. Robert Lerner et al., "Christian Religious Elites," *Public Opinion* (March/April 1989), 56. In another study, G. Richard found that 76 percent of bishops in the U.S. addressed political issues in their sermons. "Politics and Religious Authority," *American Catholics since the Second Vatican Council* (Westport: Greenwood, 1994), 78–79.

The dramatic victory of Vicente Fox in the 2000 presidential race, signaling the end of the seventy-year reign of the one-party system, extends beyond the long-term political and economic changes identified above. The general political culture, at the mass level, is also deeply altered. Indeed, Fox's election increased citizen beliefs in the actual existence of democracy in Mexico by more than 50 percent.[45] This election strongly reinforced the concept of accountability and openness among the citizenry as well as in the leadership, and 2000 will be viewed as a benchmark year in Mexico's transformation.

This leaves us with two remaining questions about Mexican power elites in the twenty-first century. First, will power elites remain a useful concept for understanding Mexico and Mexican leadership? The underlying changes in Mexican society, the emergence of new prototypical elites, and the victory of Vicente Fox do not preclude the persistence of power elites. Over the long run, a gradual decline in their importance may occur as the diversity and range of organizational and individual actors increase.

In the foreseeable future, the most remarkable change is not likely to be a decline in power elites, but their reconstitution. The barriers between the five groups, which were created and reinforced through years of semi-authoritarian rule, have now begun to crumble. The increased fluidity enabled by this shift is dramatically illustrated by capitalist and political power elites in Vicente Fox's new administration; it will also penetrate the barriers between political and military power elites in the near future.

As organizations increase in number and importance, networking will not disappear. In fact, networking is alive and well in the organizational cultures which dominate postindustrial societies. The evidence demonstrates that a vibrant informal networking system complements organizational features.

We have long assumed that "development" is synonymous with institutional growth, and that direct control over organizations therefore measures elite influence. It is apparent, however, that personal networking in Mexico is a basic means through which many power elites are connected to each other and connected across their decision-making circles. Even more significant, a major source of that personal networking remains the

45. Roderic Ai Camp, "Citizen Attitudes toward Democracy and Vicente Fox's Victory in 2000."

elite's own family, specifically wealthy and professionally successful families.

Mentors' fundamental role in Mexico is accentuated by the fact that they have used networking as a means to affect organizational culture, exerting a long-term influence on elite behavior, decision making, and policy making. Because the Fox presidency will open up new linkages, different types of potential elites will have access to influential positions in some institutions, and different types of individuals will join the next generation of mentors. The *open network*, best represented by the present cultural power elite, will become increasingly common in the next decades in the Mexican setting.

Openness in organizational structures will contribute to an increased cross-fertilization among various types of Mexican power elites. What the evidence demonstrates is how connected these elites have been through personal networks across policy circles. What Fox may introduce is a greater transparency in these inter-elite connections. This is suggested by the fact that individual power elites will actually hold organizational positions in two or more policy circles, the first examples of which will be political and capitalist.[46] This also implies that a mentor, without intending to do so, might exert a policy influence over one arena, while having operated exclusively in another arena.

The second question is what will be the role of the mentor in selecting and instructing future Mexican leaders? Some members of the power elite are not optimistic about the mentor's future, even though no decline in the presence of mentors can be detected among elite generations born after 1941. Nevertheless, there are a number of reasons to suspect that the mentor's influence may decline. One of the contributing factors is the increasing size of Mexican institutions. This is true of governmental and

46. This is illustrated definitively in Fox's first cabinet, which includes Francisco Gil Díaz, a PRI technocrat who studied under magnet mentor Miguel Mancera and worked closely with Leopoldo Solís; Mario M. Laborín Gómez, former director general of Bancomer and president of the Bancomer Brokerage firm, who has had a long career in top corporations; Ernesto Martens Rebolledo, former director general of Vitro, a leading Monterrey conglomerate; and Pedro Cerisola, director general of Aerovías de México. Fox futher crossed traditional power elite circles with the inclusion of Ernesto Ruffo Appel, a member of the power elite and a pioneer figure in the PAN, as well as Jorge G. Castañeda, a member of the cultural power elite. The reverse may be occurring in the private sector. In March 2001, Fomento Económico Mexicano (FEMSA), a top holding company, appointed former Zedillo chief of staff and energy secretary Luis Téllez Kuénzler as a member of its corporate board. *Diario de Yucatán*, March 28, 2001, www.yucatan.com.mx.

corporate bureaucracies, and equally true of traditional state-run universities. This pattern might explain why smaller private institutions may increase their influence as the locus for mentoring relationships.

A second reason to predict the decline of mentors is demographic. The number of influential Mexicans remains relatively small, but the number of Mexicans with formal educational credentials who seek success in their respective disciplines has increased at a faster pace than has the number of power elite members, expanding the number of potential disciples seeking an influential mentor. Finally, some members of the power elite admit that, given the complexity and demands of their professional responsibilities, they no longer have time to seek out disciples as their future replacements. Whether or not all potential mentors share this tendency remains to be seen.

Although they are based on sound reasoning, these speculations are not persuasive. The longstanding fundamental patterns in Mexican culture have encouraged individuals from all social backgrounds to seek out mentors. Even though it has been buffeted by many opposing influences, this pattern is not likely to change. As long as the demand remains for such figures, someone in a position to provide the mentoring responsibilities described in this work will perform those tasks. In fact, a strong counterargument can be made that in times of changing organizational settings, mentoring and networking provide a welcome stability to counter institutional unpredictability.

Mexico has shown repeatedly that its own unique informal qualities, including networking and mentoring, remain largely unaffected by institutional growth and economic modernization. A comprehensive recent study of stable democracies concludes that "national elites in these countries each contain a central circle consisting of a few hundred persons. The sizes, compositions, and densities of these central circles, and even more their cores, make for close and frequent interaction among individuals who typically hold the uppermost positions in the most important institutions and organizations of the societies."[47] As Mexican leadership marches into the next millennium, networking and mentoring will continue to be vibrant features of power elite circles.

47. John Higley et al., "Elite Integration in Stable Democracies: A Reconsideration," *European Sociological Review*, 7, no. 1 (May 1991), 49–50.

Bibliographic Essay

A well-developed theoretical literature exists on power elites. A broad assessment of these contributions which provides helpful, comparative insights across methodological approaches and substantive studies can be found in George Moyser, *Research Methods for Elite Studies* (New York: HarperCollins, 1986). The importance of the linkage between organizations and power elites is established clearly in the work of G. William Domhoff and Thomas R. Dye, *Power Elites and Organizations* (Beverly Hills: Sage, 1987). Among the most comprehensive, recent work which incorporates analyses from many types of elites and countries is that by Moshe M. Czudnowski, in his edited collection *Political Elites and Social Change: Studies of Elite Roles and Attitudes* (DeKalb: Northern Illinois University Press, 1983).

From a conceptual angle, one of the better explanations of the divisions which exist over definitions of elites is available in Alan Zuckerman's "The Concept 'Political Elite': Lessons from Mosca and Pareto," *Journal of Politics*, 39, no. 2 (1977), 324–44. Complementary to this is George E. Marcus's introduction in his *Elites: Ethnographic Issues* (Albuquerque: University of New Mexico Press, 1983). William G. Domhoff and Thomas R. Dye's "Invitation to Elite Theory: The Basic Contentions Reconsidered," in their *Power Elites and Organizations*, also offers a lucid overview. Finally, much of the debate between pluralists and elite theorists is considered by Philip H. Burch, one of the most thorough scholars on American elites, in his *Elites in American History*, 1 (New York: Holmes and Meier, 1981), 3–22.

Some of the recent literature on elites has focused on their role in contributing to societal stability and major social transformations. The work of G. Lowell Field, John Higley, and Michael G. Burton has explored many facets of these issues. Their "A New Elite Framework for Political Sociology," *Revue européene des sciences sociales*, 28 (1990), 149–82, is a good place to start.

The other crucial variable considered in my analysis of elites and networking is the mentor, about which very little has been written, with the exception of the business world. Most of the literature in this discipline, however, evolves largely from the business psychology field, not studies of power elites. Although lacking the sophistication found in the sociology and political science literature, Michael G. Zey's *The Mentor Connection: Strategic Alliances in Corporate Life* (New Brunswick: Transaction, 1990) does provide many useful insights from the American business community. A more scholarly view is available in Belle Rose Ragins, "Diversity, Power, and Mentorship in Organizations: A Cultural, Structural, and Behavioral Perspective," in M. M. Chemers et. al., *Diversity in Organizations: New Perspectives for a Changing Workplace* (Thousand Oaks: Sage, 1995), 91–132. The connection between career success and mentors is well established in the corporate world. Among those studies are Terri A. Scandura, "Mentorship and Career Mobility: An Empirical Investigation," *Journal of Organizational Behavior*, 13, no. 2 (March 1992), 169–74.

One of the most important directions in power elite studies in the last two decades is networking analysis. Much of the literature on elites since the 1980s has concentrated on this approach. A collection which explores these quantitative methods can be found in Stanley Wasserman and Joseph Galaskiewicz, eds., *Advances in Social Network Analysis* (Thousand Oaks: Sage, 1994). One of the scholars who has advanced the thesis of the importance of personal networks on decision making is Gwen Moore, who developed these arguments in her "The Structure of a National Elite Network," *American Sociological Review*, 44 (October 1979), 673–92. The most useful, detailed comparative work on networking across elite circles is a classic study of Venezuela. Allan Kessler outlines the findings pertinent to friendship ties in "The Internal Structure of Elites," in Frank Bonilla and José Silva Michelena, eds., *A Strategy for Research on Social Policy, Vol. 1: The Politics of Change in Venezuela* (Cambridge: MIT Press, 1967), 223–37.

Considerable literature exists on the specific networking concept, from an organizational perspective, among corporate, interlocking directorates. One of the most comprehensive arguments is presented in Thomas Koenig, Robert Gogel, and John Sonquist, "Model of the Significance of Corporate Interlocking Directorates," *American Journal of Economics and Sociology*, 38 (1979), 174–83. Corporate elites, as suggested in the chapters on networking, have been most studied in the literature. The work of Michael Useem is essential for understanding these linkages in the United States and their influence on governmental policy. See for example his "The Inner Circle and the Political Voice of Business," in Michael Schwartz, ed., *The Structure of Power in America: The Corporate Elite as a Ruling Class* (New York: Holmes and Meier, 1987), 143–53.

The corporate interlock has also been carefully analyzed by Beth Mintz and Michael Schwartz, "Corporate Interlocks, Financial Hegemony, and Intercorporate Coordination," in *The Structure of Power in America: The Corporate Elite as a Ruling Class* (New York: Holmes and Meier, 1987), 34–47. For the importance of financial links among corporations established through board memberships, see Joseph Galaskiewicz and Stanley Wasserman, "Social Network Analysis, Concepts, Methodology, and Directions for the 1990s," *Sociological Methods and Research*, 22, no. 1 (August 1993), 3–22. The work of John Scott, "Networks of Corporate Power," *Annual Review of Sociology*, 17 (1991), 181–203, is also valuable. Interlocks between government and the private sector, the most carefully examined of all linkages across power elite groups, is examined by Harold Salzman and G. William Domhoff, "The Corporate Community and Government: Do They Interlock?" in G. William Domhoff, *Power Structure Research* (Beverly Hills: Sage, 1980), 227–54.

Kinship as an agent of networking is not characterized by the plethora of literature available on corporate boards. Some of the leading scholars of American corporate elites, however, have explored their social origins, if not their contemporaneous kinship ties. The classic studies are those by Carl S. Joslyn and Frank Taussig, *American Business Leaders: A Study of Social Origins and Social Stratification* (New York: Macmillan, 1932), and Suzanne Infield Keller, *Social Origins and Career Lines of Three Generations of American Business Leaders* (New York: Arno Press, 1980). A more recent view of social class origins can be found in Michael Useem, "The Inner Group of the American Capitalist Class," *Social Problems*, 25 (1978), 224–40, and in Allen H. Barton's excellent work, including his "Background, Attitudes and Activities of American Elites," in Gwen Moore, ed., *Studies of the Structure of National Elite Groups*, 1 (Greenwich: JAI, 1985), 173–218. The finest comparative study of capitalist, family linkages in the Latin American region is Peter McDonough's *Power and Ideology in Brazil* (Princeton: Princeton University Press, 1981).

Networking studies which extend beyond the confines of a single power elite group, or compare more than any two groups, are far less common than studies of individual groups, excepting intellectuals and clergy, who have rarely been examined. The important connection between parents' professional careers and those chosen by successful sons and daughters has been explored within the confines of individual professions. Among the best studies of the officer corps is R. F. Schloemer's and G. E. Myers's exploration of the U.S. Air Force, in their "Making It at the Air Force Academy: Who Stays? Who Succeeds?" in Franklin D. Margiotta, ed., *Changing World of the American Military* (Boulder: Westview, 1978), 321–44, and the comparative analysis of United States government officials and the military in Lloyd Warner's pioneering work, *The American Federal Executive: A Study of the Social and Personal Characteristics of the Civilian and Military Leaders of the United States* (New Haven: Yale University Press, 1963). The most detailed work on government officials, focusing on federal judges, is Donn M. Kurtz II, *Kinship and Politics, the Justices of the United States and Louisiana Supreme Courts* (Baton Rouge: Louisiana State University Press, 1997). To understand networking patterns among intellectuals, the only comprehensive, in-depth analytical work is Charles Kadushin's *American Intellectual Elite* (Boston: Little, Brown, 1974). For comparisons with Mexico, see my *Intellectuals and the State in Twentieth Century Mexico* (Austin: University of Texas Press, 1985).

Other significant works, because of their theoretical discussions, include Gwen Moore and Richard D. Alba, "Class and Prestige Origins in the American Elite," in Peter Marsden and Nan Lin, eds., *Social Structure and Network Analysis* (Beverly Hills: Sage, 1982), 39–60, and David Knoke, "Networks of Elite Structure and Decision Making," in Stanley Wasserman and Joseph Galaskiewicz, eds., *Advances in Social Network Analysis* (Thousand Oaks: Sage, 1994), 274–94. The broadest study of American power elites is Thomas R. Dye's (including four subsequent editions) *Who's Running America? Institutional Leadership in the United States* (Englewood Cliffs: Prentice-Hall, 1976).

Some work, but not in depth, has been accomplished on power elite backgrounds in Mexico. For the Monterrey capitalist elite, see George R. Andrews, "Toward a Reevaluation of the Latin American Family Firm: The Industry Executives of Monterrey," *Inter-American Economic Affairs*, 30 (winter 1976), 23–40. The most comprehensive study on leading capitalists in Mexico, which describes their networking and background, is my *Entrepreneurs and Politics in Twentieth Century Mexico* (New York: Oxford University Press, 1989).

Socialization literature, which made such a splash in the 1970s and 1980s, has not advanced greatly, especially in relation to the formation of adults generally, and adult power elites. An excellent overview of the important issues in this literature can be found in Jack Dennis, "Major Problems of Political Socialization Research," in Jack Dennis, ed., *Socialization to Politics* (New York: Wiley, 1973). The classic study of changing attitudes among adults over long periods of time is Theodore Newcomb, "Persistence and Regression of Changed Attitudes: Long Range Studies," in Jack Dennis, ed., *Socialization to Politics*, 413–26. Some recent work has explored how ideas travel from one culture to another, a central underlying theme in this book. The work of G. John Ikenberry is instructive, including his article with Charles A. Kupchan, "Socialization and Hegemonic Power," *International Organization*, 44, no. 3 (summer 1990), 283–315.

Some of the specific variables which influence elite socialization include place of origin and adult residence. Allen H. Barton has explored the role of geography among United States elites in B. A. Rochman and R. H. Linden, eds., *Elite Studies and Comparative Politics* (Pittsburgh: University of Pittsburgh Press, 1984). Parents, and the careers they pursued, have also been influential in the socialization process. Most interest in this variable can be found in the socialization literature on politicians. The work of Robert D. Putnam, because it is comparative, is insightful: *The Beliefs of Politicians: Ideology, Conflict, and Democracy in Britain and Italy* (New Haven: Yale University Press, 1973). Some understanding of the influence of family on military officers can be found in an early examination of future army officers, in J. P. Lovell, "The Professional Socialization of the West Point Cadet," in Morris Janowitz, ed., *The New Military: Changing Patterns of Organization* (New York: Russell Sage, 1964), 119–57, and in a recent work by Serge Guimond, "Encounter and Metamorphosis: The Impact of Military Socialization on Professional Values," *Applied Psychology: An International Review*, 44, no. 3 (1995), 251–75. The impact of family ambience on elite formation is explored among American politicians in the pioneering work of Alfred B. Clubok, Norman M. Wilensky, and Forrest J. Berghorn, "Family Relationships, Congressional Recruitment, and Political Modernization," *Journal of Politics*, 31 (November 1961), 1035–62.

The role of education in the socialization process of power elites is a central focus of this book. Some valuable literature exists on the impact of differing institutions on student attitudes. Among these studies are Reo M. Christenson and Patrick J. Capretta, "The Impact of College on Political Attitudes, A Research Note," *Social Science Quarterly*, 49 (1968), 315–20, and W. Paul Vogt, *Tolerance and Education: Learning to Live With Diversity and Differences* (Beverly Hills: Sage, 1997). For some comparative data from Latin America, the only major study is that by Arthur Liebman, Kenneth Walker, and Myron Glazer, *Latin American University Students, A Six Nation Study* (Cambridge: Harvard University Press, 1972). The most focused study on the impact of education on elite socialization remains Rupert Wilkinson, *Gentlemanly Power: British Leadership and the Public School Tradition: A Comparative Study of the Making of Rulers* (New York: Oxford University Press, 1964). For a detailed analysis of the role of the Autonomous Technological Institute of Mexico on the new generation of technocratic economists, see Sarah Babb's *Managing Mexico: Economists from Nationalism to Neoliberalism* (Princeton: Princeton University Press, 2002).

The military has received some attention in the past in the area of educational socialization. Among the more insightful work, providing findings which are helpful across cultures and services, are T. M. McCloy and W. H. Clover, "Value Formation at the Air Force Academy," in C. C. Moskos and F. R. Woods, eds., *The Military: More Than Just a Job?* (Washington, D.C.: Pergamon, 1988), 129–52, Gary L. Wamsley, "Contrasting Institutions of Air Force Socialization: Happenstance or Bellwether?" *American Journal of Sociology*, 78 (1972), 399–419, and Serge Guimond's work, cited above.

Nothing empirical is available about the Mexican military's educational socialization, but new trends are discussed in detail in my "The Educating and Training of the Mexican Officer Corps," in Elliot V. Converse, ed., *Forging the Sword, Selecting, Educating, and Training Cadets and Junior Officers in the Modern World*, vol. 5, Military History Symposium Series of the United States Air Force Academy (Chicago: Imprint Publications, 1998), 336–46. For data on the impact of the United States on the military education of foreign officers, including Mexicans, see John A. Cope, *International Military Education and Training: An Assessment* (Washington, D.C.: Institute for National Strategic Studies, 1995). A broader assessment of the decline of United States influence on the Latin American military is analyzed carefully in the work of J. Samuel Fitch, especially his "The Decline of U.S. Military Influence on Latin America," *Journal of Inter-American Studies and World Affairs*, 35 (summer 1993), 1–49. The most comprehensive analysis of the impact of United States training on foreign military officers can be found in Jennifer M. Taw's "The Effectiveness of Training International Military Students in Internal Defense and Development" (Santa Monica: RAND, 1993).

The changing trends in higher education, especially the importance of private universities and technically oriented training, is fully explored in

Daniel Levy's *Higher Education and the State in Latin America* (Chicago: University of Chicago Press, 1986). The only serious examination of other cultural institutions, specifically foundations, across the region, is Levy's *Building the Third Sector, Latin America's Research Centers and Non-Profit Development* (Pittsburgh: University of Pittsburgh Press, 1996), a pioneering effort on this subject.

To understand the broad, changing patterns in global education, it is helpful to peruse Mary E. McMahon, "Higher Education in a World Market: An Historical Look at the Global Context of International Study," *Higher Education,* 24 (1992), 465–82. The importance of foreign graduates as mentors to repeating generations of students who study abroad is analyzed in Hans N. Weiler, "The Political Dilemmas of Foreign Study," in Elinor G. Barber et. al., eds., *Bridges to Knowledge: Foreign Students in Comparative Perspective* (Chicago: University of Chicago Press, 1984), 184–95.

Unfortunately, almost no literature exists on the socializing impact of foreign education abroad. Most of what does exist is speculative. The exception to this typical pattern includes Xinshu Zhao and Yu Xie, "Western Influence on (People's Republic of China) Chinese Students in the United States," *Comparative Education Review,* 36, no. 4 (1992), 509–29, and Gerald W. Fry, "The Economic and Political Impact of Study Abroad," *Comparative Education Review,* 28, no. 2 (1984), 203–20. For a highly critical dependency argument of the impact of foreign education, see the work of E. F. Fuenzalida, "The Contribution of Higher Education to a New International Order," in B. Sanyal, ed., *Higher Education and the New International Order* (Paris: UNESCO, 1982), 124–44.

The way in which ideas are actually spread globally has only begun to receive some recent attention, some of it quite sophisticated theoretically. Among the more useful work for this study is G. John Ikenberry and Charles A. Kupchan, "Socialization and Hegemonic Power," *International Organization,* 44, no. 3 (summer 1990), 283–315.

The role of the technocrats in Mexican policy making, and the degree to which their characteristics correspond to those found elsewhere in the region, receives the most comprehensive treatment from Stephanie Golob's "Making Possible What Is Necessary: Pedro Aspe, the Salinas Team, and the Next Mexican 'Miracle,'" in Jorge I. Domínguez, ed., *Technopols: Freeing Politics and Markets in Latin America in the 1990s* (University Park: Penn State University Press, 1997), 95–143, and her Ph.D. dissertation, "Crossing the Line: Sovereignty, Integration, and the Free Trade Decisions of Mexico and Canada," Harvard University, 1997. For understanding their emergence from lower levels of the federal bureaucracy, see Miguel A. Centeno, *Democracy within Reason, Technocratic Revolution in Mexico* (University Park: Penn State University Press, 1994). My own early "The Middle-Level Technocrat in Mexico," *Journal of Developing Areas*, 6 (1972), 572–82, provides the first empirical analysis of the early version of these future economist governors.

Latin American technocrats are not typically comparable to their Mexican counterparts, but the best comparative work nonetheless suggests important shared theoretical concerns; see Miguel A. Centeno and Patricio Silva, eds., *The Politics of Expertise in Latin America* (New York: St. Martin's, 1997), and Jorge I. Domínguez, ed., *Technopols, Free Politics and Markets in Latin American in the 1990s*, cited above. Two of the best case studies in Latin America, from which much can be learned, are Juan Gabriel Valdés, *Pinochet's Economists: The Chicago School in Chile* (Cambridge: Cambridge University Press, 1995), and Eduardo Silva, *State and Capital in Chile: Business Elites, Technocrats, and Market Economies* (Boulder: Westview, 1996). However, the best work on the role of economists in policy making, and their evolution in the macroeconomic policy of Latin American countries generally, is found in the essays and articles of Verónica Montecinos and John Markoff. See especially their "The Ubiquitous Rise of Economists," *Journal of Public Policy*, 13, no. 1 (1993), 37–68, and their essay "From the Power of Economic Ideas to the Power of Economists," in Miguel A. Centeno, ed., *The Other Mirror: Essays on Latin America* (Princeton: Princeton University Press, 2001).

The relationship between networking, organization, and decision making is among the most explored at the formal, institutional level. Some of the major contributions in this field are those by Mark S. Mizruchi and Joseph Galaskiewicz, "Networks of Interorganizational Relations," *Sociological Methods and Research*, 22, no. 1 (August 1993), 46–70. Michael Useem's work, cited above in the context of business elites, provides important contributions on inner circle relations in his *The Inner Circle* (New York: Oxford University Press, 1984).

The case study of organizational influences in the Mexican federal economic bureaucracy is best understood in general terms by reading John Bailey's early work, "Presidency, Bureaucracy, and Administrative Reform in Mexico: The Secretariat of Programming and Budget," *Journal of Inter-American Economic Affairs*, 34 (1980), 27–59. Other, more recent insights on the evolution of Mexican economic technocrats are Judith A. Teichman, *Privatization and Political Change in Mexico* (Pittsburgh: University of Pittsburgh Press, 1995). The most detailed analysis ever published of technocratic networking in these selective agencies is Eduardo Torres Espinosa's *Bureaucracy and Politics in Mexico: The Case of the Secretariat of Programming and Budgeting* (Brookfield: Ashgate, 1999).

The case study of the organizational relationships among Mexican capitalists relies on two excellent, focused analyses: Ben Ross Schneider, "Why Is Mexican Business So Organized? unpublished paper, Northwestern University, March 1999, and Alicia Ortiz Rivera, "Consejo Mexicano de Hombres de Negocios," unpublished M.A. thesis, Instituto Mora, Mexico City, 1998. For general background and specific details on capitalist organizational and networking linkages, and their general setting in the Mexican context, see my *Entrepreneurs and the State in Twentieth Century Mexico*, cited earlier.

Finally, generationally focused analyses of Mexican elites exploring the last decade are sparse. My own work on political leadership, through the beginning of the Salinas administration and extending back to the late nineteenth century, can be found in my *Political Recruitment across Two Centuries: Mexico, 1884–1991* (Austin: University of Texas Press, 1995), which devotes a lengthy chapter to this topic. My predictions of future leadership credentials can also be placed into a larger context of Mexico's own social, economic, and political situation as forecasted by Michael J. Mazarr, *Mexico 2005, The Challenges of the New Millennium* (Washington, D.C.: CSIS, 1999). The electoral victory of Vicente Fox in July 2000 will have numerous profound structural implications on political leadership, including recruitment, networking, and socialization.

Index

Abedrop Dávila, Carlos, 85n62
Academia Hispano-Americana, 117n71
adult residence: changes in trends in, 236, 249; effects on power elites networking contacts, 49–50, 63–64, 66–72, 93; socialization effects of, 110–12, 120
Aeroméxico, 273n38
Agency for International Development (AID), 155n6
Aguayo, Sergio, 84n59, 158n17, 188–90, 206, 263n10, 272n35
Aguilar Camin, Héctor, 83n55, 116n67, 241–42
Aguilar Monteverde, Alonso, 85n62
Aguilar Zinser, Adolfo, 158n17, 232n7, 267n18
Aguirre Velázquez, Ramón, 217n20
AID (Agency for International Development), 155n6
Alcalá-Zamora y Castillo, Niceto, 117n74
Aldrich, Nelson, Jr., 104
Alemán Valdes, Miguel: economic policies of, 232; as mentor, 72; mentors of, 102–3n19, 102; Mexican Council of Businessmen and, 220n25
Alemán Velasco, Miguel, 83n55; educational networking contacts of, 44n26; lawyers in administration

of, 272n33; as mentor, 72; mentors of, 102–3n19
Alemeida Merino, Adalberto, 68n13
ALFA, 248
Alfaro Siqueiros, David, 45n28, 83, 113–14
Alianza Cívica, 189
Alvarez, Luis H., 68n13
ambassadorships, as networking source, 88, 88n71
Amigos de Fox, 267
anti-Americanism, 140
anti-capitalism, as theme in public education, 128
anti-clericalism, as theme in public education, 128. See also Cristero rebellion
Arango, Jerónimo, 54n53
Aranguren Castiello, Ignacio, 70n20
Aranguren family, 70n20
Arce, Miguel, 30n22
Arévalo Gardoqui, Juan, 78n42, 88n70
Arévalo Vera, Gustavo, 78n42
Argentina, 213, 216, 216n16
armed forces, numbers in Mexico, 139n58
Army National War College, 193
Aron, Raymond, 105
Artigas Fernández, Mario, 47n30
Aspe Armella, Pedro Carlos, 182, 257; as academic, 183; economic neoliberalism and, 135, 172–74; as tech-

291

Compositor:	Binghamton Valley Composition
Text:	10/13 Aldus
Display:	Aldus
Printer and binder:	Thomson-Shore